Reform and Resistance
in Schools and Classrooms

REFORM AND RESISTANCE IN SCHOOLS AND CLASSROOMS

An Ethnographic View of the Coalition of Essential Schools

DONNA E. MUNCEY AND PATRICK J. MCQUILLAN

YALE UNIVERSITY PRESS NEW HAVEN AND LONDON

Designed by Sonia L. Scanlon
Set in Sabon with Copperplate display by
The Composing Room of Michigan, Inc.
Printed in the United States of America
by BookCrafters Inc., Chelsea, Michigan.

Library of Congress Cataloging-in-Publication Data
Muncey, Donna E.
    Reform and resistance in schools and
    classrooms : an ethnographic view of the
    Coalition of Essential Schools / Donna E.
    Muncey and Patrick J. McQuillan.
        p.   cm.
    Includes bibliographical references and index.
    ISBN 0-300-06108-0
    1. High schools—United States—
Administration.   2. Education,
Secondary—Social aspects—United States.
3. Ethnology—United States.
4. Coalition of Essential Schools.
I. McQuillan, Patrick J.   II. Title.
LB2822.2.M86   1996
373.12'00973—dc20   95-43603
                            CIP

A catalogue record for this book is available
from the British Library.

The paper in this book meets the guidelines for
permanence and durability of the Committee on
Production Guidelines for Book Longevity of
the Council on Library Resources.

10 9 8 7 6 5 4 3 2 1

CONTENTS

This book is distinctive in several respects. It is very rare in the arena of school reform for the principal investigator courageously to seek and support an independent, systematic, several years' long description and analysis of an intervention effort. Besides courage there was also wisdom in selecting two social scientists who are extremely well trained in anthropology, one of them a former schoolteacher and the other very knowledgeable about education. Theodore Sizer deserves our respect and gratitude for encouraging the writers of this book to give us no-holds-barred ethnographies of the interventions' life histories in all their complexities.

Efforts to reform and improve an organization as traditional and complex as a high school—embedded as it is in a larger school system, and related as it is to a state department of education—are fantastically difficult, far more difficult than our policymakers and educational theorists have realized. I cannot decide whether Theodore Sizer's decision to undertake this task says as much about his masochism as it does about his recognition that our society can no longer afford to let schools continue as they have been. Personal diagnosis aside, he deserves the title of statesman because he not only had an overarching vision of what schools should be in terms of our national interests and purposes, as well as in terms of the meaningfulness of schooling for students over their lifetimes, but also because he committed himself to bring the matter to public attention and to instill in that public the resolve to do what needs to be done. He knew what he was getting into—that there would be successes and failures and that we had to deepen our understanding of the enormity of the task. In asking Drs. Muncey and McQuillan to do ethnographies of several schools he ensured that our understanding would be deepened, that the maxim "the more you know the more you need to know" would be confirmed again. And indeed it has been.

In this book we find compelling description and analysis of the excitement, perturbations, and dynamics that are the inevitable consequences of the institutional-change process. We get these with a clarity, comprehensiveness, and forthrightness that may well be unique in the educational literature. Only those imprisoned in a utopian optimism—or abysmally ignorant of the culture of schools—would expect a Hollywood success story. The inadequacies of our schools, like the devastations of cancer, are and should be puzzles for which there is no one simple explanation and certainly no one solution in the sense of "cure." What we get in this book is not only superb description in the best ethnographic tradition but also a kind of compass directing the attention of future interveners to what does and does not help desired changes. Not everyone will read that compass in the same way, but no one will finish this book without having an enriched understanding of what we are up against in school reform. We have had a surfeit of simple formulations and simple answers justifying the wisdom of Mencken's remark that for every social problem there is a simple answer that is wrong.

I am grateful for the opportunity to thank Sizer, Muncey, and McQuillan for a book with which everyone in the arena of educational reform will have to contend. With this book the literature on school reform—its rationale, methodology, and balanced assessment—has taken a giant step to maturity.

Seymour B. Sarason

ACKNOWLEDGMENTS

When we entered into formal research agreements with the Coalition of Essential Schools and with the individual schools we studied, we agreed to use pseudonyms for schools and for any and all individuals (except Theodore R. Sizer, the Coalition's founder) represented in our writings. This is a common practice in ethnographic research and writing, but it has the unintended consequence of rendering it impossible to properly thank the very people who made the work possible and useful. Nevertheless, we gratefully acknowledge the support and encouragement of teachers, staff, and students at the eight study schools who gave fully of their time—a very precious commodity—so that we could learn about their work and their impressions of the reforms taking place or under consideration. We also thank all the staff members of the Coalition of Essential Schools, who freely and graciously gave of their time and insights throughout our research.

Theodore R. Sizer and Holly M. Houston (two-thirds of the Coalition staff at the time we began our research) welcomed the suggestion that a long-term ethnographic study of the fledgling Coalition could shed light on how and why change happens. Given the high rate of failure that exists among educational reform initiatives, their decision to encourage our work was a brave one. Throughout our work, we appreciated the Coalition staff's openness to our inquiries and support of our research, not only when our attention was focused on the schools but also when we turned our attention to the staff's work.

The Exxon Education Foundation made possible our research with a generous series of grants to Brown University and the Coalition of Essential Schools on our behalf. We thank Exxon and our two program officers, L. Scott Miller and Philip Merchant, for their interest in and support of our work.

Throughout the analysis and writing phases of our work we received useful and much-needed advice from an advisory board of educational researchers that included Philip Cusick of Michigan State University, Mary Metz of the University of Wisconsin (Madison), Arthur Powell of Cambridge, Massachusetts, and Hervé Varenne of Teachers College, Columbia University. Seymour B. Sarason spent hours with us reviewing our writings and probing us to think further about its consequences. We thank these individuals for encouraging us and supporting our work.

Many thanks are also extended to the following people who read and commented on multiple drafts of the manuscript: Liliana Costa, Martha Gardner, Elaine D. Gustafson, Robert Hampel, Emily Mathis, and Sarah C. Uhl. Two anonymous reviewers for Yale University Press gave us helpful suggestions about the manuscript. Gladys Topkis, Eliza Childs, and the staff at Yale University Press carefully guided and assisted us through a long revision process with patience and tact, and we thank them for all their work on our behalf.

We also thank our spouses, Israel Ruiz and Jody McQuillan, for their support, encouragement, and understanding during the many years we have been involved with the research study and the preparation of this book.

We dedicate this book to the teachers, administrators, and students at our study schools to honor the work they do every day and their commitment to improving education for all children.

I

INTRODUCTION

1

THE COALITION OF ESSENTIAL SCHOOLS

Horace knows that the status quo *is* the problem. It forces him to compromise in ways that cripple his teaching, his ability to create thoughtful students. Compromises are always necessary in the real world, Horace admits; and the issue, then, is which compromises will serve the students best. Only by examining the existing compromises, however painful that may be, and moving beyond them to better compromises, can one form a more thoughtful school. And only in thoughtful schools can thoughtful students be hatched. —THEODORE R. SIZER, *Horace's School*

A sure alternative is not self-evident. Trial is needed. Experiments must be ambitious and long range; schools are complicated places and attitudes—those of teachers, students and others—must change as well as do the structures of the schools in which they work. This takes time, political protection and patience. —THEODORE R. SIZER, "Précis of the Statement on the Improvement of American Secondary Schools to the National Governors' Association"

This is a book about change in schools—the challenges of creating and shaping change; the rationales offered for mandating change; resistance and other obstacles to change; and the role of dialogue, action, and reflection in nurturing, sustaining, redirecting, and assessing efforts at change. We look at the struggles for power and control that accompany and largely define educational reform work and the negotiations that reform advocates and opponents engage in to direct, protect, interrupt, or challenge it. The educational reform movement we focus on is the

Coalition of Essential Schools (CES), an increasingly prominent participant in the national discourse about educational reform and in policy
making on the state and national levels.

The Coalition of Essential Schools is a school reform movement
based on the nine common principles listed below:

Common Principles of the Coalition of Essential Schools

1. The school should focus on helping adolescents learn to use their
   minds well. Schools should not attempt to be "comprehensive" if
   such a claim is made at the expense of the school's central intellectual purpose.

   academic emphasis

2. The school's goals should be simple: that each student master a
   limited number of essential skills and areas of knowledge. While
   these skills and areas will, to varying degrees, reflect the traditional academic disciplines, the program's design should be
   shaped by the intellectual and imaginative powers and competen-
   cies that students need, rather than necessarily by "subjects" as
   conventionally defined. The aphorism less-is-more should dominate: curricular decisions should be guided by the aim of thorough
   student mastery and achievement rather than by an effort merely
   to cover content.

   less is more

3. The school's goals should apply to all students, while the means to
   these goals will vary as those students themselves vary. School
   practice should be tailor-made to meet the needs of every group or
   class of adolescents.

   *no tracking
   meet all needs*

4. Teaching and learning should be personalized to the maximum
   feasible extent. Efforts should be directed toward a goal that no
   teacher have direct responsibility for more than eighty students. To
   capitalize on this personalization, decisions about the details of
   the course of study, the use of students' and teachers' time and the
   choice of teaching materials and specific pedagogies must be unre-
   servedly placed in the hands of the principal and staff.

   *personalized
   80:1*

5. The governing practical metaphor of the school should be student-
   as-worker rather than the more familiar metaphor of teacher-as-
   deliverer-of-instructional-services. Accordingly, a prominent pedagogy will be coaching, to provoke students to learn how to learn
   and thus to teach themselves.

6. Students entering secondary school studies are those who can show competence in language and elementary mathematics. Students of traditional high school age but not yet at appropriate levels of competence to enter secondary school studies will be provided intensive remedial work to assist them quickly to meet these standards. The diploma should be awarded upon a successful final demonstration of mastery for graduation—an "Exhibition." This exhibition by the student of his or her grasp of the central skills and knowledge of the school's program may be jointly administered by the faculty and by higher authorities. As the diploma is awarded when earned, the school's program proceeds with no strict age grading and with no system of "credits earned" by "time spent" in class. The emphasis is on the students' demonstration that they can do important things.

7. The tone of the school should explicitly and self-consciously stress values of unanxious expectation ("I won't threaten you but I expect much of you"), of trust (until abused), and of decency (the values of fairness, generosity, and tolerance). Incentives appropriate to the school's particular students and teachers should be emphasized, and parents should be treated as essential collaborators.

8. The principal and teachers should perceive themselves as generalists first (teachers and scholars in general education) and specialists second (experts in but one particular discipline). Staff should expect multiple obligations (teacher-counselor-manager) and have a sense of commitment to the entire school.

9. Ultimate administrative and budget targets should include, in addition to total student loads per teacher of eighty or fewer pupils, substantial time for collective planning by teachers, competitive salaries for staff, and an ultimate per pupil cost not to exceed that at traditional schools by more than 10 percent. To accomplish this, administrative plans may have to show the phased reduction or elimination of some services now provided students in many traditional comprehensive secondary schools (Coalition of Essential Schools 1985).

This set of ideas about what constitutes better schooling for today's youth was formulated by Theodore R. Sizer, professor of education at Brown University, on the basis of several years of research in American secondary schools. Sizer's writings, including *Horace's Compromise*,[1] and subsequent public presentations brought his view of the inadequacies of secondary schooling in the United States to prominence in the education community. The enthusiasm teachers and school administrators expressed for his ideas encouraged Sizer to collaborate with interested schools and to put together a small staff based at Brown University in Providence, Rhode Island. The staff and schools became the Coalition of Essential Schools, an effort committed to locally defining and implementing the common principles. As chairman of the Coalition, which was founded in 1984, Sizer also raised more than $30 million by 1991 and more than $100 million by 1994 for this reform effort.

Many view Ted Sizer as the charismatic leader of the Coalition.[2] A report by the Coalition's Committee on Evaluation, a group of prominent educators charged with assessing the earliest efforts of this reform program, suggests something of Sizer's appeal:

> Why did [schools] join? Commitment to or attraction towards the [common] principles was undoubtedly the major reason why most schools rallied to the Coalition banner. It is probably impossible to draw a clear line between principles and personality, however . . . the personal qualities of Ted Sizer were the most critical factor for many of the schools who joined. Many of them single out a specific occasion when they met Ted or heard him talk about the Coalition as a precipitating event. . . . Sizer embodied a sane rebirth of progressive education principles combined with a rigorous emphasis on better standards in the form of exhibitions. He brought a Harvard dean's status, a historian's confidence and a boyish charm to discussion of educational reform. He inspired trust and he demonstrated the ability to connect diverse audiences and create networks of support. . . . He created the discourse that is the Coalition. (1988: 9–10)

In contrast to much rhetoric of the early and mid-1980s, Sizer's

---

1. The planning for this research, "A Study of High Schools," began in 1979. Fieldwork was conducted during the 1981–82 academic year. In addition to *Horace's Compromise*, two books were produced by Sizer's colleagues in this effort: *The Shopping Mall High School* (1985) by Arthur Powell, Eleanor Farrar, and David Cohen and *The Last Little Citadel* (1986) by Robert Hampel.

2. See, e.g., the Coalition of Essential Schools, Committee on Evaluation (1988) and Muncey and McQuillan (1993b).

approach to school reform did not include criticizing teachers. Instead, he sought to illuminate how the "mindlessness" of American secondary schooling forced even well-intended teachers to compromise their ideals: "Most jobs in the real world have a gap between what would be nice and what is possible. One adjusts. The tragedy for many high school teachers is that their gap is a chasm, not crossed by reasonable and judicious adjustments" (Sizer 1982: 37B). Further setting him apart was his insistence, in *Horace's Compromise,* that teachers had to be at the heart of school reform: "As effective teaching absolutely requires substantial autonomy, *the decentralizing of substantial authority to the persons close to the students is essential.* 'Downtown' continues to set goals, but decisions about how teacher and student time is organized, the materials and the approaches used, and the way staff are deployed must be at the school level, or, in large schools, at house (or other subschool) levels" (Sizer 1984: 195; emphasis in original).

Emphasizing the difficulties and constraints that surround teaching, Sizer nonetheless challenged teachers to address these problems. In his view, many aspects of traditional schooling needed critical reexamination. At a 1987 gathering of faculty, administrators, and students from Coalition schools, Sizer discussed various dimensions of the Coalition's reform platform, especially the goal of creating thoughtful students who would become thoughtful adults:

> We believe that the primary purpose of school is to develop students' intellect; that is essential for everybody in society . . . [and] this applies to all children without exception, every single last one. . . . Since intellectual education is very difficult, only a simple program can present it—thus, less-is-more. That is, it's better to understand a few essential things well than [have] trivialized knowledge of lots of things. . . . We believe that one learns best by doing, not by being told, but by being engaged. The same is true for students; to learn well, they must be engaged. . . . So the students need to be the workers, not the teachers. . . . Also, we need to respect [students'] differences. . . . The teacher has to know her/his students. You can't have 175 students, like [in] most big [city schools]. You can't know their minds and understand how they make mistakes. We want 80-to-1 [student:teacher ratios], at a reasonable price. . . . We need to develop students' minds and

character. Thoughtful people in algebra class are thoughtful people in life . . . decent people, inclined toward fairness, generosity, and tolerance. (Sizer 1987)

For Sizer, educational reform meant not only rethinking schooling at the local level, but also taking on larger political and philosophical issues: "That word 'essential' in the name of our project has a double meaning. On one hand it is essential that we restructure overloaded and ineffective schools. And our project also involves figuring out what is essential in the way of education. The toughest part is 'the politics of subtraction.' . . . You have to decide what is fundamental" (Sizer, quoted in Brandt 1988: 34–35).

Consistent with his assertion that to improve schooling power had to be decentralized, Sizer also believed strongly in local interpretation of the ideals he promoted. Thus, the common principles that undergird Coalition reform are ambiguous by design; each member school interprets them within its own cultural and institutional context and determines its specific approaches to change. The Coalition central staff does not offer member schools a model or even a suggested starting point for change but rather emphasizes local control and autonomy. Nonetheless, in their first reform endeavors, Coalition central staff focused their efforts on the *triangle of learning* (the relationship between student, teacher, and subject matter), locating the individual classroom at the center of schools' reform efforts. The assumption was that changing the relationships, incentives, content, and pedagogy in individual classrooms could guide the change process schoolwide.

At its inception, the Coalition was viewed as a partnership among its twelve charter member schools and a small central staff. The earliest member schools usually were drawn to the Coalition after the principal, a group of teachers, or someone in the district office read *Horace's Compromise* or heard Sizer speak during his promotional tour for the book or at an educational conference. The three-person central staff was formed to help give shape to a university–secondary school collaboration that was guided by a philosophy, not by a program or set of membership expectations. When the first schools began implementing Coalition ideas, there were three central staff members, one being a part-time graduate student assistant. The staff visited member schools, assisted with fundraising, organized and staffed professional development workshops for teachers, and wrote and reflected upon the implications of making the common principles central to teachers' daily work. The perception of the small staff was that they were supporting, not directing, the work of twelve schools committed to experimenting with change guided by the common principles.

Fundraising was an important aspect of the central staff's and, most particularly, Sizer's early work. Membership in the Coalition did not entail paying fees to the Coalition central staff or to Brown University, nor did it entitle a member school to funding to assist with reform work. The Coalition did fundraising to support research and development work by the Brown-based staff and to underwrite travel to meetings and to schools. Further, on a case-by-case basis, schools were assisted in their searches for external funds to support their reform work. Some schools received thousands of dollars in foundation grant money as a result of their affiliation with the Coalition; others funded travel to Coalition events and any school-based reform work largely from existing school budgets.

From an initial membership of twelve charter schools in December 1985, the Coalition grew in two years to fifty-six schools nationwide. In fall and winter 1987, the central staff faced what they saw as a major turning point. Despite the Coalition's growth in membership and its increasing prominence in school reform, some advisory committee members and some funders argued that the Coalition would lack credibility unless it could include more schools and replicate its successes in a wider range of educational settings (Coalition of Essential Schools, Committee on Evaluation 1988). They worried that the Coalition lacked the requisite scale to make a national impact, even if a significant number of the existing member schools changed fundamentally as a result of Coalition-based reforms.

The central staff was also open to expanding the reform network because of a growing realization that many Coalition schools were finding schoolwide change difficult to implement. Schools that the central staff thought had the leadership and faculty commitment to initiate substantive change were running into problems. Creating change was proving neither predictable nor straightforward. Further, the central staff began to feel that focusing on classroom-based change might not engender the scope of change they considered necessary. Consequently, though still emphasizing the need for students to be at the center of a school's rethinking of its mission, structure, and curriculum, the central staff came to advocate a wider range of strategies, including seeking political affiliations intended to create top-down support for grassroots reform and promoting broader conceptions of school restructuring, such as changing the schedule and the bureaucratic atmosphere of many schools. In the opinion of some central staff members, expanding Coalition membership would likely lead to a sizable number of changed schools, and this would help them better understand the change process.

With these concerns in mind, in 1988 the Coalition formed a partnership with the Education Commission of the States (ECS)—a "non-profit, nationwide interstate compact formed to help governors, state legislators, state education officials and others develop policies to improve education" (Re:Learning 1989: 6). The partnership, which came to be known as Re:Learning, sought to link school change "from the schoolhouse to the statehouse." According to this plan, states would join Re:Learning and underwrite reform work in a number of schools throughout the state; the Coalition would focus on school-site reform; and ECS would work with state and local governmental agencies to develop policy environments conducive to school-site change (for example, procuring waivers if faculty felt restricted by existing regulations) and to encourage state-level support for schools interested in Coalition membership (Healey 1988).

The new partnership helped to leverage funds for reform work—not simply from legislatures and departments of education in Re:Learning states, but from additional sources that were drawn to its ambitious national agenda. The Coalition hoped that Re:Learning would encourage schools to join because they would have access to state-allocated funds and support that CES central staff alone could not provide. When it became apparent that many schools in states that were unlikely to join Re:Learning for a lack of support among state legislators nonetheless wanted to join CES, the central staff hired regionally based coordinators to work with the schools and to organize regional conferences and workshops.

As the number of member schools grew and the scope of Coalition reform expanded, the Brown-based staff increased from three persons in 1985 to twenty-eight full-time employees by 1990 and to forty-two by

1992.[3] The original staff members had secondary school teaching experience and formal expertise in policy or curriculum development. As the central staff expanded, personnel with experience in teaching and administration were recruited, but they increasingly hired support personnel to handle administrative responsibilities, particularly membership inquiries and conference planning. By 1992, there were approximately two administrative staff for each person involved with program research, development, and outreach.

The Re:Learning partnership together with the creation of CES regions decentralized much of the central staff's work, offered the potential for more direct support for member schools, and promoted growth in membership. In October 1990, for instance, there were 74 CES member schools, which were implementing new practices based on the common principles and had formally applied for membership; 6 Re:Learning states; 9 states considering Re:Learning membership; and 6 CES regions with funded coordinators working to recruit schools and nurture them through the change process. By January 1992, there were 120 CES schools, 21 "networking" schools (schools that were planning for change but had not yet applied for membership), 151 "exploring" schools (schools researching and discussing the common principles), and nine Re:Learning states. Forty member schools were in Re:Learning states, as were most of the networking and exploring schools. Most of the Coalition schools were secondary schools, although some middle and primary schools had joined.

Although the Coalition's growth has been continuous since its inception, expansion has accentuated a tension between depth and breadth that runs through the entire reform movement. For the central staff, this tension has translated into questions such as: How many member schools must the Coalition have in order to be taken seriously by funders and the general education community? How big is too big to be effective in supporting schools in understanding and making the changes necessary? Some staff members felt that schools would change more rapidly and genuinely if the Coalition staff spent more time working with them and deepening the classroom-based work. Others argued

---

3. For further discussion of the growth and expansion of CES central staff, see Muncey and McQuillan (1993b).

that the staff should limit their time in individual schools and focus on broadening the audience for Coalition ideas and assist schools' efforts more indirectly—through conferences, workshops, and symposia.

In the Coalition's history, both perspectives have played key roles. For instance, certain projects have been designed to help faculty in CES schools deepen their understanding of Coalition philosophy and practice. The IBM project, for instance, allowed the central staff to work with a select number of CES schools to help them promote change by utilizing computer technologies—from using CD-ROM databases to expand their research facilities to exchanging ideas with other Coalition schools through a computer-based network. In contrast, indirect efforts by the central staff to promote Coalition reform include professional development opportunities for teachers in CES schools, workshops organized to educate school personnel and district- and state-level personnel in school reform strategies, conferences to introduce Coalition ideas to interested schools, and the creation of categories of premembership for schools considering CES affiliation. The allocation of resources, however, has always favored approaches that led to steady growth in the number of Coalition member schools, Re:Learning states, and Coalition regions. In part this stems from funders' belief that the Coalition would be taken seriously only if there were more member schools. It also reflects the central staff's recognition that it is difficult to isolate and nurture the most promising schools—precisely for the same reasons they maintained that each school must design its own reform agenda. That is, local community factors, intraschool politics, and such unexpected events as turnover of key administrators can affect a school's progress in reform implementation. With these concerns in mind, the staff opted for a safety-in-numbers approach to general membership while continuing to select promising schools for projects designed to deepen Coalition ideas.

This policy of continued expansion had specific consequences for central staff members and influenced the nature of the Coalition. For one thing, as the organization grew, the responsibilities for central staff increased. For example, early in its history staff members often supported fledgling efforts by working directly with member schools. As a consequence of program expansion, however, they had to devote more time to recruiting new schools and addressing related political concerns. Expanding CES membership, the geographical spread of the movement, the growing variety of member schools, the increased emphasis on university–secondary school collaborative projects, and the perceived need to incorporate more actors into the school reform process have all contributed to central staff members' shifting perceptions of their appropriate roles.

In our research we found that discussions at the member schools about what—if anything—needed to change in member schools and how and why change should occur often reflected substantive differences among school faculties. Yet, this was initially masked for the central staff, who often worked most closely in their workshops and symposia with those interested in change. As a result they sometimes developed an impression of greater unanimity about the need for change than existed at our study schools. Site visits, the one dimension of CES work that best revealed the differences within schools to the central staff, were gradually restricted because of increasing workloads. This lack of consensus about the need for change had long-term effects on the change process at each of our study sites.

STUDYING THE COALITION

The Coalition represents only one of many school reform efforts in the United States, but it offers a productive perspective for viewing school reform more generally. For instance, the first member schools joined in 1984, shortly after the publication of the National Commission on Excellence in Education's *A Nation at Risk* and Ted Sizer's *Horace's Compromise*.[4] In addition, Coalition schools represent a cross section of American education and include public, private, parochial, urban, suburban, and rural schools. The Coalition's reform platform embraces many practices common to other reform initiatives. Some of the study schools, for example, have been restructured into teams of students and teachers; others have reorganized their schedules to provide longer blocks of time for classes. Many schools implemented some measure of site-based management, and a number have organized professional-

4. *A Nation at Risk* (1983) was one of a series of reports published in the early 1980s that emphasized how ill prepared U.S. high school graduates were for either higher education or the world of work, the country's growing inability to compete internationally, and the potential long-term consequences of these ills for American society.

development activities. The schools we studied also experimented with alternative assessment and redesigned their curricula in terms of fundamental or "essential" questions—all with the goal of making students more active learners (see Wiggins 1987a, 1989, 1991). Further mirroring broader developments in school reform, the Coalition has encountered difficulties implementing its ideas beyond the limited experimentation in individual classrooms and pilot projects and in the larger arena of schoolwide change (see Firestone et al. 1989; McQuillan and Muncey 1991, 1994; Muncey and McQuillan 1990, 1992a, 1992b, 1993a; Wehlage et al. 1992).

The Coalition of Essential Schools initiated its reform effort with the intention of "creating schools where the rigorous use of the mind for all kids, without exception, is the highest priority" (Sizer 1988a). To achieve this goal, the Coalition proposed changing many aspects of traditional school life—including student-teacher relations, classroom pedagogy, departmental structures, and budget priorities. To help them understand what did and did not change and why, we were enlisted by the central staff and member schools to create an ethnographic record of their efforts. The research design we adopted focused on three aspects of the Coalition's reform movement in eight of the twelve original member schools: (1) central staff activities and their role in the development of the reform movement; (2) interaction between the central staff and individual schools; and (3) the efforts undertaken at some Coalition schools.

Our work was not a formal educational evaluation of the Coalition of Essential Schools. Rather, because of the Coalition's emphasis on local interpretation of the common principles, we conducted most of our research in individual schools and sought to document broadly what occurred by focusing on two general questions: How are the common principles interpreted by students, teachers, and administrators in Coalition schools? And, how are they implemented? The research entailed observing classes, various school events, faculty and administrative planning meetings, and other school-based activities. We interviewed students, teachers (both Coalition supporters and opponents), and administrators about their work, about proposed or implemented changes, and about their future plans. We conducted a survey of fifteen hundred students in Coalition schools and collected such related data about the schools as newspaper articles, yearbooks, faculty memos, and correspondence between the schools and Coalition central staff. Our research focused on the school sites, but we also attended Coalition staff meetings, conferences, and workshops; interviewed central staff members; attended many Coalition-sponsored professional development activities; and stayed abreast of developments within the central staff. We began our work in August 1986, when the study schools were in the initial stages of restructuring and the Coalition itself had been in existence for about a year and a half. Data collection concluded in June 1991.

The eight school sites were selected to represent the diversity among Coalition members at that time, including schools from different geographic regions (New England and the Mid-Atlantic), schools with differing racial and ethnic compositions, and whole-school reform efforts and school-within-a-school projects. School-within-a-school (SWAS) programs, designed to pilot CES ideas with some faculty and part of the student population, were common. Half of our study sites selected this approach to change, as did half of the original twelve member schools. Using a SWAS approach allowed a school to encourage willing faculty to experiment with reform ideas without committing all faculty to the changes being undertaken.

Six of the eight are public high schools, one is a private high school, and one is a newly created secondary school in a district of choice. Three of the public schools are urban schools with enrollments of approximately one thousand students, with two of them serving mostly students of color. Two schools were suburban high schools with substantial per pupil expenditures and reputations as excellent schools; one enrolled two hundred fifty students and the other nearly one thousand. One school was a small rural school. The private school, too, was small, with fewer than two hundred students. Before joining the Coalition, the schools varied in their commitment to change. Only two held faculty referenda on whether to join the Coalition; the others joined at the initiative of a principal, headmaster, or superintendent. Administrative turnover was common at these schools. During our research, each study site experienced a change in the principal, the headmaster, or the Coalition coordinator (an administrative position commonly created by CES schools to oversee their programs). Changing demographics were at issue in most of our study schools as well. For example, at one school the student population fell by nearly 30 percent over the course of our research. Pseudonyms are used for the schools and for the individuals mentioned at each site. (Our methodological approach is discussed in more detail in the Appendix.)

ETHNOGRAPHY AND EDUCATIONAL CHANGE

Although educational change is difficult to study because one does not see it happening, our five-year ethnographic research design helped us to understand the forces associated with change (or resistance to change) in an ongoing fashion. Most Coalition programs began with enthusiasm and fanfare, but over five years these efforts became more routine and, in some cases, more representative of typical school life. Further, since no one could predict the consequences of directed change at the outset, the long-term approach allowed us to identify key developments as they emerged and to adjust our research foci as activities and priorities shifted at our study sites.

Ethnography was also well suited for studying educational change because of its holistic orientation. That is, we assumed that systemic connections exist among myriad aspects of school life. To advocate intentional and directed change, as any reform movement must, was necessarily to suggest altering the relations among component parts. Change in any aspect—whether structural, curricular, or ideological— introduced the potential for change in all facets of schooling. Moreover, the common principles targeted multiple aspects of school life for change. Our ethnographic perspective, then, helped us to see how changes attempted in one facet of schooling influenced other areas of school life.

We also adopted a holistic approach to understanding how the various participants in school reform (students, teachers, and administrators) interpreted Coalition philosophy and reacted to change. Whether we were studying a recent innovation adopted by a school or a more routine part of school life, we sought to understand how all participants were interpreting these events. Further, when we looked at specific changes schools had implemented, we sought to understand how various school personnel viewed the process by which the innovation had emerged, as well as the implementation and subsequent reactions to the reform itself. We also looked at multiple levels of the educational system (Cusick 1991; Sarason 1990). For instance, when examining the effects of a specific pedagogical reform, we considered how change affected individual teachers, students, and administrators, the school as a whole, and, finally, the central staff and the Coalition more broadly.

As with most ethnographic research, our task was not to evaluate these efforts but to watch closely what happened in the study schools and between them and the central staff. Over time, our interest in the professional lives of those we studied and our nonevaluative stance helped us to develop rapport with many who collaborated in our research. By exploiting the flexibility of ethnographic field research—in particular, its long-term nature and its commitment to seeking multiple points of view—we gained a broad sense of what changed at each school site as well as a detailed understanding of why people said they felt and acted as they did.

Throughout this book we focus attention on two levels of the educational system: the school-based and the classroom-based change efforts undertaken in Coalition schools. Our five years of ethnographic research have made it clear to us that contemporary school reform efforts in the United States are both institutional and individual phenomena. That is, most reform platforms, whether explicit or implied, have implications for both the structure of schools (the schedule, administrative responsibilities, and graduation requirements) and the roles and responsibilities of individuals within that structure (students, teachers, and administrators). We have therefore organized our book according to these two perspectives, as they can reveal very different understandings of change, often within the same reform effort at the same site. For instance, whereas many schools we studied found it difficult to effect schoolwide change, some individual teachers and teams of teachers changed their pedagogy, classroom organization, curriculum, and assessment practices in novel ways. At other sites where schools were restructured in apparently significant ways, classroom instruction still seemed quite traditional. Thus, school reform could look markedly different depending on whether it was examined from an individual or a schoolwide perspective.

Finally, aside from the concluding chapter, our writing is embedded in our informants' worlds. The descriptions, explanations, and analyses use largely the terminology, beliefs, and explanations of those we studied. Although this approach may make us appear overly sympathetic to our "natives," our goal is to provide descriptions and explanations that serve as plausible understandings of others' lived experiences. We immersed ourselves in the worlds of those we researched, not as a means to validate their actions, but as a means to appreciate the complexity of their lives—an understanding that we hope will inform ongoing and future efforts at school change.

Observing the Coalition reform effort has shown that creating and sustaining school change is a complex process with many constraints—political, social, cultural, and financial, to name a few. American secondary schools have existed in their present state for nearly a hundred years. Changing such structures and practices as departmental divisions, a hierarchical bureaucracy, dominant pedagogies, and an overall schedule structured according to a 180-day school year, a five-, six-, or seven-period school day, and forty-five-minute periods requires changing the habits of many different actors with often widely differing interests. And to attempt to change an institution while simultaneously running it generates additional concerns—for one, learning new roles as one is trying to unlearn old habits.

We hope that this book will help clarify why some Coalition reform efforts have been sustained while others have stalled or been disbanded, why change efforts divided some faculties while others found common ground and a sense of shared purpose, and how all our study schools were somehow changed as a consequence of their collective reflection about whether current practices were in students' best interests.

One final point we wish to make in this introduction concerns the book(s) we did not write. Other analytic frames could be used to understand what occurred at these schools: for instance, gender, race, class, and conflict-driven perspectives come to mind as analytic orientations that could generate valuable insights into school life. Although we respect these approaches, we chose an interactionist perspective and attempted to move between micropolitical (Blase 1991; Ball 1988) and structural (Cusick 1991; Metz 1990; Powell, Farrar, and Cohen 1985) explanations that kept our focus on educational change or the lack thereof.

ORGANIZATION OF THE BOOK

Educational reform can look quite different depending on whether one adopts an institutional or individual perspective. So that the reader can appreciate these two sides to educational reform, we present the material in two sections. The first section looks at specific schools undergoing change. The second offers more narrowly focused studies that describe the efforts of individual teachers and administrators to promote reform.

In chapters 2 through 6 we take a broad view of educational reform and offer case studies of five study schools as they attempted to implement change. We included these cases, first, because demographically they are representative of the schools that joined the Coalition in its earliest years and, second, because they illustrate the range of experiences our study schools encountered during their efforts at change. Generalizing from these five case studies, in chapter 7 we offer a comparative analysis of what can be learned by looking at the school as the unit of change.

In chapters 8 to 12 we consider how schoolwide reform initiatives supported individual efforts at change. In chapter 8 we examine one teacher's attempts to change his pedagogy, curriculum, and assessment techniques over a four-year period. Chapters 9 and 10 use the classroom as the unit of analysis. A course in which resistant students negotiated the quantity and quality of work they would be expected to do is the focus of chapter 9. In chapter 10 we use a day-in-the-life approach to examine some of the ways teachers sought to promote more active learning among their students. In chapter 11 we contrast the leadership styles of principals in two study schools and examine differences in how they defined their role in the school change process and how these differences influenced their schools' effort at reform. Some generalizations derived from considering these individual efforts at change are set forth in chapter 12. In conclusion, in chapter 13 we situate Coalition reform in some larger contexts, moving outside the Coalition's ways of talking about itself to look at school reform in American society more generally.

II

SCHOOL-BASED CASE STUDIES

2

"STUDENTS FEEL THAT THIS IS *THEIR* PROGRAM"
LEWIS HIGH'S ESSENTIAL SCHOOL PROGRAM

> In the larger school, classes were so large that teachers
> could only lecture. In the Essential School we're able to de-
> velop a real relationship with our teachers. We're almost
> like a family. —AN ESSENTIAL SCHOOL STUDENT

> Observers talking to students, in small groups and one-
> on-one, find that they [students] have a special sense of en-
> thusiasm about the [Essential School] program and their
> place within it. They appear to be more interested not only
> in the schoolwork they are currently doing, but in going to
> school in general. Their aspirations in life are high. —A
> FOUNDATION REPORT

Lewis High, located in a mid-Atlantic city with 750,000 residents, enrolls an entirely African-American student population. Approximately
three-quarters of the faculty are also African-American. Lewis is one of
nine "zoned," or neighborhood, comprehensive schools among the
city's seventeen high schools. Generally, the top students in the city
attend one of five academic or three vocational-technical magnet
schools, for which students must apply and meet entrance requirements. The remaining students enter the comprehensive high schools,
which, as one foundation report observed, usually serve areas of the city
that "many of the higher achieving children have left for city-wide [aca-
demic and magnet] schools. . . . Of all the high schools, the lowest
attendance, worst scores, and the highest dropout rates are found in the
comprehensive high schools."[1]

1. For issues of confidentiality, we offer no references for the foundation reports
cited in this chapter.

In 1985, when Lewis first became involved with the Coalition of Essential Schools, the school enrolled nearly two thousand students. The school, however, was forced to relocate while structural repairs (asbestos removal) were undertaken, and from 1988 through 1991 Lewis High shared a building with another city high school. This relocation had several ramifications. For one, enrollment decreased by approximately nine hundred students, precipitating a concern with job security among the faculty. Also, the times of the normal school day were changed; it began at 10 A.M. and ended at 4 P.M.

In some respects, Lewis is very much an inner-city high school. School doors are often locked or chained to restrict the entry of outsiders. To limit vandalism, many windows are made of Plexiglas. Before students are allowed into the building, teachers and administrators check their identification cards and make certain that they have regulation mesh book bags so they cannot conceal weapons. The school's dress code forbids students to wear baseball caps, leather jackets, or gold jewelry—both to avoid the theft of valuable items and to distinguish Lewis students from outsiders. Security guards and administrators all carry walkie-talkies. Most classes enroll more than thirty students. And collectively, students fail more than one-third of the courses they take.

Yet Lewis has a comfortable, "small school" feel as well. In the classrooms and hallways, students, teachers, and administrators seem at ease with one another. Violence is rare. Staff and students alike openly acknowledge pride in their school. An indicator of this pride, the classrooms and hallways are clean and graffiti-free. Lewis also offers many extracurricular activities, including a range of athletic teams and music and drama groups. In its permanent location, Lewis is unquestionably a "neighborhood school," and many families choose to send more than one child there even though they could apply to the academic high schools or vocational-technical magnets.

These two sides of life at Lewis High were especially apparent during basketball games. Before entering the gym, students had to show an ID from one of the participating schools; students from other schools were not allowed to attend for fear of what interschool rivalries might generate. Throughout the games a few administrators scanned the crowd for potential problems. At one game, a Lewis teacher pointed out a student whose younger brother was killed in junior high because he resisted an attempt to steal his warm-up jacket. At another game, a teacher explained that a student observed walking with a limp had been a prominent athlete but could no longer play sports because he had been shot with a Saturday night special, a homemade gun often used by gang members. Another faculty member said of a young man in a silver Peugeot, "There's a successful Lewis grad who's working in the 'service economy'"—he was dealing drugs.

In contrast to these stereotypically urban aspects of the basketball games, elements of school and community life commonly associated with what Sara Lawrence Lightfoot termed "the good high school" (Lightfoot 1983) were also apparent. At both boys' and girls' games, school spirit was pronounced as spectators and cheerleaders enthusiastically supported the teams, and both sides were always well represented. The games were also community events attended by all ages—from babies in snowsuits to adults. The spirit and camaraderie among spectators made the security precautions and accounts of violence seem incongruous.

LEWIS HIGH AND THE COALITION

Lewis High School became affiliated with the Coalition through the initiative of a superintendent familiar with Ted Sizer's work. After considering a number of schools where the city could pilot a Coalition program, the superintendent found a more-than-willing volunteer in David Johnson, Lewis High's principal. Through an informal application process—the superintendent and principal expressed interest in the Coalition and Sizer and his staff wanted to include a number of urban schools in this effort—Lewis High became a charter member of the Coalition, and Johnson recruited faculty willing to participate in the program.

Lewis's first Essential School program involved a team of four teachers (English, social studies, science, and Latin) who volunteered to share a group of 150 ninth-grade students (a normal teaching load in the school system) and had common planning time for one school year (1985–86). Aside from the common planning time set aside for this team, the school department made no special provisions for the Essential School. During this year the team explored various teaching and assessment strategies and regularly shared their experiences with one another. The following summer (1986), teachers from the Essential School and other faculty attended Coalition workshops and a conference on helping teachers promote critical thinking among their students. They held workshops at Lewis with Coalition staff members as facilitators. In addition, they created a two-week lab school as an alternative to summer school for students from the Essential School who had failed courses that first year.

For the 1986–87 academic year, the city school department provided Lewis with additional funding. The Essential School staff could then expand to include one teacher from each of the school's academic departments—math, English, social studies, foreign language, and science—and hire a full-time coordinator, Carla Dobson, who oversaw the operation of the Essential School. This entailed, among other things, recruiting students, chairing meetings of the Essential School team, and helping faculty implement Coalition practices in their classrooms.

This team created a block schedule that allowed them to vary class length according to their curricular needs. In the morning, there was a two-hour time block for Essential School classes, followed by a ninety-minute period during which students ate lunch and attended an elective course. For the final two and a half hours, students returned to the Essential School. Most commonly, Essential School faculty structured these four-and-a-half hours each day so that this time was equally divided for students among their five Essential School classes. Teachers typically taught the equivalent of four class periods each day and used what had been a fifth teaching period for collaborative or individual planning. The Essential School also created its own curriculum that required students to take one more year each of science, social studies, math, and a foreign language than students in the larger school.

During this second year, the program enrolled only 116 students, a special provision the school department made for the Essential School so that the program could come closer to the eighty-to-one student-teacher ratio promoted by the Coalition. Despite its additional funding, the program could support only one team that year. Consequently, the Essential School did not keep the students who had previously participated in the program but selected a new group of ninth-graders with the understanding that, if successful, the school department would continue to fund the program so that it would include increasingly more of the school. As the program expanded in the ensuing years, the team set admission requirements. Prospective students were required to write an essay explaining why they wanted to join the program, to submit teacher recommendations, and to have had a 95-percent attendance rate the previous year. They could also be no older than fifteen (ensuring that they had failed a grade no more than once) and were no more than one level below grade in reading.

The next year (1987–88), the Essential School followed its students from the previous year into tenth grade and added a new group of ninth-graders and new faculty. The Essential School recruited teachers considered skilled and committed to their profession—aided by David Johnson's overt support and involvement. During the next two years (1988–90), the program continued to expand, adding both students and faculty, so that the Essential School encompassed all four grades. However, one unforeseen factor restricted the degree of expansion: the closing of Lewis High's original building for three years for asbestos removal. In June 1991 (the end of our research), the Essential School enrolled roughly 425 students, slightly less than half the total school population. Lewis High returned to its original site during the 1991–92 school year and planned to continue expanding its Essential School to include the entire school.

SOME CRITICAL ELEMENTS OF LEWIS'S COALITION PROGRAM

One of the objectives of Lewis's original Essential School team was to create a schedule that would allow faculty to adjust instructional time to meet their educational priorities. For instance, the team members decided that they wanted at least 75 percent of the students to pass mandatory state exams in reading, writing, math, and citizenship by the end of the sophomore year. The schedule they created helped them exceed this goal by providing time to prepare for each exam. As David Johnson explained: "A lot of city schools have had difficulty with [the state comprehensive exams], but I feel that if we put a lot of emphasis on those and get them out of the way right at the start of students' high school experience, then we're not saddled with having to worry about passing those tests later on. The students and teachers are then free to go on with regular course work. That's why we're able to do humanities with Essential School students, why we're able to put them in physics and trig." In addition to providing opportunities to prepare students for these exams, the flexible schedule allowed the program to hold graduation exhibitions, host guest speakers, and sponsor assemblies.

The schedule also complemented a related goal of the program: to personalize students' education. Outlining the rationale, David Johnson explained in a newspaper article: "I believe that if you give students individual attention, bolster their self-confidence and let them know that you expect them to perform, and perform well, they will usually give you what you expect." In a later interview Johnson elaborated: "I think that the most positive aspect of the program is the self-concept of the students. They have great expectations of their teachers and the teachers have great expectations of them. And I think that when you're dealing with urban children, that's half the battle. If you can get the expectations right, then you can start to get the priorities right."

Commenting on the Essential School's efforts to personalize student learning, the coordinator discussed how this goal required teachers to approach students differently: "Some teachers probably see us as being soft on kids . . . as giving kids unnecessary chances or opportunities to play games. . . . But you just have to rethink the whole process of assessing students' needs—about sharing with them your expectations . . . [or having] a certain amount of trust or expecting a certain amount of decency. . . . Being able to talk with kids about their strengths and weaknesses and planning to accommodate those takes time and it takes a different way of thinking." An Essential School teacher stressed how the program's structure promoted personalization: "We're closer to our students simply because we have fewer of them. We know more about individual students because we have more parental contact and individualized instruction. We know what students really can do." A third faculty member maintained that the more personalized approach significantly transformed student attitudes: "The students feel that this is *their* program. . . . We tell our students, 'You are special,' so they feel better about themselves and they want to do their best."

In some teachers' opinions, this more personalized approach to student learning led to one especially noteworthy development: a shift in expectations by both faculty and students. As an Essential School teacher commented: "Our expectations are different . . . and students know it. They know they would do less in the larger school but they feel pride in being part of the Essential School. . . . Students used to be happy doing drills in workbooks, but they don't want that anymore. Now they want to work and be stimulated."

Personalizing students' educational experiences in Lewis's Essential School has taken many forms. Students receive midterm as well as final grades each quarter. Faculty hold conferences with parents. The Essential School also sponsors assemblies intended to address student interests and needs. Discussing this aspect of the program, the coordinator, Carla Dobson, explained: "We did one session we called 'Growing Up Male and Black in the Eighties,' and we looked at the need for education. We looked at the criminal justice system and how it impacted upon your life if you get involved in it. . . . We invited younger . . . black folks so that the kids would identify with them. . . . people they would listen to. . . . We're also going to do something more with career choices and work choices. . . . We tried to look at other areas of need, not just academics, because we have as part of our goal to develop . . . the whole child."

Essential School faculty also decided to promote the benefits of a college education among their students. For instance, some program funding was used so that all students could take the Preliminary Scholastic Aptitude Tests (PSAT) at no expense to them. The faculty also held a PSAT orientation session. To give students some knowledge of college life, the Essential School sponsored tours of local colleges and universities. As Johnson explained: "You have a significant group of kids with good potential who didn't even take the PSAT because you've got to inspire them toward college and the college entrance process. . . . We're dealing with a lot of kids who have no history of college anywhere in the family. So, as a result, they're not highly motivated toward the college entrance process. That's something we're trying to deal with in the Essential School. . . . We take them on tours of college campuses. . . . I would not insist that they go to college, but I want the door to be open when they get there."

Many Essential School students concurred with these teacher and administrator perspectives. During a question-and-answer session at a Coalition symposium, for example, a student remarked: "I hadn't experienced education that was this personalized before. In the larger school, classes were so large that teachers could only lecture. In the Essential School we're able to develop a real relationship with our teachers. We're almost like a family. . . . [And] teachers not only teach facts. . . . We learn to be leaders, we learn to work in groups, and I, personally, have come to realize that learning is a constant process, not something that just takes place in classrooms." In another Coalition workshop, an Essential School student reflected on student-teacher relations: "[Teachers] are like your parents. . . . We know what to expect from them, and they know what to expect from us. We can't just turn in anything and get a [grade]. They make me really learn and they reassure me that I can learn."

Some students enjoyed the Essential School so much that they persuaded friends to enroll as well. Carla Dobson explained: "We've had a lot of kids . . . who we took in the program who were recommended by friends already in the program. . . . And we did it for one reason: we felt that if they thought enough about the kind of academic experience they were having that they wanted to share it with friends, then that was some very positive PR for us. So we took those kids in. And we haven't been sorry."

Lewis's Essential School gradually implemented an assessment innovation promoted by the Coalition: the exhibition—public, performance-based displays of academic mastery by students. In the first years of the program, some teachers developed exhibitions for their courses. Often, these replaced final exams and combined in-depth research with class presentations. By the 1989–90 school year, Lewis made the exhibition a graduation requirement. To prepare for the exhibition, in their junior year students identify a topic and begin preliminary research. During their senior year, they take a one-semester course, "Contemporary Affairs," in which faculty assist students in their research and help them develop their exhibitions. As Carla Dobson explained in a narrative to a funding agency, through this assessment strategy students should "demonstrate mastery of communication skills, written and oral, and of research skills . . . includ[ing] the use and knowledge of resources, the compilation and computation of statistical data, the relations between and relevance of facts, and the development of hypotheses and thesis documentation." The Essential School sets aside two to three weeks early in the second semester to present student exhibitions. Parents, administrators, faculty from local colleges, and other Lewis teachers are invited to attend. Committees of Essential School faculty grade the exhibitions.

The Essential School's flexible schedule, the effort to personalize students' education, and the graduation exhibition are all interrelated. The schedule provides a framework that allows faculty to individualize learning, while the exhibition—because it is largely student-defined and allows students to draw on their academic strengths—embodies this more personalized education.

CLASSROOM TEACHING AND ASSESSMENT

Although the Essential School structure differed significantly from that of most secondary schools, much classroom teaching seemed traditional, which is not to imply that it was inadequate. For instance, while studying the classification of living organisms, a biology class worked in the computer lab on drill-and-practice exercises that developed student understanding by testing their recall ability. For the class period, students answered questions posed by the computer program:

This animal is bilaterally symmetrical but is not a worm. (Answer: *mollusk*)

When an organism is classified, biologists observe its physical characteristics to assign various *(taxons)*.

As the taxonomic levels become *(smaller)* in size, the characteristics of the organisms become more similar.

Students had three chances to arrive at the correct response before the program provided the answer.

Some math classes also seemed rather typical. A geometry class began, for example, with students doing a series of problems listed on the board. The first problem asked students: "Using the diagram below, name the relationship between the following pairs of angles, given that M is parallel to L and N is parallel to P." Students identified such geometric relations as vertical, complementary, and congruent angles for ten questions. The next section (twelve examples) provided students with the measure of two angles of a triangle and asked them to determine the third. (Because the sum of the angles of a triangle equals 180 degrees, this was essentially a subtraction problem.) Students then worked on twelve problems that offered slightly more complex relations among the angles formed by transversals while the teacher assisted those who had difficulty. When students completed the work, they exchanged papers, and the teacher read off the answers and urged students to ask questions. No students asked any.

In another math class, similarly, the teacher introduced students to algebraic fractions by having them manipulate regular fractions—identifying how they determined common denominators, for instance. He then told the class how similar processes were applicable to algebraic fractions, demonstrating by doing the first example on the board. Students then worked on problems from a worksheet as the teacher provided individual help. When this work was completed, students went to the board and explained, step-by-step, how they arrived at their answers.

A midterm exam from a junior English class further illustrates how aspects of Lewis's Essential School remained traditional. The first eleven questions, all multiple choice, assessed student understanding of Plato's *Republic*—for example, "Plato's *Republic* deals with creating: (1) the good life, (2) utopia, (3) the good state, (4) the good earth." There followed four matching questions—for example, "Myth of the Metals: a lie told to the citizens of Athens to convince them that the positions given them were best for them." Students were then asked to respond to the following items:

List four virtues that would be needed by the citizens in order for the state to be perfect.

What is Socrates referring to when he gives the definition "a sort of natural harmony or agreement"?

Socrates divided the mind into three parts. List these.

The section on Plato ended with an essay question: "Both Socrates and Plato believed that in order for a state or society to be a 'good' state or society, the citizens must be trained to perform only one function, be trained from birth for that function, and be limited to strict guidelines in reference to education, social life, occupations, etc. Would you agree or disagree with this thinking? Write a five-paragraph paper in which you either defend or dispute this thinking."

The second section of the exam dealt with the novel *Great Expectations*. After six multiple choice questions, students were asked to match speakers with specific quotes. They also had an essay question: "Choose a character in *Great Expectations* who undergoes change in the novel and one who does not. Tell how life (education, experience, trials, and the like) changes the first character. Describe the static character, and explain why he or she does not change." The final section involved an analysis of the novel and included fifteen reading-comprehension questions (similar to those on the Scholastic Aptitude Test [SAT]) based on three selections from *David Copperfield*. All questions in the final two sections came from standardized tests.

Even some exhibitions appeared rather mundane. In one class, students gave presentations about ancient Greece and the Elizabethan period. For each period, students spoke about history, architecture, art, literature, music, and drama. Although students alluded to such rich topics as the universal themes evident in Shakespeare's plays, they read directly from prepared essays; there were no spontaneous questions from their classmates or teachers. Assessments in all these cases relied extensively on students' ability to recall discrete facts. Only the two essay questions from the midterm exam required them to formulate opinions, apply knowledge, or synthesize their understanding of course materials.[2]

In addition to conventional approaches to pedagogy, curriculum, and assessment by Essential School faculty, students at times responded in traditional ways to the work presented them. When teachers gave students challenging assignments, students sometimes complained, loudly and openly. When an English teacher had his class work with original sources to understand the social context for *The Scarlet Letter,* for instance, students reacted with frustration and confusion: "What are they saying? I can't understand anything." "This is stupid. It makes no sense." "I can't do this. I don't even know what they're talkin' about."

2. Other researchers who have visited Lewis High's Essential School have made similar observations. One study funded by the U.S. Department of Education suggested that this trend was tied to the nature of Lewis's student population: "Ideally, there ought to be sufficient flexibility in Coalition philosophy to allow all students to have an appropriately challenging education. But in practice, many of the classes at Lewis seem organized to help the many students who have had to overcome the myriad obstacles to learning and academic achievement endemic to our inner cities, just to stay in school and get a diploma. At Lewis, high ability students are accommodating to a curriculum designed for students who are struggling. Lewis's central goal is to not write off any students, but to help them through, if they have the courage and willingness to work."

Describing his English class in a journal, one Essential School student wrote:

> Today was the same old thing: We just came into class and the teacher told us to do any work for class that we were missing. So we sat there quietly and worked, but most of the students began to fall asleep, including me. The teacher just sat at the desk and graded papers. Two people were sent out of the class because they were talking too loud. . . . Then later in the class, the class got louder. Two days later, we saw a film about what we had been reading in class. The room was cluttered and hot and the movie put almost everyone to sleep. Some of the students were very loud at some points in the movie. After the movie, we discussed how it related to our class but the people who did not pay attention to the movie had to see it again.

Further, students sometimes left the classroom to get a drink and never returned, or forgot their textbooks, or put on makeup or perfume. When sizable numbers of students did not complete their work on time, the Essential School occasionally provided makeup periods.

BUCKING THE TREND: A SCHOOL-WITHIN-A-SCHOOL PROGRAM THAT EXPANDED

Our study schools included four school-within-a-school (SWAS) programs. Although the size, structure, and student composition differed among the schools, each SWAS program included a team(s) of teachers that worked with a particular group of students. Each program was also committed to implementing its interpretations of the Coalition's common principles. However, of these four schools only Lewis continued to expand its SWAS program throughout the five years of our research—adding more students and faculty every year but the second. Perhaps the most prominent factor promoting this continued growth was leadership. Although the superintendent who had sought Coalition membership left the position two years after Lewis had joined and her replacement had an uncertain commitment to Coalition philosophy, at the school site administrative support for Lewis's Essential School remained consistent. Many Coalition programs we studied experienced substantial administrative turnover—including principals and coordinators—

which jeopardized administrative commitment to Coalition practices and philosophy. Lewis's Essential School never faced a disruption in administrative commitment to its efforts, even though David Johnson spent one year working in the superintendent's office and was temporarily replaced by an assistant principal.[3] From the program's inception, David Johnson provided considerable support—recruiting teachers, seeking foundation grants, assigning disinterested teachers elsewhere, and reallocating staff positions. For instance, when more than thirty Lewis teachers were about to be reassigned because of decreased enrollment—a consequence of the move to a new building and citywide demographic shifts—the Essential School held meetings with faculty, and Johnson then kept those who expressed a willingness to teach in the Essential School and transferred some who were unwilling or uninterested.

Moreover, Johnson was instrumental in securing "special program" status for the Essential School. In effect, this allowed the Essential School to retain faculty with limited departmental tenure since their tenure was assessed in terms of the program, not in terms of the number of years they had been in a specific department. Although Johnson was temporarily appointed to the superintendent's office in summer 1989, he remained in close contact with the program, and his temporary replacement shared his enthusiasm for the Coalition. Commenting on his staffing plans, for example, this principal noted: "I need people who are committed and receptive to Coalition philosophy. If I get the right support—that is, if I get the staff I want—we can do some good things here at Lewis. But . . . I need to be able to say, 'This person doesn't want to be with us. Can I have a replacement?' That's just a few people— those not willing to work with the program. If I get that flexibility, there's no question that Lewis will be a model school for the city." The following year (1990), Johnson returned as Lewis's principal.

In addition, Carla Dobson, the Essential School coordinator, held a full-time administrative position throughout our research. In our other study schools, all coordinators had teaching as well as administrative responsibilities, and none held the position throughout our research period. Dobson oversaw program development, assisted with fund-

---

3. In every case where turnover occurred, it proved disruptive to the school's reform efforts.

raising, and participated in professional development efforts within Lewis and nationally as a representative of the Coalition.

A second dimension of Lewis's restructuring efforts seems tied to the growth and viability of its Essential School: Lewis made professional development a priority. Relative to other research sites, the school staff regularly attended and sponsored professional development activities, many of which were connected to the Coalition. For instance, David Johnson and Carla Dobson attended semi-annual meetings of the Principals' and Coordinators' Council, where administrators from Coalition schools discussed their work and considered strategies for future efforts. Because Lewis consistently expanded, restructured its Essential School program, and implemented various Coalition-related innovations, the Coalition central staff identified it as a school that had taken the "second step" toward schoolwide restructuring and selected Lewis to participate in the Five Schools Project, which promoted reform by providing participating schools with some additional funds and encouraging close contact with other project sites and the CES-based central staff. Lewis also participated in the Coalition's joint project with IBM, an initiative that used various computer technologies to help schools promote change.

In addition to these schoolwide Coalition projects, individual Lewis faculty and administrators participated in other Coalition-sponsored efforts. David Johnson, for example, was a Thomson fellow. In this role, he attended conferences, symposia, and workshops, most being Coalition-sponsored, where he discussed Lewis's reform efforts and its Coalition affiliation. Two Lewis teachers served as Citibank faculty, Coalition teachers who are schooled in promoting educational change and who serve as consultants to restructuring schools. Furthermore, Lewis faculty and administrators were often asked by central staff to make presentations at Coalition workshops and symposia.

Lewis also sponsored its own professional development activities, often with the assistance of the central staff. These included weeklong summer institutes and half-day workshops during the school year. Carla Dobson described the first summer workshop (July 1986): "We looked at different teaching styles. We looked at different curricula. We looked at coaching. We looked at how we would implement student-as-worker. . . . We did interdisciplinary curricula. . . . And we did practical applications of what it was we were doing. . . . In the final week we had a laboratory school . . . [where] we used the integrated curriculum approach. We combined math and science and we did humanities, which included foreign language, English, and social studies. We also adopted a thematic approach with our curricula." These activities served multiple purposes: they provided the Essential School with a forum to collectively consider changing aspects of their program, they introduced new faculty to aspects of the Essential School, and they offered experienced teachers opportunities to reassess their understanding of Coalition philosophy.

A third factor that contributed to Lewis's continued program expansion involved the indicators of success to which the Essential School could point. Whereas other comprehensive high school students in the city had trouble passing the mandatory competency exams in reading, writing, math, and citizenship, for three consecutive years (1986–89) and in all four areas of competency, Essential School students outperformed both their Lewis counterparts and the systemwide average in all but one exam, where they equaled the citywide score.[4] In terms of attendance, dropout rates, and college acceptances, the Essential School had a relatively impressive record as well. Although figures varied from year to year, throughout our research Essential School attendance was regularly about ten points better, and its dropout rate lower, than the larger school and also the systemwide average. Moreover, nearly 60 percent of the graduates of the Essential School consistently go on to higher education; the larger school generally sends about 40 percent of its students to college, and citywide, about 20 percent of high school graduates go to college.

These signs of success were widely touted. For example, Lewis's Essential School was featured in local and national newspapers. As a

4. It is important to note that the Lewis program's success is a relative phenomenon. That is, Lewis is one of nine comprehensive high schools serving students who are most likely to be disenchanted with or disinterested in their schooling. (For instance, while roughly a third of the junior class took the PSAT exams in fall 1989, only three students scored above the 50th percentile nationally—the highest being in the 57th percentile.) Lewis has shown gains relative to these schools—in attendance and dropout rates and performance on state competency exams. But, as we discuss later, in schools where student attendance and dropout rates are already exemplary, it was more difficult to convince people that Coalition philosophy offers a more effective approach to teaching and learning, and test-score comparisons were not used to measure success.

Thomson fellow, David Johnson traveled widely and promoted his program—its philosophy and performance—in many settings. In recognition of Lewis's efforts, the central staff often included their teachers, administrators, and students in workshops and public presentations. These opportunities to promote the program reassured parents who were considering enrolling their children. Since the Essential School was funded in part by private foundations, these data also proved useful in reports to philanthropic organizations and efforts to elicit support within the city school system.

Although these indicators of academic achievement seem impressive, Essential School faculty readily acknowledged that their flexible schedule allowed them to prepare students intensively for competency exams, an opportunity unavailable to other Lewis and city faculty. Furthermore, as the authors of an independent study conducted by a local university wrote: "The evidence shows that *going in* the students begin with sizable advantages over other Lewis students; they are younger, thus more likely to have been promoted on time at each earlier grade in their respective histories; and second, the students turn out to have had much better attendance rates historically than their non–Essential School counterparts at Lewis. An objective observer might argue, then, that the Essential School students are in fact the most likely students to succeed anyway—in whatever enrichment environment they are in or not in." The study also questioned whether student performance was a consequence of improved teaching and learning or other factors, such as smaller class size or enrolling students who had better attendance records and histories of superior performance. Nonetheless, the study added that, after controlling for differences in student characteristics, "the thrust of the evidence is that participation in the Essential School program at Lewis increases a student's school attendance and promotion rates, which are important behaviors linked to school academic achievement and graduation."

Lewis faculty who did not teach in the Essential School also raised questions about the program's effectiveness. They maintained, for example, that the Essential School manipulated its dropout figures by enrolling its troubled students in the larger school before they officially dropped out. Signs of skepticism were also apparent in Lewis's professional development activities. During one Essential School–directed workshop, faculty openly questioned whether the Coalition philosophy was right for all students. In another session, teachers questioned the validity of comparing Essential School students with those in the larger school. One faculty member who visited Essential School classes looking for ways to improve his teaching found that although their pedagogy was "touted as revolutionary, . . . nothing very different was going on." Another teacher remarked, "I came to the workshop—took a week out of my summer vacation—because I knew I was going to come and hear something so different, so profound, and . . . I didn't learn anything that I didn't already know or that we weren't already doing."

Although administrative support, an emphasis on professional development, and opportunities to promote signs of academic success aided the expansion of Lewis's Essential School, three related factors contributed as well. First, no existing organizational structures restricted Essential School expansion. At other Essential Schools, faculty were committed to existing curricula and school programs—such as honors and advanced placement (AP) courses or magnet programs—which made expansion problematic. Although Lewis offers a naval Junior Reserve Officer Training Corps (NJROTC) program, there were no conflicts between the programs, possibly because NJROTC required only one period a day, and many Essential School students enrolled in the program.

Second, the teachers' union did not oppose Lewis's Coalition-related efforts. When declining enrollments caused the transfer of faculty to other city schools, for example, some relatively inexperienced Essential School faculty retained their positions even though other teachers in their departments who were transferred had more tenure. When Lewis faculty filed grievances about their reassignment, the transfers stood because the superintendent had accorded the Essential School special program status, effectively making it comparable to a department. Johnson attributed this union support to the grassroots nature of Lewis's reform efforts combined with signs of improved student performance: "We've presented our Essential School program as a bottom-up approach to change and the union personnel liked that. They support that kind of change. I've found that they'll support new programs if the programs look as though they'll improve instruction. We also have our track record going for us."

And third, the administration never created any context in which the entire school could discuss the appropriateness of Coalition membership. As our other case studies reveal, some faculties were offered opportunities to collectively deliberate Coalition affiliation. In retrospect, these forums helped those opposed to or skeptical of their school's Coalition-related work to coalesce and oppose the action—in some cases with considerable success. At Lewis, such potential sources of resistance as teacher unions, competing programs, and skeptical faculty had no formal opportunity to resist program expansion.

From its inception, the goal of those associated with the Essential School was that the program would continue to expand. Yet it is noteworthy that as the program came to include more and more of the school, aspects of the Essential School experience became somewhat diluted. For example, Lewis's first Essential School team spent an entire year experimenting with teaching and had six weeks during the summer to create its program. Subsequent members received a less intensive introduction to Coalition philosophy. One year, because of uncertainty about whether the program would expand, the team had no preliminary introduction. Also, an assistant principal who initially served as an instructional leader gradually spent less and less time working with the program because of other responsibilities. Further, as Lewis's Essential School expanded, so did the average class size. During the 1986–87 school year, teachers averaged about twenty students per class. By the 1989–90 school year, the average was closer to thirty students.

INTRAFACULTY TENSIONS

Throughout our period of research, various tensions, tied largely to developments associated with the Essential School, reverberated throughout the school. One common criticism of the Essential School was that those involved, both students and faculty, received preferential treatment. Noninvolved faculty maintained that students had privileges and opportunities unavailable to other Lewis students—such as taking overnight field trips, having more classes in a foreign language (most foreign language teachers were in the Essential School), and being allowed to make up incomplete work over holidays and the summer (rather than failing or attending summer school). Discussing the use of additional funding the Essential School received, one larger-school teacher stated: "The Essential School has been given a lot of money—grants—and they can do just about anything they want to do. I think it's unfair to leave out your other students. I think [these students] should be able to do some of the things that the Essential School does."

Larger-school faculty also expressed resentment for the student attitudes and strains among the faculty that they felt such privileged treatment engendered. As one teacher recalled: "The students—not all of them—have an attitude, an air, as if they are the top students. They look down on other students. . . . And these students resent the authority of what we are called—'traditional school teachers.' I don't feel that these students have learned this on their own. I think they've been prompted. . . . In other words, we see people . . . doing things and we learn to do the same thing. We take on the same attitude as the adults. And I believe the students have taken on attitudes."

As in other SWAS programs we studied, faculty from the larger school at Lewis also felt that Essential School teachers received favored treatment—reduced student loads, additional planning time, and higher-quality students (because of the program's entrance requirements). They pointed to the professional development activities Essential School faculty could afford because of their grants as further signs of inequity. Noninvolved faculty also felt that they were often forced to accommodate the interests of the Essential School. For instance, when teachers were added to the Essential School just before school started one year, their original students were distributed to other classes. When Lewis High relocated for asbestos removal, the Essential School received its own section of the building; all other faculty shared rooms with teachers from that school.

The tensions apparent in these claims of preferential treatment were heightened by concerns with job security. The business department, for example, noted that with the advent of the Essential School its faculty decreased—from eleven to four full-time teachers. In the opinion of one department member, the Essential School's curriculum played an integral role: "My concern about the Essential School is that . . . the program does not involve vocational education. . . . The structure that I see here is that the student will be locked into four years of English, four years of math, four years of science, four years of social studies. Then a practical art is a must and a fine art is a must. The only place it leaves [the business department] is for one credit. . . . We had 85 students who came to me and indicated, 'We want to pursue data processing.' That's a two-hour credit. So they were told [by the administration that] it was impossible. . . . I'm not saying that the Essential School is not a good program, but I think there have to be more opportunities for students and parents to make selections."

Noninvolved faculty also had philosophical differences with the Essential School, mainly whether the program's college-oriented curriculum was appropriate for all students. In the words of one teacher: "My concern is that every child in Lewis High School is not going to college. We know this. And yet the program is set up as strictly academic, with little or no room for electives. [The neighborhoods] where our students come from, most of these students go to work. They're looking for immediate employment. We would like to see them do something other than fast food, which is fine to a point but, once they graduate, it hurts to see them slinging hamburgers when they could be operating a computer. But they must be proficient in those areas. They must have marketable skills."

Another faculty tension concerned communication. From the perspective of some noninvolved faculty, there was little effort to establish a schoolwide forum to discuss developments within the Essential School or future plans for the program. Further, the faculty did not vote on approving the creation of the program. A teacher's initial remarks in an interview suggested something of this perceived lack of dialogue: "I appreciate the fact of being able to talk with you simply because you're the first individual who has ever come to me to ask [for my opinion] about the school or the program." Another Lewis teacher had a similar reaction: "[The administration] needs to do what you're doing. They need to ask teachers [about the Essential School]. They leave the teachers out."

Although it seemed likely that the Essential School would eventually encompass the entire school, Lewis faculty sensed a we-they division within the school. One larger-school teacher said: "My concern about the Essential School is that it does not appear to me that there's total school involvement—that from the very beginning teachers were selected. It was not a voluntary thing. We were not really a part of it." An Essential School faculty member was also aware of the division. As she explained: "We have people who are a little bit jealous. We had a program last year that Essential School students participated in and they wanted to know why our kids were the only kids who participated.

[They said] 'It should have been a Lewis project. All kids should have been given this opportunity.' And I say, 'no.' One thing: whatever I'm responsible for, I give it all I've got. I'm not responsible for the remainder of the school, so I'm not looking for programs for those kids. And I'm not saying the kids shouldn't have them. . . . It's those teachers who are responsible for them."

Although teachers elaborated on these issues in interviews, the problems were seldom publicly acknowledged. In some teachers' opinions, declining student enrollments citywide combined with Lewis's drastic reductions in faculty as a result of the school's move created job insecurities among faculty. Consequently, few teachers wanted to be seen as dissidents and risk being assigned to another school and possibly needing re-certification to keep their jobs. In the words of one faculty member: "The Essential School is the 'fair-haired child' in this building, and no one's going to question the principal on it."

FUNDING THE ESSENTIAL SCHOOL

Beyond the school site, the most pressing problem facing Lewis's Essential School was financial. In its first five years the program was awarded nearly $250,000 in outside grants, which defrayed the cost of field trips with students, professional development workshops, and conferences attended by Essential School faculty. But during the program's first year the principal told a visiting teacher that start-up costs, rather than being 10 percent above existing expenditures—as suggested in the Coalition's common principles—were closer to 30 percent. In the fall of the program's second year (1987), a local newspaper article observed that David Johnson had secured a $50,000 foundation grant and a $15,000 state grant to support the Essential School during its first year and that the foundation had provided similar funding the second year. The writer then noted: "In the city, where secondary schools average at least 30 to 35 students per class, [reducing the class load to 20 students, the approximate size of most Lewis SWAS classes when the article was written; subsequently this number increased] would mean the addition of hundreds of teachers in a system with limited resources. [The] chief financial officer for the city school system said it would cost approximately $12 million to reduce the average class size in grades 9 through 12 to 20 students per class." A financial report by a foundation involved with

Lewis's program addressed the same issue: "The question about class size raises an important point: to reduce all high school class sizes to 20 would be prohibitively expensive within existing resources."

Lewis's Essential School was the only one of the four SWAS programs among our study schools that consistently expanded the size of its program and simultaneously attempted to deepen its efforts to restructure the school and to implement Coalition reforms. Moreover, in doing this, the Essential School made professional development a part of school routine and made exhibitions based on students' original research a graduation requirement. That the school has done these things is even more impressive given that it has encountered many of the same problems as other SWAS programs (McQuillan and Muncey 1991).

Although the validity of Essential School success was questioned by outside researchers as well as larger-school faculty—both of whom maintained that the program enrolled the best and brightest of Lewis students—the Essential School has welcomed all opportunities to adapt its structure to a fully representative sample of Lewis students. In addition, the Essential School's efforts to personalize their education had a positive effect on many students. As one foundation report observed: "If student interest in, and enthusiasm for, the program is proof of how well the program works, it appears to work well. . . . [Students] appear to be not only more interested in the schoolwork they are currently doing, but in going to school in general. Their aspirations in life are high. Of seven Essential School students asked to indicate what they would do on graduation, all seven say they intend to go on to college."

3

"DIFFERENT PEOPLE WITH DIFFERENT AGENDAS"
RUSSELL HIGH'S ESSENTIAL SCHOOL

While teaching in Russell's Essential School for the last two years, my influence has perhaps been the greatest. Because we meet with students in tutorial periods and in advisory groups, and because we have extra planning time together as teachers, we are able to really know many more of the students as persons. There is a very real opportunity to help the students learn that they must invest time and effort in their education and that there are benefits to be derived from that. —EXCERPT FROM AN ESSENTIAL SCHOOL TEACHER'S WINNING APPLICATION TO THE NATIONAL TEACHER OF THE YEAR PROGRAM

It's a charade that the faculty is changing the school. . . . We got someone with the charisma of Ted Sizer who charmed the faculty into believing that they were capable of changing the school. He got teachers excited and got them to the point where they dared to hope, and then he disappeared from our world. —A TEACHER NOT IN THE ESSENTIAL SCHOOL

Russell High is one of four magnet high schools in Deesport, an eastern city with 150,000 residents. The school serves an ethnically diverse student body of approximately one thousand students. In September 1987, African-American students formed the largest student group, 45 percent of the school; 21 percent were Hispanic; 15 percent white; 8 percent Portuguese; 6 percent Asian; and 5 percent Cape Verdean. This ethnic distribution remained consistent throughout our research. Within the city's secondary school structure, Russell is an arts and communication magnet, offering courses in theater, chorus, art, photography, and dance. All Deesport students are eligible for this program, which during our period of research enrolled roughly 15 percent of Russell's students. Russell also has a Coalition school-within-a-school, generally referred to as the Essential School, which is open to all city students and which came to enroll about 30 percent of the student body by the end of our research. In addition, the school offers programs in special education (6 percent of the school), English as a second language (ESL) (25 percent), and a tracked, comprehensive high school curriculum (25 percent).

In the 1950s and early 1960s, Russell was a neighborhood school that competed with the city's College Preparatory High School for Deesport's top students. Most students were white residents of the affluent Nelson Park neighborhood, although the school always had a core of African-American students (approximately 15 percent). In the late 1960s, as the city's demographic profile shifted, increasing numbers of low-income students and students of color enrolled at Russell. In spring 1969, as events nationwide highlighted the inequities experienced by many persons of color in America, African-American students at Russell began to protest their treatment by the school and school system. At first, students—with support from community activists—sought to pressure the city's school department into hiring more faculty of color and adding African-American writers and perspectives to English and history courses. When the school department resisted certain requests—maintaining that it could not act as quickly as students wished—some African-American students initiated a violent protest.[1]

The Deesport school system reacted to this turmoil by implementing programs and policies to address concerns that had been raised. For instance, efforts were made to create multicultural curricula, parents were encouraged to become active participants at the school, and faculty and students were offered workshops to improve interethnic relations. But for many Deesport residents this event culminated what they

1. Although the press and the community referred to this event as a "riot," many participants point out that it began as a protest against perceived inequities perpetrated at Russell High by the city school system. Still, substantial property damage occurred.

perceived as an ongoing decline of the school. Increasing numbers of families in Russell's feeder pattern withdrew their children and enrolled them in private schools or College Preparatory High. To bolster enrollment, the city bused students to Russell from the Heights, a low-income neighborhood with many persons of color and non-English-speaking residents. These students—who came to constitute the majority of the student body—had to take two buses to get to school each morning. Consequently Russell was no longer a neighborhood school. Moreover, the enthusiasm that followed the violent protest gradually waned, and the school's reputation within the city declined.

In the decade before Russell's involvement with the Coalition of Essential Schools, the school was beset with problems, including high principal turnover (twelve in thirteen years), building disrepair (the local newspaper wrote one article entitled, "Walls of School Literally Tumbling Down, Some So Bad Emergency Repairs Have to Be Made"), a dropout rate of nearly 50 percent, and falling attendance rates. Student course failures numbered about eighteen hundred annually—on average, nearly two per student. In "Russell Essential High School: Year One Report" of 1987 the coordinator, who held a joint administrative-teaching position created for the program, discussed how the school's reputation influenced its student composition:

> The image of the school . . . both in Nelson Park as well as in the less affluent neighborhoods, is that Russell is a rough school and you'll be lucky to learn much as a student.[2] . . . As coordinator I have met with many different groups and visited the many public middle and Catholic intermediate schools. The general theme is that the counselors and teachers put the top students almost into a pipeline for the College Preparatory School, or . . . the Catholic and private high schools. The next level of students is pegged for the business-vocational magnet. The next level of ambitious students is encouraged to go to the other magnets, including Russell's arts magnet. And then there are the many other students who are not headed into any program or magnet school. . . . In many cases these students do not wish to come to Russell, partly due to what

2. Although the school has a poor reputation, many Russell students who began their freshman year with trepidation discovered that the school was neither as chaotic nor as violent as they expected.

rumors they've heard, definitely because it's too far away from their homes, and also because the school can't teach them a specific trade. (1)

Situating Russell High within the Deesport school system provides another perspective on the school's reputation. Although persons of color compose only 20 percent of the city's population, they constitute 57 percent of the public school population—in effect, Deesport is a white city with a minority school system. In November 1987, the city enrolled a student body that was 43 percent white, 25 percent African-American, 20 percent Hispanic, and 11 percent Asian. Because of racial imbalances at all its high schools, in the 1970s the city instituted its magnet system to voluntarily address desegregation issues through choice. This system includes a science magnet and a business-vocational magnet that, as does Russell, have open enrollment. The fourth magnet, the college preparatory high school, restricts enrollment through an entrance exam.

Although the magnet system was intended to provide quality education to all city students while adhering to federal desegregation guidelines, issues of race, ethnicity, and socioeconomic status are evident in the system's structure. For instance, although persons of color (who are disproportionately likely to represent lower-income groups) compose nearly 60 percent of the secondary school population, they represent only 22 percent of the school population at College Preparatory High; at Russell, students of color constitute 85 percent of the student body.[3] Student scores on the Metropolitan Achievement Tests (MAT) from spring 1987 are also revealing of how the magnet structure mirrors these divisions. The cumulative average of math, reading, and language scores at Russell was the lowest in the state, the twenty-fourth percentile nationally. The business-vocational and science magnets scored in the twenty-sixth and thirty-first percentiles, respectively. In contrast, College Preparatory High School scored in the eighty-fourth percentile, nine points higher than any other school in the state.[4] Scholastic Apti-

3. In part, this difference reflects the fact that College Preparatory High offers no ESL or special education programs, programs that enroll sizable numbers of students of color.

4. The MAT scores in 1989 followed virtually the same pattern. The tests are administered every two years in this state.

tude Test (SAT) scores revealed a similar breakdown. In 1989, the combined mean SAT scores at College Preparatory High was 1028. At the science magnet the combined mean was 653; at the business-vocational magnet, 650; at Russell, 679. Thus, in Deesport, white and more affluent public school students are disproportionately likely to attend College Preparatory High, the school with the most widely accepted signs of student achievement.

THE COALITION AT RUSSELL HIGH

As with many of the earliest Coalition members, Russell's involvement began with a visit from Ted Sizer (in March 1984). Russell's principal, a self-described skeptic of "university types who think they have all the answers," invited Sizer to address the faculty after hearing him speak at a conference on school reform and being impressed by his understanding of and commitment to educational change. Following this visit, a faculty committee was established to consider Coalition membership. Concurrently, a second committee with representatives from a local university that had a history of involvement at Russell, the Deesport teachers' union, and two Russell teachers met with the principal and the superintendent of schools to address systemwide issues related to the proposed reform: how Essential School faculty would be selected, how the program would award credits, whether Essential School teachers would work outside their certified disciplines, what the coordinator's official status would be, and so on.

The faculty committee recommended that Russell join the Coalition, and the school approved the program by a two-thirds majority. The collaborative committee proposed that the school begin implementing Coalition practices by creating a SWAS program, a strategy that seemed to offer a safe, noncontroversial approach to school change. This was deemed necessary because, even though the faculty voted to accept the program, not all teachers wanted to be directly involved. The SWAS structure, therefore, could involve those who were interested without forcing others to participate. Nonetheless, many associated with the program expected that it would expand to include most of the school. As the principal commented on numerous occasions, "Russell is taking the Pac Man approach to school reform. We expect that the Essential School will eventually swallow up the entire school."

A team of four teachers (representing English, math, social studies, and biology) and a coordinator who administered the program and taught one class were selected to design the program through an application process open to all Russell teachers. For the half year before the Essential School's implementation, these persons were relieved of their teaching responsibilities so they could develop curricula, interview student applicants, and create a program structure. The basis of this structure was the team of four teachers who shared 104 students.[5] Classes met for double periods (approximately an hour and forty minutes) every other day. Teachers taught two double periods a day, supervised study halls for Essential School students three times a week, and had seven nonteaching periods a week. During its initial year (1986–87), the Essential School enrolled freshmen and sophomores. To enroll, students were required to have solid attendance records, to submit recommendations from two teachers, to write personal statements explaining why they wanted to join the program, and to have at least a sixth-grade reading level.

When the Essential School began in fall 1986, another dimension was added to the program: in conjunction with the Coalition, educators who specialized in social studies, English, and biology were hired jointly by the collaborating university and Deesport school system to work with the team and to teach in the education department at the university and supervise student teachers. The university paid three-quarters of their salaries; the school department paid the remaining quarter. One of the more prominent aspects of their work at Russell occurred during planning periods, twice weekly meetings where Essential School faculty and the professors discussed topics ranging from program policies to student performance to teaching strategies. In this context the professors served largely as sounding boards and provocateurs for issues that confronted the Essential School. They also helped interested teachers develop curricula and explore alternative teaching styles. In general, they sought to promote various reforms at Russell in whatever manner they could.

In each of its first four years, Russell's Essential School added new freshman students, a few upper-class transfers, and additional teachers.

---

5. This number reflects union guidelines that set the maximum teaching load for any one class in the Deesport school system at 26-to-1.

By September 1990, the program enrolled nearly three hundred students from all four grades and had a staff of a dozen teachers, roughly three-quarters being Russell veterans and one-quarter new to the school.

EDUCATIONAL CHANGE AT RUSSELL HIGH

In creating the Essential School, Russell High initiated a number of changes at the school. There was, for instance, the SWAS structure itself and such related developments as teacher teaming and the joint teaching-administrative position of coordinator. Essential School faculty also implemented a grading policy that allowed for no grades below 80, instead assigning students incompletes until work was satisfactorily completed. As part of its Coalition affiliation, faculty from a local university worked to promote change throughout the school. In addition, a second university-related initiative, the 1992 Committee, sought to encourage reform schoolwide. Some aspects of these changes were viewed positively by faculty, administrators, and students, while others generated tensions and controversy and created divisions within the school.

Same in other schools

THE SWAS STRUCTURE

Through the SWAS structure they adopted, Essential School faculty were able to personalize students' education by teaming four teachers and a group of students, often for more than one school year. In talking with a group of visiting educators, a faculty member commented: "The most obvious strength of our program is that [the SWAS] allows us to get to know our students well and they come to know us. . . . So we can deal with some problems that you might not even know about if we didn't have the program. . . . With most of our kids, we also have communication with the home. . . . And because we have team planning meetings, we can share information on our students and get to know them that much better." Another Essential School teacher at the same meeting added: "The most important aspect of our program is the sense of community we feel, teachers and students. We know our students better so we can be much more creative with them. Now the students come to school and they want to learn. And so that motivates us to further sharpen our creativity to meet their needs. . . . I know we don't meet all their needs but it feels less futile than before."

Later that day, some Essential School students met with the same group of educators and reinforced many of the teachers' observations. For example, in response to the question, "How do your Essential School teachers differ from other teachers you've had?" one student remarked: "They don't write you off. They really care about how you're doing. And since you may have the same teachers for a number of years, they know your capabilities. You can't BS them." To the same question, a second student said: "They don't forget that you're a person. If you come to school in a bad mood, they'll give you a break. Other teachers just give you a grade." A third student added: "The teachers will call me at home if I'm sick so I can stay caught up. That never occurred at my other high school. I had the chicken pox in my junior year and was out for a long time, and the teachers all called to check up on me. And they weren't just telling me to do the work. They really cared."

Other aspects of the Essential School may have contributed to this sense of personalization. An advisory system was part of the program, and a faculty adviser met periodically with his or her advisees to discuss concerns ranging from Essential School policies to teenage pregnancy to college admissions. Essential School students received midterm performance reports as well as quarterly grades. A parent advisory group met monthly. In addition, some teachers adapted pedagogical and curricular interpretations of personalization to their classrooms. Collaborative student work was common in a number of classrooms, and some teachers encouraged students to draw on personal interests in completing school work—for example, undertaking oral history projects in social studies classes and writing autobiographies in English classes. These efforts to personalize students' school experience promoted some noteworthy developments. Essential School attendance was consistently higher than in the larger school, generally by about 10 percent. Ninety percent of the Essential School's first graduating class (1989) attended college. Moreover, applying to college became a common expectation among Essential School students.

Despite its perceived benefits, the SWAS structure generated tensions within the faculty. Some faculty claimed, for instance, that Essential School teachers received preferential treatment—they had extra planning periods and taught a somewhat select student population. Others maintained that the Essential School received a disproportionate share of school resources. As one noninvolved teacher told a visiting reporter:

"They have their rooms painted, and they get more resources than we do. The Essential School gets all the trappings, they get preferential treatment. It is discriminatory, although I voted to set it up here."[6] Halfway through the program's first year, perceptions of preferential treatment intensified when Essential School teachers were released from study hall duty three times a week for program planning, and their students were added to classes taught by larger school faculty.

Tensions were heightened when the first-year Essential School report noted that much intrafaculty skepticism emanated from a "bunch of naysayers." Those who felt they were the target of this reference responded by hanging a sign on the door of their department office: "Naysayers Inc. All Others Stay Out." After this incident, no one from the department applied to the Essential School. In the first-year report, the coordinator, Paul Carroll, reflected on faculty rifts and resentment: "When teachers work hard they have little time left to socialize. No doubt that's why 'Horaces' make 'compromises.' . . . For us in the Essential School . . . there is no time for socializing amongst the faculty or even amongst ourselves. So there is little casual conversation. We are a pretty serious, goal-oriented group with lots of papers to correct, so 'coffee-time' discussion with faculty outside, or even inside, the program is hard to come by" (4).

Many points of tension emerged, but Essential School faculty focused on their program and did little to address these issues. With time, many nonaffiliated teachers grew indifferent or opposed to the effort, even some who had voted to create the program. Moreover, few Russell teachers applied to join the program. When other reforms were undertaken at the school they were often lumped together with the Essential School—especially if they included Essential School teachers or university faculty—and were approached with skepticism.

TEAMING

Rather than working in relative isolation and serving a random selection of students, Essential School teachers were teamed and each team taught the same one hundred or so students. By working more closely with colleagues and students, many teachers felt they were able to maintain consistent academic standards and to reach students who might

6. To preserve confidentiality, we provide no specific references.

have gotten lost in a larger school setting. As one teacher explained, "Because we're in a team, things *will* get done. Kids can't just get by because they will get incompletes." Teachers appreciated the opportunities to discuss professional matters with colleagues and to develop better understandings of their students through the planning meetings. The following remarks typify these perceptions:

> The greatest benefit to being part of the Essential School is having the opportunity to exchange ideas with other teachers. Usually, you close your door and have little to do with other teachers. You never realize that you share many of the same problems. . . . Usually, when you're with other teachers you talk about anything but school. Now we discuss our teaching methods. We have professional exchanges.

> I'm much closer to the other teachers in the program—personally and professionally—than I have been in twenty years. . . . We have a real professional relationship because we all share the same students. Here, I know all my students' teachers so I know who to go to if there's a problem with a student. . . . I could never do that before.

> [Teaming] offers teachers a sense of not being alone . . . of being committed to each other and working with students. We have time to talk with each other. . . . It helps you focus better on what to do.

To explain how teaming had influenced her teaching, an Essential School teacher described a project her team devised: "We did an interdisciplinary unit on nuclear energy. . . . We relied on team teaching and had a common exhibition. Mr. Davis did 'Four Futures,' which is a look at the relationship between the United States and Soviet Union and what some possible future scenarios might be. In English, students read *Hiroshima*. In chemistry we looked at nuclear energy as a possible source of energy, as something that could be positive. The students' final exhibition was to write a letter to 'an important person.' The idea was to support their arguments about nuclear energy and weapons with facts. Students had to show that they had learned something in English, chemistry, and history."

Being part of a team also enhanced some teachers' sense of professional responsibility—in part, a consequence of the interdependence promoted by the team relationship. As one teacher explained:

> When you're part of a team, you come to depend on a group of people. I see [the team] as depending on me to be there—to attend school, to do a good job, not to cop out [on our standards], not to just give lip service to what we're trying to accomplish, to be supportive of one another. . . . I can't say that I've become really close friends with any group members, but I have a good working relationship. For instance, Marilyn needed support and reassurance today in the meeting, and I think she got a very supportive reaction from the other team members. . . . Being in a group can also mean that you have more responsibilities. It can mean more work, time, and energy. But I can tell you I don't know what I'd do without the group.

Teachers also described an increased sense of responsibility in their relations with students. Comparing the Essential School to his previous experiences, a teacher noted: "I like having responsibility for my curriculum and the program overall. I think it allows me to better evaluate my students' progress because I get to see my students as individuals. It's also led me to work harder and made me more resourceful. . . . You're still teaching kids, but there are more kinds of problems because you know the students better. . . . Not only are you a teacher but you're a social worker. . . . It's not enough to disseminate information. You need to get to know the students."

Teachers attributed many positive developments to teaming, but they also identified some disadvantages, one being increased workloads. As one teacher noted, program success also meant more work: "I guess this shouldn't be a drawback, but I'm finding that there's lots more day-to-day work that has to be done. The kids are doing work and that gives you lots of tedious work that you have to do. . . . Last year [before joining the Essential School], in a class of twenty-five students, five might turn the work in and there was no pressure to chase kids who didn't do it. . . . Now, in a class with twenty-nine students, twenty-seven will show up and twenty-five will turn in papers, and then you've got some students who are still completing incomplete work. It becomes really wild." Acknowledging the benefits of teaming, another Essential School teacher questioned whether the increased workload was realistic: "I look forward to being part of a team. There is mutual support and feedback. We're involved with collaborative planning, and I have a greater sense of achievement and purpose when working together. Of course, it's a lot more work. I don't believe we can keep this up with all of our after-school commitments. . . . If the program demands this much time, any program would be successful. We need to be more efficient or there won't be many teachers willing to give so much of their time."

As with teaming, faculty saw advantages to common planning time, but there was a sense that meetings could be unproductive and frustrating—in particular, that logistical matters often took priority over educational concerns:

> I don't feel that we address anything . . . thoroughly. We go off on too many tangents. I don't see it as planning. I don't feel we solve anything. I don't think that we get to plan. We should be discussing how our lessons interconnect and what skills we can work on to reinforce one another's teaching. . . . I'm sick of seeing the same lists and agenda items over and over again. It's frustrating. . . . We do nothing as a team.
>
> The kind of planning that I envisioned doesn't go on. . . . Sometimes we get to discussing logistics . . . and in reality we had discussed [certain topics] for hours already. . . . I thought we'd be talking about specific subjects and skills and coordinating our efforts but that's not what we do.

For some Essential School faculty, teaming led to disillusionment when philosophical differences arose within teams. For instance, some Essential School teachers filed a union grievance to secure three additional planning periods, rather than overseeing study halls for their students.[7] Other team members disagreed, saying that these study periods provided students with individual attention and offered a means to reduce some of the incompletes they had accumulated. Philosophical divisions also emerged when the Essential School considered initiating an advanced placement program. Some teachers saw this as improving

7. In their contract, Essential School teachers were provided five additional planning periods each week. Initially, the team used only two of these periods; the other three served as study halls for their students. As the year progressed, some teachers felt overwhelmed by their workloads and decided to file a grievance to secure the additional periods.

program quality, but others considered it a form of tracking, a policy the Essential School's first team sought to eliminate.

Tensions generated by these disagreements could make collaboration difficult. After two years in the Essential School, one teacher noted: "Sometimes I get discouraged because I feel that the Essential School philosophy is not the core of people's beliefs. Instead, it's being broken down by different people with different agendas. . . . When I joined the program I thought that those who were in the program agreed to go along with the philosophy of the Essential School program but that has not turned out to be the case." Another Essential School teacher described her frustration with how one program policy was translated into practice: "I don't think our program encourages consistent, good behavior by our students because the teachers are too slack. We all seem to have different philosophies, and we aren't consistent. We agree in our meetings that we're going to try and get students to stay in their homerooms after the bell rings, but that only lasted two weeks. I went crazy trying to keep kids in the room. We're not consistent so . . . I eventually gave up."

Teaming offered both benefits and drawbacks. Although most teachers enjoyed the collegial interaction offered by the SWAS structure and many felt it promoted more effective teaching, teachers also found that teaming could mean more work. In addition, philosophical differences within the program—some of which were highly charged— caused some teachers to feel disheartened.

ESSENTIAL SCHOOL LEADERSHIP

As part of Russell's plan to implement Coalition philosophy, an effort was made to reinvent administration in the SWAS program. For instance, those who designed it—representatives from Russell High, the city school system, the teachers' union, and a local university—sought to blend teaching and administration in the position of coordinator. By teaching one class while administering the program, the coordinator could, it was hoped, use classroom-based insights to inform program policy. Both persons who filled this role during our research found the blending difficult. Teaching responsibilities could interfere with administrative duties. As the first coordinator, a man with considerable experience at Russell, explained: "It was enjoyable but it was difficult to make the shift between what I had to plan for administratively and what

I had to plan for and get done to be ready for class. . . . Teachers have to be in a certain place at a certain time, and things would come up. And one of the unfortunate facts of life is . . . if something comes up and you don't deal with it right away, things take longer to finish off. Or, you have to deal with them at some other time that's even more inconvenient or inappropriate. . . . I found that putting the time together to adequately plan for the teaching plus running the program itself really made it difficult." Similarly, the second coordinator, a woman from the first Essential School team, discussed how administrative duties often could not be postponed: "It's funny because I was the one at the beginning who really wanted this position to be a teacher position—not just an administrative position—and I think in theory it's real important. But it's hard. . . . I always feel like I'm working in a crisis situation. . . . I feel like I'm working in an emergency room, but it's at a school instead of a hospital. . . . We've had everything from runaway kids being beaten up by police to girls running away with their boyfriends who were accused of a crime. I've had judges call me. I've had social workers call me. . . . Parents come in crying. Then you come back from class, and there are three people in the office and ten messages waiting for you."

They both also found it difficult to be educational leaders. For the first coordinator this was due, in part, to some uncertainty as to how aggressively he could promote change. As he explained: "It was hoped that the coordinator would be a supervisor, to work on teaching with people. One problem I saw with that responsibility is that I was not officially an administrator, so it was not . . . within my position to do that. . . . I felt that there would be an automatic grievance situation [if I did]. . . . I saw the relationships within the program as collaborative, as working together . . . [and myself] as one person within the team. Then to turn around and begin to criticize their teaching . . . sets you off as not a team member."

Addressing the same issue, the second coordinator discussed how administrative concerns often precluded her from promoting classroom-based change: "I thought I was going to be an educational leader. I thought I'd be able to use my skills as a teacher. I thought I would be helping people write exhibitions, work on cooperative learning—helping change what goes on in the classroom. I thought I'd be a resource person . . . and work more with teachers in the larger school and be a liaison. . . . [Instead,] I spend so much time responding to gossip, responding to rumors, responding to mixed messages, responding to memos, responding to letters, responding to complaints." Like the first coordinator, this woman found that her ambiguous status made it difficult to be an educational leader: "I have absolutely no power. I'm in the teachers' union. I can't tell people what to do, even if a parent calls and complains about a teacher, when kids come in and complain about a teacher. It puts me in a really difficult position. Those . . . things I have to refer elsewhere."

Essential School teachers also sensed that the coordinator role lacked definition. As one teacher remarked: "The notion of the coordinator as a teacher, leader, and peer is not a reality. The coordinator is in no-man's-land—between teacher and administrator. . . . It's a *huge* position." Another teacher offered a similar observation: "[The coordinator's] role needs to be better defined. It seems to me that there's a bit of confusion as to what he should be with regard to being a teacher equal to us, and what he's really called upon to do. He seems to do things that are mostly administrative—75 to 80 percent of the time. . . . The coordinator doesn't know what he's supposed to be doing, so he does whatever has to be done. . . . He's forced into doing some things he did not expect and, in a sense, chastised for doing these things. . . . It's a tough position."

The coordinator position, then, proved to be a difficult synthesis to realize. Both coordinators intended to be educational leaders within the Essential School, but their roles put them in precarious positions and neither person worked extensively with teachers on classroom-based matters.

THE POLICY ON INCOMPLETES

The first Essential School team instituted a grading innovation—the "incomplete." Believing that students too often moved on to succeeding grades because compromising teachers awarded low Cs and Ds on the basis of "seat time," the team decided to award only three grades—A, B, and incomplete. Students who failed to earn a grade of at least 80 received an incomplete and were then expected to complete all work satisfactorily. In practice, this grading system proved problematic. Rather than redoing work, many students ignored their incompletes, even those from previous quarters. Further, the numerous record-keeping procedures required for incomplete makeups drained faculty energy and time and strained patience. Attending to the multiple problems associated with this grading shift took time from planning meetings; it required teachers to devise makeup plans with students; and it caused the Essential School to adjust its schedule each semester to accommodate students who had incomplete work. After the first year the grading system was expanded to include the C (75) because many students had argued they could finish their work if allowed a 75. Two years later the faculty made another change. Initially, students had received incompletes for any unsatisfactory work. As the number of incompletes grew, Essential School faculty decided that incompletes should be a privilege, not a right. Students therefore had to petition teachers and defend their need for additional time, and teachers decided whether to allow them an incomplete.

Even after these changes, Essential School teachers felt they faced increased workloads. One teacher explained: "I am still trying to figure out ways to cut down on my paper work. By trying to hold students to standards of 75-or-better, it's overwhelming in terms of returning papers to be corrected. . . . Initially, I returned everything and got some papers three, four, or five times. I went crazy with time. . . . Now I'm chasing kids and calling parents to get them to help." A second teacher provided another perspective: "Initially, I was to have only one preparation. I saw that as a great advantage. But in the second semester, with all the failures, I had two preparations [because one group of students was redoing the entire first semester]. And next year, I might have three. It seems that the incomplete policy was simpler in its conception than practice. . . . I began to see not student-as-worker but 'student-as-conversationalist' and 'teacher-as-secretary,' keeping student affairs in order."

A third teacher felt the incomplete allowed students to "postpone reality" and could provoke student resentment: "I feel we're teaching kids to procrastinate and not to do the best they can because there are no deadlines. It caters to bad work habits—why do it now if you can do it later? For a few kids, it works. But with the majority of students, it causes resentment. They say, 'This is the third time you've given this back! What do you want from me?'"

Student reactions also raised concerns as to whether the grading shift promoted mastery or whether teachers eventually accepted exactly what they intended to avoid—shoddy work. As one teacher remarked to colleagues in a planning period: "We did an essay question and students were handing in things that weren't even sentences. . . . It's hard to deal with. . . . They exhaust us and wear us down." Another teacher maintained that the incomplete promoted disjointed student work: "I feel that many students don't follow through on the assignments. Most are done late, and they [students] forget material when they don't want to do it [the assignment]. Consequently, information becomes very fragmented. And once it's fragmented, it's tough to be effective as a teacher." In reference to exhibitions—the cumulative, performance-based assessments promoted by the Coalition—another teacher alluded to a similar tendency: "I like the idea [of exhibitions] but . . . students put things off to the last minute and they can't get by that way. . . . It has us all confused. What I end up getting is a bunch of last-minute pieces of exhibitions from students, and they are not what I wanted. I wanted them to be developed over time. . . . Students need to submit drafts of the exhibition for it to be meritorious. It needs shaping."

Within the Essential School a tension occasionally arose over whether to maintain standards or to limit the number of incompletes. In a letter to the coordinator, a math teacher complained of being pressured to lower his standards:

> I felt that six "statistics" assignments addressed the performance objectives I intended. . . . [However,] many students had problems with this mind-set. . . . Students were frustrated and were not able to get by on attendance alone. Some were frustrated by having to work within the given framework. Others felt they weren't doing math. And so on. . . . When the end of the quarter drew near, I was tempted to ignore the "incomplete problems" *many* individuals had and eventually went that route and started algebra and geometry. I continued to work at making up work when possible. As "makeup week" started, everyone became aware of what I knew—*most* people hadn't completed "statistics." I felt pressured (mostly by you) to "produce" a bigger group of people who were caught up. I worked at it. I gave people who only had "one more thing to do" the benefit of the doubt (on their promise that the second part of the exhibition would be completed). When work was handed in I made *no* promises. All was contingent upon *successful* completion of the work, not just doing

it! Now I have many students with short memories and a couple with staff representatives [the coordinator and a university professor, who the teacher felt were overly supportive of students]. I feel betrayed. I also feel that it's impossible to do this job to the expected level of success while being pushed and pulled in as many different directions as I (we) have been.

The Essential School never did away with incompletes, and tensions from this policy reverberated through the program. For many teachers, it meant more work. It could strain student-teacher relations. As faculty spent considerable time trying to resolve the matter, philosophical differences within the Essential School were often revealed, thereby straining relations among the faculty and disillusioning some teachers.

UNIVERSITY INVOLVEMENT

The university that established a partnership with Russell through the Essential School had a history of involvement with the school that took many forms. The education department consistently placed several student teachers at Russell. During our research, the cognitive science department undertook a study of the implementation of hypertext technologies in English and social studies classes, and a dean's office sponsored a drug abuse prevention program. Although these were different university entities, Russell faculty tended to generalize and refer to them all as "the university."

Faculty perceptions of these interactions were mixed. In conjunction with creating the Essential School, for example, the university helped Russell secure a grant of $215,000. These funds helped pay the salaries of the coordinator, the university professors, and an Essential School secretary, as well as the cost of refurbishing a teachers' workroom, a few classrooms, and the school library. Although people associated with these programs generally appreciated them, the projects also generated ill will. Some faculty benefited from involvement with the university, but others resented what they perceived as privileges and claimed that those with university connections received favored treatment.

In addition, some Russell faculty viewed the university as opportunistic, as becoming involved with the school only when it suited its interest. For instance, Russell was a site for student teaching and for university researchers; it was now part of a school reform program.

Clearly these projects benefited the university, but some Russell teachers questioned whether they helped the school. As one faculty member stated in a department meeting, "We're just a lab [for the university]. That's all." Those skeptical of the university's intentions saw the Essential School as one more instance of the university imposing its interests on Russell.

University involvement at Russell grew especially contentious in the Essential School's fourth year (1989–90) when the coordinator position became available. In a letter to the superintendent, one applicant articulated some common faculty perceptions:

> I hereby withdraw my application for the position of coordinator of the Russell Essential School. I am doing this because . . . I believe that one individual used the prestige and the financial clout that the university enjoys to impose their(?) choice on the Essential School program. It seems that little or no consideration was given to the mandate of the Russell High School faculty. The most frustrating aspect of this process is the fact that while [the university] brags that this is a "bottom-up" plan, "the power that is" has circumvented the "bottom," the real workers. That this most basic tenet has been ignored renders the Essential School program no longer credible. Furthermore, I and perhaps others, no longer feel a sense of "ownership" of Russell Essential High. . . . My resentment comes from a feeling that I have been manipulated and, to an extent, made to play out a farce.

Faculty had mixed reactions to the presence of university professors at Russell. Those who worked closely with them generally appreciated the professors' expertise. As one teacher commented while developing lesson plans with a professor, "Give me more. This is great. I love it." Another teacher remarked: "I am very pleased and feel lucky to work with [the professor]. He's been a tremendous help. He provides me with excellent comments on my teaching. He helps me conceive of alternative ways of teaching. He's provided me with materials that allow me to move away from traditional ways of teaching and he gives me direct support for my classroom activities." Acknowledging the ambivalence associated with the professors' work, a third teacher also praised their efforts: "I think [the professors' involvement at the school] is fine. They offer us a different point of view. I have no problem capitalizing on their involvement. . . . I've never felt that they're trying to force their opinions on us. I find it hard to believe that anyone feels that way."

Not everyone at Russell agreed. In part, faculty disaffection stemmed from the ambiguous nature of the professors' work. The Coalition stressed grassroots reform and local autonomy, but the university professors had to strike a balance between advocating change and respecting faculty autonomy. Contrasting remarks by one professor are illustrative: he described the position as being "helpful 'insiders' rather than outside consultants coming in and telling people what to do and pretending to know better. Eventually, [the faculty] has the final say. That's how it has to be. Otherwise, the whole thing's a farce." Yet recalling one planning meeting, the same professor acknowledged an urge to challenge teachers to reassess the status quo: "I'd prefer to deal with tough issues first . . . often key issues get obfuscated. . . . If I'm not confrontational, I have . . . to accept the team's policy, and the issue never gets dealt with. . . . So I pay a price whether I put it off or deal with it. My relationship with Joan is a perfect example of this bind. I want to say, 'You've got to be kidding me. You haven't been successful in getting work done. You know the standards are slipping, and still only 50 percent of the students are passing. How can you say there's no more work to do?' . . . And she'd portray this as the university professor forcing her to go with my ideas."

Tensions faced by the professors also emanated from a general skepticism of change held by many experienced teachers. For some, promoting change implied criticism. One veteran teacher explained why she never joined the Essential School: "I would not be too willing to have anyone from the university start telling me how to teach, although I know that is technically not what happens. . . . But you know, the strong suggestions and the 'do it our way or else' kind of thing. I like a little bit more freedom in teaching."

Other teachers had seen reforms come and go, with few having any lasting beneficial effects. Moreover, some opposed aspects of Coalition philosophy. A faculty member remarked in an interview: "When anything called 'new' or 'innovative' comes along, it's usually perceived as something to be wary of. . . . From my own experience . . . I've seen that many lack substance: [just] change for the sake of change. . . . The question in my mind is: If it ain't broke, why fix it? . . . And I'm not sure if the method . . . is right. Who's to say that the Coalition's program is the right one?"

In general, teachers interested in change welcomed the professors' assistance, and those who questioned the need for change, the appropriateness of Coalition philosophy, or the university's presence at the school were often skeptical and did little to assist them. In turn, the professors felt they had some positive input into school life—helping revise curricula, offering another perspective when developing program policies, and supporting faculty committees. They also acknowledged limits to their influence and some frustration with faculty cynicism, which contributed to a shift in their responsibilities and involvement at Russell. During the Essential School's first two years, the professors were at the school almost daily. In the ensuing three years, their involvement steadily declined. By June 1991, they were seldom at the school. Their jobs were redefined by the university so that their responsibilities at Russell were limited, and they began working in other, more receptive city high schools. At this point the positions were funded entirely by the university.

THE 1992 COMMITTEE

During the Essential School's first year (1986–87), Russell faculty and administrators, personnel from the local university, and some educational consultants created the 1992 Committee, a schoolwide effort intended to help faculty "rethink the education provided students." Hoping to involve a broad cross section of teachers from Russell's various programs in collaboratively defining future directions for the school, the 1992 Committee sought to address two questions: "What will Russell High look like in five years?" and "What should be the relationship between the Essential School and the arts magnet?" The committee initiated its work with a well-attended, university-sponsored dinner meeting, which stirred faculty interest and led to voluntary, ongoing meetings to address the two questions.

In its first year and a half of existence, faculty involvement with the committee was sporadic. The initial meetings of the committee generally brought together at least half of the school's faculty. By spring 1987, however, most meetings included no more than seven or eight teachers (from a faculty of about seventy), a university representative, and perhaps someone from an educational consulting firm that became involved with the effort. During the 1988–89 school year, the 1992 Committee received an influx of funds and enthusiasm when the Coalition of Essential School's joint initiative with the Education Commission of the States, Re:Learning, was undertaken. As a potential Re:Learning school, Russell received $20,000 from the state department of education to help the school investigate the feasibility of Re:Learning membership, a potentially controversial development as Re:Learning membership would require, in theory, that the entire school embrace Coalition philosophy and practices. Through a steering committee, the 1992 Committee solicited faculty proposals and funded those it considered appropriate. The committee also published a newsletter and created subcommittees on such issues as school governance and departmental restructuring.

During the 1989–90 school year, Re:Learning funding ran out, and interest in the 1992 Committee also declined. By 1990–91, the steering committee and subcommittees no longer met, and the newsletter was not published. Faculty attributed this inactivity in part to the fact that Russell had expected an accreditation study during that year (although the study was postponed). Because they planned to combine the 1992 Committee with accreditation work, they had set aside no time for the committee per se. It also appears that faculty frustration contributed to the decline in interest. As one committee member said at a meeting in fall 1987: "What we're saying is that we've got to focus. . . . We haven't focused on a direction so we have no goal. Therefore, we need consensus on an acknowledged goal, one we subscribed to last spring [at the first 1992 Committee meetings]. Maybe we're missing committee commitment, a . . . direction that we've all agreed upon. What is our goal? It was articulated and endorsed last spring—that is, by example and instruction to educate young people in good citizenship and academic areas as they apply. But we are not educating kids. There's no instruction going on. . . . We're suspending and punishing kids but not educating them. We need a consensus, a goal."

Overall, the committee had a limited effect on the school. Faculty visited restructuring schools, attended professional conferences, and reported their findings to the steering committee. With their funding, Russell High bought books, subscribed to education journals, and purchased a copy machine. Proposals aimed at curricular or structural change, however, had little enduring influence. A team of teachers, for example, were to develop graduation exhibitions for four subject areas: English, math, social studies, and science. The committee met, but no changes were implemented. There was also an effort to foster communication between Essential School and arts magnet faculties—to identify common interests and possibly connect the programs—but they remained separate organizational entities. In addition, projects intended to coordinate biology and health curricula, to develop an interdisciplinary game that linked the central themes of Western civilization, and to create a "house" for ninth-grade, at-risk students were initiated but never implemented.

After five years Russell's Essential School program remained a "specialty shop" in a "shopping mall high school" (Powell, Farrar, and Cohen 1985). Although Russell's principal had touted the program as embodying the "Pac Man approach to school reform," such comprehensive expansion never occurred. To some degree, this reflected the controversial nature of the program. The SWAS structure proved divisive; faculty were skeptical of university involvement. Moreover, opposition to the Essential School and Coalition philosophy was tied to the principal. The principal supported the Essential School, and faculty who had prior feuds with him sometimes made it known that they would oppose the program because it might make the principal look good.

Expansion was also restricted because the Essential School and other Russell programs never found common ground. Early on, Essential School and arts magnet faculty met to consider collaborating or merging programs—both programs stressed active learning and performance-based assessment, both sought to personalize learning, and both involved teams of teachers working with the same students. Yet the programs remained separate, and to some extent hostile, as the following letter to faculty and administrators written by a Russell music teacher implies:

> Once again the people at Russell High go in another direction without considering what *is*, before considering what *will be*. For the last eleven years, Russell High has been an arts magnet school. . . . One must understand that these students *must* have

eight to ten periods a week of arts classes to have any meaning to the term ARTS MAGNET.

Without question, the Essential School has been detrimental to the music portion of the arts program. Students have been unable to continue in the music program due to the Essential School insisting on them taking a foreign language outside of the four Essential School periods. . . .

SINCE OUR SCHOOL IS AN ARTS MAGNET SCHOOL, THERE SHOULD BE A REPRESENTATIVE FROM THE ARTS MAGNET WITHIN THE GROUP OF THE HOLY FOUR (ENGLISH, HISTORY, MATH, AND SCIENCE). IF RUSSELL HIGH IS TO CONTINUE OFFERING A MAGNET PROGRAM, IT MUST NOT BE WEAKENED FOR THE SAKE OF ARTIFI-CIAL REFORM.

Although this example pertains to the arts magnet program, the issue was especially key at Russell because, in contrast to Lewis High, the principal had no opportunity to transfer uninterested or unwilling faculty.

Funding was another factor that constrained efforts to expand Russell's Essential School. Although the common principles maintain that Coalition-related change should not exceed a 10-percent increase, the start-up costs for Russell's SWAS exceeded normal expenditures by more than 10 percent, based on per capita expenditures. To fund the program, Russell required support from philanthropic foundations, the Deesport school department, the state department of education, and Chapter II. Since Essential School faculty taught one less class per day than noninvolved faculty (four rather than five), Essential School teachers were about 20 percent more expensive than teachers with five-class loads. Thus, for every five Essential School teachers, the school department had to hire an additional teacher to cover the five classes they did not teach. If the entire school adopted this structure, it is uncertain whether the school department could cover the expense incurred by providing all teachers with an extra planning period each day. Further, since foundation grants and the university assume a portion of the salaries for the professors, the SWAS secretary, and the coordinator, if the school system adopted the same structure more broadly and did not have the additional foundation and university support, these salaries would represent another significant cost increase.

4

"A STRUGGLE THAT HAD TO PLAY ITSELF OUT"
ELLISTON HIGH SCHOOL

People said, "Sure. If folks want to go out and if they want to experiment and get involved in this, that's okay, they should be able to do that." But then all of a sudden we joined the Coalition. I think people had a difficult time with that. All of a sudden we're a Coalition school. What does it mean if we're a Coalition school? Does that mean we *have to* make these changes? I think there was some uncertainty . . . and uneasiness with that. —A TEACHER

I think that we were up against people who were cast in cement. It is a terrible thing to say about colleagues, but it is true. My real opinion is that I see people who are reluctant and afraid to change anything. As someone said it— "Obviously, it's going to mean more work." . . . Some people have gotten [their jobs] down to a science where they don't have to carry anything home . . . the phrase is, to make the job "do-able." It's the truth. . . . I don't mean to level charges, but some people don't want to change what they're comfortable with. And I think that some people felt that this was going to be a bigger commitment than they wanted to make . . . and they read "change" as "more work." —A TEACHER

We never use the word Coalition anymore. It's like it's a dirty word. —A TEACHER

The school we examine in this chapter joined the Coalition of Essential Schools, and then its faculty began the long process of determining what, if anything, they wished to change about their current practices. During this time, changes in their interpretation of what Coalition membership entailed and concerns about local control of the reform agenda—coupled with political, philosophical, communicative, and personal differences—led Elliston faculty to reconsider their involvement with the Coalition, after three years of membership but before a formal program was established. Eventually, after discussing the school's philosophy and what constituted good schooling, the faculty affirmed much of what they were currently doing and rejected Coalition membership. Many issues from the previous chapters about school-within-a-school programs and school change arose here, suggesting that these issues are endemic to the change process rather than to a specific form of implementation.

ELLISTON HIGH SCHOOL

The town of Elliston is a sprawling suburban community bordering a city of approximately 240,000. Many who live in the town are executives in local divisions of several large corporations. The school district serves two communities—Elliston and Parkview—and people often purchase homes in these towns expecting that their children will receive a quality public education. Many parents are actively involved in their children's education.

Elliston High School has an excellent reputation. In 1988, the school was ranked first in the nation in an independent survey of public high schools. The school offers its one thousand students an array of courses—including electives in foreign languages, business, unified arts, music, and theater, to name a few—all organized according to several tracks. The school also offers many advanced placement courses. About one-fifth of all seniors enroll in one or more AP course, and three-quarters of these students score high enough on AP exams to receive college credit. There are also extensive extracurricular activities. To accommodate the electives and the different configurations of time these classes can require (for example, seminars and labs), the school has a modular schedule that divides each school day into twenty-two modules of eighteen minutes. During our research the majority of classes lasted for three "mods," or fifty-four minutes.

Most Elliston students are white and can be characterized as "privileged," although some low-income urban students—mostly African-American—are bused to the school as part of an educational opportunities program. The school accords its students substantial autonomy and responsibility. During their unscheduled periods, for instance, they are free to work unsupervised in several locations throughout the building. In line with this, students are expected to come to class prepared—commonly having two to three hours of homework at night—and to contribute to the day's lesson. In turn, many Elliston students expect to work hard, do well, and attend respected colleges and universities. Virtually all students graduate and most (85–90 percent) pursue higher education.

In 1985, when Elliston High first considered Coalition membership, the school's enrollment was declining. The number of students decreased from thirteen hundred in that year to a low of between nine hundred and one thousand students in the 1990–91 academic year. As a consequence, debates about Coalition membership were often tied to concerns about the impact of declining enrollments.

THE COALITION AT ELLISTON HIGH

Elliston's contact with the Coalition of Essential Schools began in December 1984 during an informational meeting held by Ted Sizer for interested schools in the region. Afterwards, in a letter of December 19 to Sizer, the outgoing principal wrote that given the issues Elliston faced (declining enrollments and the need for continuing self-examination), the school was interested in pursuing the next steps of testing "the concepts advanced in your book." On December 20, the incoming principal, Ken Wallace, wrote Sizer, outlining plans to raise his staff's awareness of the Coalition: "As you can imagine, the next few months at Elliston High School will be ones of great challenge. In the next few weeks we will be planning informational and awareness meetings for other administrators and teachers. Hopefully, these will result in opportunities for our faculty to meet with you and your staff at Brown or here at Elliston High. . . . [We] hope that, as we discuss and clarify our own thinking, our deliberations will result in a rather natural step toward our more formal involvement as a member of the Coalition."

Between 1984 and 1986, Wallace and interested faculty engaged in various activities to increase their understanding of Coalition philosophy. They held faculty seminars to explore Coalition philosophy and practices. Ted Sizer visited the school. Faculty participated in Coalition workshops, and the school created the Sizer Study Committee to consider the implications of Coalition affiliation for their school. In a letter written later, one person involved in the exploration process noted that after reviewing *Horace's Compromise,* the faculty "came to the conclusion that the Coalition offered us the framework to work on a reform movement without compromising all of our local control."

In February 1986, the Sizer Study Committee distributed a proposal for Coalition membership to faculty. This proposal emphasized six of the nine common principles—intellectual focus, simple goals, personalization, student-as-worker, graduation by exhibition, and atmosphere of respect and decency—but it made no mention of the other three principles. It also summarized what the principles might mean for Elliston and what participation in the Coalition would allow:

> These principles represent a shared set of goals for the schools that participate in the Coalition. These principles provide a framework for reference while permitting local schools to adapt them to their own needs. Elliston's participation in the Coalition of Essential Schools will:
>
> 1. Allow small groups within the school to apply the Coalition's basic principles. *The same level of commitment will not be required of the entire faculty.* While some faculty members participate directly, all will observe the effects of the program.
> 2. Encourage further work on issues of concern to Elliston High School students and faculty, such as the creation of interdisciplinary programs and ways to foster in the students a sense of responsibility and respect.
> 3. Promote the sharing of ideas among colleagues.
> 4. Formalize and make systematic a way of evaluating what happens at a school over time. The Coalition will provide

consultants to work with us cooperatively in implementing and evaluating the basic principles.

5. Allow wider recognition for what we are doing as a school.

Often in education, people expect immediate definitions of goals and outcomes. There are no prescribed, formalized outcomes in the Coalition. The group recognizes the need for gradual formulation of outcomes and the need for at least a year of careful planning before any changes are undertaken (emphasis added).

The committee also suggested that the school's involvement in the Coalition could take many forms, including a SWAS program or clusters of interested teachers.

The first facultywide discussion of membership was held in March 1986. Soon after, a survey/vote was taken to ascertain faculty interest in the Coalition.[1] The results (shown below) were distributed to faculty and administrators in a memo of April 11 and affirmed faculty support for the six principles emphasized by the Sizer Committee, as well as for allowing interested faculty to implement these principles through Coalition membership. Yet almost half the faculty expressed no interest or indicated they had no time to participate in proposed Coalition work.

Responses to the Survey/Vote of Elliston Faculty, April 1986

1. I support the general principles outlined by the Sizer Committee in their proposal.

   yes 75   no   14   not sure   3

2. I would be willing to support a group of faculty members planning ways to implement those common principles in the everyday life of the school.

   yes 73   no   21

3. I would support the joining of the Coalition of Essential Schools as a method of implementing those common principles.

   yes 53   no   29   blank   6   unsure   1

4. My level of interest at this time is:

   not presently interested in this idea   22

1. We use the term *survey/vote* because this became part of the debate about Coalition membership, with different factions maintaining that it was one or the other.

interested but don't have the time   22
would like to find out more about what it is   15
interested and would like to help plan   31

In July, the membership proposal was presented to the Elliston School Board, which spent the summer reviewing it. Wallace expressed optimism about Coalition efforts at Elliston in a letter he wrote on July 1 to the Coalition: "While Elliston . . . might be the 'slowest' of the schools to join the Coalition, we hope that proceeding carefully will result in broad teacher and community support for our efforts. . . . Thirty-three members of our professional staff are on the Sizer Committee, . . . more than a third of our staff. This high level of commitment will be of great benefit as we begin our deliberations."

In November 1986, the school board voted to join the Coalition. Two coordinators were appointed to direct this effort. In a letter of January 1, 1987, to the Coalition, Ken Wallace outlined plans for the first year and the proposed structure of Elliston's Coalition program. "As a school, we are still stumbling out of the starting blocks. This semester will be spent on a variety of organizational activities, including discussions of the principles, identification of current programs that address the principles, and development of a two to three year plan of activities. In addition, we will [plan] local seminars and curriculum writing projects for this summer. . . . Our organizational structure will include a steering committee representing teachers, administrators, parents, students, and the Board of Education. Initially, I will be chairing this committee. Hopefully, . . . leadership will shift to faculty as we develop specific plans and have adequate funding."

The 1986–87 school year was primarily used to plan because Elliston was on double sessions at the junior high while the high school was renovated. Although the coordinators felt the school as a whole was progressing in its Coalition-related work, opposition to Coalition affiliation also emerged. When a Coalition central staff member visited the school in late March, faculty questioned their school's Coalition membership. Some worried that electives would be eliminated and jobs lost. Some felt that they had little time to devote to the project (in part due to the double sessions). Others expressed a lack of trust in the administration and concern about the faculty's ability to collaborate effectively. Still others felt union issues might arise, especially regarding equity. The staff member's field notes included two direct quotes about issues he felt needed immediate attention: "A lot of us are thinking this is a pig in a poke. . . . We are now good—if it ain't broke, don't fix it." and " 'Election' is a misnomer. . . . Do you hear us? This [was] pushed down our throats. There's not much support for this in the faculty room."

These two issues—whether change was needed and whether Coalition membership was imposed in a top-down manner—remained unresolved at Elliston throughout its brief, turbulent membership in the Coalition. They were most prominent when change at larger-than-the-classroom level was attempted and when discussions about the school's mission and philosophy emphasized Coalition principles. These tensions, articulated at the start of Elliston's membership, sum up the political and philosophical opposition that would force the vote that led to the school leaving the Coalition two years later. It would be misleading, however, to suggest that opposition was, from the start, unified and aggressive. The resistance actually comprised various factions, each of which objected to Coalition affiliation for different reasons.

The following academic year (1987–88), the coordinators organized a school and community project based on Coalition practice, created a steering committee to oversee Coalition work, provided teachers with opportunities for professional development tied to Coalition philosophy and practice, published an occasional newsletter, and considered developing a pilot Coalition program for implementation in 1988–89. In addition, one coordinator wrote, "We have decided to narrow our scope to three of the nine common principles . . . (1) less-is-more, (2) student-as-worker, and (3) decency." Beyond this, the coordinators continued to experiment with their own interpretations of Coalition pedagogy in their classrooms and presented their work at Coalition symposia. A few other Elliston teachers also experimented with their teaching, and several faculty and administrators attended Coalition workshops.

In fall 1987, a teacher, who described himself as philosophically opposed to Sizer's ideas and skeptical of their practical feasibility, circulated to all faculty copies of an article that derided the "process approach" to learning as ignoring content and questioned whether the Coalition might have similar problems. Some faculty again challenged the procedure used for joining the Coalition—was there a vote or was it a survey of faculty opinion? As faculty divisiveness intensified, one teacher wrote to the coordinators and suggested: "Don't use the words 'close-knit group' in any article. This may be true as a practical concept but destructive when it comes to the egos of the faculty, i.e., the Sizer Club." Further, many faculty resented the coordinators' providing support to change classroom practices because such offers seemed to imply that their teaching was inadequate. In interviews, both coordinators stressed how much they were learning; they had no idea how political things were at the school, nor were they prepared for the resistance they encountered.

In late October a Coalition staff member spoke with one coordinator about the steering committee and reported a sense of frustration at the school site. According to the coordinator, Wallace was trying to keep his "hands off," to allow the steering committee ownership of the budget and program. But the principal was also anxious to see an agreement reached in time to submit a budget to the school board in early February. Despite faculty resistance and the principal's concerns, the coordinators felt that there were positive developments that fall. One wrote in a journal that the steering committee was evolving and that the principal and many department heads seemed interested in a thematic, interdisciplinary project about American society, which the coordinators were trying to organize.

The steering committee was indeed getting off the ground: a group of interested faculty, administrators, and parents met in late September to establish guidelines. They decided that teacher representation on the committee would be by discipline and that the administration, school board, parents, and students would each have one representative. A total of eighteen volunteers served on the committee. The committee also outlined its responsibilities. As recorded in the minutes of an October meeting, these were "to meet as needed [to resolve ongoing issues], to represent each special interest group, to act as a sounding board, to regulate schoolwide programs, to share information and aid in communication, and to formulate [a] budget for next year." Some representatives to this committee opposed the Coalition and attended meetings in large part to monitor, and in some cases to impede, Coalition efforts.

In late spring 1988, the steering committee suggested a SWAS format as an appropriate structure for piloting Coalition ideas. Debate about a SWAS pilot began the following fall and continued until December. At a committee meeting in December—more than two years after the school had joined the Coalition and with little in place except the committee and individual efforts in a few classrooms—the issue of what being a Coalition school meant for Elliston was raised again, and the committee decided that a SWAS program would not be acceptable. The committee's report ended by raising a larger concern: "What we don't know . . . is what being a Coalition school could mean for us. What do we want it to mean? The steering committee feels that we as a staff and school community have to define what the Coalition principles mean for our school and for us as teachers. It is the hope of the committee that this process can be an open one which does not preclude the possibility of rejecting some of the principles or even all of them."

Eventually the committee, the principal, and the Coalition coordinators determined that the school would vote in the spring about continued Coalition membership. As part of the debate, throughout the 1988–89 school year several strongly worded memos were circulated among the faculty. The following excerpts from these memos address some of the key issues:

Memo 1: Membership in the Coalition steering committee should be changed. It is my understanding that the responsibility of the steering committee is to promote, foster, and implement the Coalition principles at Elliston High School. As we all have heard many times, the perception of many faculty members is that the Coalition would eliminate . . . electives. Therefore, jobs and departments will be cut or eliminated. People volunteered (or were appointed) to make sure this didn't happen (protect my turf). This has created a no-win situation for both the committee and the school. The committee is charged to carry out a task that its members do not want to see accomplished.

Recommendation: If we continue in the Coalition two committees should be established: One consisting of people who want the Coalition to succeed and one to be a "watch dog" to make sure the rights of individuals and departments are protected.

Memo 2: Our joining the Coalition was due to the interest of some of the faculty in looking at itself in the light of changing times, called for by many studies of American schools and completely in accord with an ongoing study of a vibrant and vital institution. These reasons for some sort of evaluation are quite valid and it seems to be incumbent on those who might vote nonsupport of the Coalition to offer an alternative.

Another aspect to be aware of is that a vote of nonsupport will give a clear message to those who have been involved that their efforts can be undone by others who for whatever reason, well founded or frivolous, are not interested in doing things that particular way.

Memo 3: When I attended a conference at Brown to learn about the Coalition, I thoroughly enjoyed it. It was stimulating to sit around with other members of our profession and discuss educational issues—to present problems that we all encounter and try to arrive at innovative solutions. I agree wholeheartedly with [the authors of other memos] that teachers need and benefit from these precious moments of reflection. However, upon my return to Elliston, reality set in. [My] department was and is in the midst of a complete revamping of our program. The funding that we needed for our curriculum writing was reduced. In my own conscience I cannot justify spending money at a conference at Brown when money is needed for our own programs right here at home.

I *am not* going to sit down and write down my definition of the nine principles. What I need is enough money to make sure that we have the necessary materials for our new curriculum and time in the summer to continue . . . revisions. If the school board wants to give me additional time in the summer for discussion and reflection, I will gladly take it. But if it comes down to a choice, the moneys will be better spent on . . . immediate needs.

One memo included a letter from Ted Sizer to all member schools strongly encouraging a commitment to schoolwide implementation of Coalition philosophy. This excerpt from his letter proved problematic for Elliston staff: "It is virtually impossible to pursue one of the nine Common Principles without ultimately engaging with them all. . . . Improving the work in conventional classrooms is a wonderful thing but insufficient for this particular Coalition's work. Our goal is more ambitious—to effect a new, demonstrably higher level of educational quality by breaking out, where necessary, of existing constraining structures" (Sizer 1989a). The February (1989) faculty meeting at Elliston included a lengthy debate about Sizer's letter, particularly about whether the school had to implement all nine principles to remain a Coalition member. Although this had been a concern from the start, it came to dominate discussions about membership, and one coordinator wrote to Sizer to ask for clarification about some of the issues that had arisen within the faculty.[2]

Other events affected discussion of the school's relation to the Coalition. During 1988–89, Elliston High received a national award from one of the teachers' unions—based on an application that highlighted the school's Coalition-related work. The award was announced while debate about Coalition membership was intensifying, and some of those opposed to membership viewed this award as résumé-building by the coordinators, not as an achievement the entire school could embrace.

At the end of March, in preparation for a faculty vote on continued Coalition membership, the steering committee raised four questions: "(1) Does Elliston have to implement all nine principles in order to remain a member of the Coalition? (2) What does each principle actually mean? What do we currently do with each principle? (3) How do the principles apply to our [proposed] new mission statement? (4) Should Elliston continue its affiliation with the national Coalition?" Numerous communications with Coalition central staff requested clarification on the first point and inquired about the boundaries of local interpretation—for example, could individual principles be completely

---

2. When Sizer received this letter, he circulated it among members of the central staff and requested their input. One person responded with a memo that emphasized, in part, what the Coalition might learn from the Elliston experience: "Many of these questions are unspoken in other schools we're involved with because a lot of the faculty simply don't see their lives being affected by the Coalition and therefore see no need to raise these questions. So, on the positive side, the fact that these questions are raised indicates that the faculty at Elliston has seen the future in terms of the nine Common Principles and are now beginning to pay attention. . . . The letter [also] . . . drives home to me how much more work we have to do in spelling out for our schools with examples of what are our interpretations of the playing out, in the school setting, of comprehensiveness, less-is-more, teacher-as-generalist, and of one-to-eighty. We must spell these out in ways that go beyond the legitimate concerns about 'giving up subjects.' We must encourage teachers to recognize the . . . difficulty of becoming more accountable with the curriculum in their own hands. We must spell out the notions of teacher-as-generalist . . . and . . . attempt to spin out examples of how achieving a ratio of one-to-eighty does not necessarily mean the loss of jobs but much work."

rewritten? The underlying question always remained: Why did Elliston need to change? In late April, Sizer responded to the coordinator's earlier letter with a ten-page letter in which he elaborated on his earlier comments but still emphasized that all nine common principles were interrelated.

In May, the faculty received a survey listing each of the nine common principles and the proposed local interpretation. Faculty were asked to indicate the extent of their agreement with the steering committee's interpretations, which were identical to only three of the nine Coalition principles: universal goals, exhibitions of mastery, and values of unanxious expectation. There was an explicit redefinition of the principles concerning the comprehensive high school, student-as-worker, and teacher-as-generalist. The remaining principles (simple goals, personalization, and budget) were reworded but not completely challenged. Generally, there was strong agreement with the common principles *as rewritten*. The comment section of the survey, however, included strong disagreements and criticisms, indicating that previous interpretive differences had not been erased by what seemed to be greater consensus about the committee's interpretation of the common principles. Among the comments were: "Less is not necessarily better"; "We are losing our comprehensiveness when we drop courses and programs in the elective areas"; "I am opposed to Sizer's concept of teachers being generalists"; and "Student-as-worker is not palatable." Two faculty comments addressed wider issues: "If we want to rewrite so many of these, why are we in the Coalition?" and "What *are* the school's goals?" Just before the vote, the principal and the coordinators each summarized their views in memos to the faculty.

In June 1989, on the statement, "Elliston High School should continue its formal affiliation with the . . . Coalition of Essential Schools," faculty voted fifty-five opposed and thirty in favor. The school requested permission for interested faculty to attend Coalition-sponsored activities, and that summer a few teachers took part in workshops. No further participation in Coalition activities has occurred since.

COMMENTARY BY PARTICIPANTS, NOVEMBER 1989

Six months after this decision was made, we interviewed several Elliston faculty and administrators. In their remarks, no one attributed opposition to the Coalition, the heated debating, or the final vote to withdraw solely to one factor. Most listed several, as did a Coalition proponent: "I think there was a 'three *P*s kind of [thing]. . . . There were pedagogical questions throughout; there were political issues; and then there were some personal, personality, things." Respondents also frequently mentioned that a fear of change, a lack of interest in change, or an unwillingness to change contributed to the tensions that enveloped the school. As one respondent noted: "A lot of our staff feels very competent in what they've been doing, and they feel that their students have been successful. . . . They just feel there wasn't a strong need for change." Overall, then, people identified four factors as contributing to the tension, debate, and eventual vote to withdraw: political issues, personality conflicts, philosophical differences, and questions of the need for change.

POLITICAL TENSIONS

The political tensions that arose subsumed four interrelated issues: the possible loss of jobs if Coalition philosophy were implemented, questions of whether this was a grassroots or top-down reform effort, concerns with membership in the reform-minded group, and equity issues. Given the declining enrollment in the district at the time, it is not surprising that job security became an issue. One teacher recalled: "Some people were opposed to [Coalition membership] because they very much felt threatened. An essential part of the Coalition is the idea of a core curriculum, and Sizer's idea that a school's purpose—central purpose—should be the intellectual improvement of kids' minds . . . threatened people in physical education, for example, . . . people teaching shop courses . . . people in any of the . . . courses that don't really fit into that core." The principal offered a different perspective:

> Were jobs ever threatened? Now my own view of that is no, they weren't. A person never lost a position here because of a decision about the Coalition. . . . Generally speaking, a reduction in staff occurs as a result of declining enrollment . . . and kids' selections of courses. But in people's minds, I think, jobs were lost because of the Coalition. . . . We lost the home economics program. We didn't lose it because of the Coalition, but it happened to cease to exist as a program here. . . . We've had reductions and people were laid off . . . and I think that some people attributed that to the

Coalition. But what they don't realize is that we went through a serious decline in enrollment from 1,350 students to 950 students, and . . . minimized the faculty loss over that time, and improved the teacher-pupil ratio . . . and part of that is because I could use the leverage of the Coalition . . . when talking to the superintendent about achieving our objectives. We made a commitment to 1-to-80 [faculty-student ratio].

A second political issue was whether this reform effort was a top-down or grassroots initiative, and many related issues—whether faculty had voted to join the Coalition, whether a vote to determine continued membership would be scheduled, how much the principal controlled the program, and so forth—reflected this tension. One teacher, skeptical of the Coalition from the start, observed: "A lot of people felt that it was not a bottom-up movement, as it was advertised to be, but a top-down . . . movement . . . [driven by the] principal. . . . People were very skeptical of the process. When we joined the Coalition a survey was used as a vote . . . and people weren't told that the survey was going to be used as a vote. So people were unclear as to what the purpose of the survey was when they filled it out . . . and when people realized how the survey was used, it created some anger. . . . So, right off the bat, there was some bitterness about the way in which we joined."

A faculty member who felt that a vote had been taken still acknowledged that top-down concerns were at issue: "There was a feeling all along by a percentage of the staff that [Coalition membership] was rammed down their throats . . . even though the faculty was involved and votes were taken and decisions were made very openly and publicly. . . . I don't think that's an accurate perception, but yet I think that was felt here by a fairly good percentage of the faculty. So there's always been that kind of feeling, 'Well, we just had no choice in this. It is another one of their administrative mandates that has been played upon us.'"

Another teacher suggested that the question of voting to determine continued membership deflected attention from academic issues:

At some point certain people on the faculty thought that they were going to have the option to vote, so there then existed a power struggle concerning, "When are we going to vote?" And a lot of people—instead of putting their effort and energies into the ideas and what was being learned—just really pressed heavily onto Ken,

"When are we going to vote?" and "We want to vote," and it made it very difficult for him because he doesn't want to dictate. . . . He wanted to have input and he tried to foster that. He's an excellent facilitator, [but] what happened was that the faculty was on a head hunt—"I want to vote and I want to vote now." And I don't think people were voting on the Coalition-of-Essential-Schools-as-a-method-of-reform. They were voting on Coalition-of-Essential-Schools-I-don't-want-to-lose-my-job, and that bothers me. That bothers me a lot.

Factionalism within the faculty represented an additional political concern. One coordinator addressed this issue:

Very clearly it became a question of politics. . . . If you're in the [Coalition] group, you're in the in-crowd. If you're not, you're in the out-crowd. And only good people: principals, buddies . . . are the good people and are interested in doing a good job for children. So if you were "in," you were a good teacher. If you were "out," you were a bad teacher. That's political. I know it was a we-they kind of a thing in the sense that [the Coalition] was from on high, [as] it was perceived [by many]. [Here it] was really Ken's baby, and he wasn't going to let it die in any way, and he'd do anything in his power to keep it. And [the out-group] has all kinds of examples of how he did that. How it took three years, for instance, for a vote to finally come about.

Offering his perspective, Wallace framed the issue of factionalism in terms of the reform-minded group not including traditional school leaders, which made winning and losing within the faculty as much a concern as Coalition philosophy: "You get these kinds of ins and outs of who has control and new blood versus old blood—all those kind of classic issues related to change. This was not something that came out . . . but the people who were most associated with the Coalition were not what I would call the traditional faculty leaders. . . . [And] eventually [it] gets to the point where . . . you forget what the issues are . . . and it becomes winning and losing, and we and they. That bothered me a bit because it wasn't so much them versus me [the principal]. It was an intrafaculty discussion. Although it was played out in a very professional way."

The final political issue involved concerns with equity. As a Coalition proponent observed, many Elliston teachers were apprehensive: "Some people saw [the Coalition] as an elitist thing—that there were only a few of us who wanted to do it and that others were going to be dragged kicking and screaming into it, whether they wanted to or not. Or that it would be, even worse, a school-within-a-school, and there would be some privileged group. . . . That's kind of a natural response, I guess . . . people here really guard their turf. We want to make sure everything's equitable in this place and sometimes to the detriment of the school. . . . But sometimes people get petty."

A faculty member who opposed Coalition affiliation connected his concerns directly to how Elliston allocated its discretionary funding:

> A lot of people . . . wondered why we needed to join the Coalition to make educational reform. Why can't we do it on the local level? Why do we need to join a national group when we get into an issue of spending money? Why are we spending money sending people here and there and everywhere when we could maybe spend the money better. . . . [Then the state] changed our curricula around, so why weren't we spending more money rewriting our curricula versus sending people all over the place and getting teachers release time? So, it was very hard to get answers as to how much money we were actually spending. The standard line was, "Well, the Coalition is paying for all these people." Okay, they're paying for all those people. Who's paying for their substitutes when they're missing classes? And there weren't answers on that. If they're going to take a teacher, two teachers out of a classroom, that's going to cost money. Could that money be better spent developing math curriculum, and developing social studies curriculum?

PERSONALITY CONFLICTS

Personality conflicts at Elliston High also influenced this reform effort. Specifically, within the faculty there emerged concerns about résumé building as a motive for involvement in Coalition reform, distrust of the principal and his reasons for becoming involved with the Coalition, resentment toward the coordinators for the benefits others felt they received, and criticism of the leadership styles of the principal and the coordinators. Some felt Wallace would leave the faculty with a program they had never agreed on. As one teacher said: "Some people felt that Ken was imposing this on us, whether we wanted it or not. That he'd made a decision up front." A Coalition supporter noted how skeptical faculty reacted: "You hear that all the time . . . 'Ken's building his resume. He's onward and upward, and as soon as he leaves he's going to leave us with this thing that no one wants. [But] we can wait him out. If we just prolong it long enough, we'll get out of it.' And, of course, they were successful. They did."

In part, faculty mistrust of Wallace stemmed from his decision to take a hands-off approach to Coalition membership. As one of his supporters said, there was "a great sense of distrust, of not knowing what Ken really was about." Wallace himself said: "My personal dilemma was whether or not to become more involved in the actual work of the steering committee . . . and whether to be more involved in the political strife. I chose—and evaluated that decision a number of times with a number of people—to not become actively involved in those things because I felt that if the Coalition was going to survive here, it had to survive because the faculty had a broad-based support for it, [not simply] because the principal wanted it. Now I took a lot of lumps. And I know that. It's kind of an easy way for people . . . to say, 'Well if the principal had been more active, he could have saved it.' I chose not to do that."

Addressing the same issue—Wallace's level of involvement with reform—one teacher suggested that it may have been a no-win situation: "[Ken] tried to take a very low-key, hands-off approach. I think some people were suspicious of that. They said, 'We all know down deep that he wants it and that he believes in it and that he would like to see it implemented, so . . . the fact that he's not [directly involved], there must be a reason.' . . . And then there were other people, like myself, who suggested that he should just say 'Yeah. We're going to do it. It's my idea. Tough if you don't like it. But that's the way it is. It's the best thing educationally that we have going for us.' . . . *So it was kind of a dammed-if-you-do and dammed-if-you-don't situation.*" Regardless of his actions, Wallace could be accused of résumé building. If he imposed reform on the school, he would have violated his hands-off policy, as well as the Coalition's emphasis on local autonomy. If he let the faculty vote and lived with their decision, the question became: Did he really care about the Coalition or his own advancement?

A similar sense of mistrust was directed toward the coordinators, and this further complicated the situation. As Wallace recalled:

[The coordinators] published things, and then people would take potshots at them through newsletters. I think they were viewed to some degree as trying to create this image of the Coalition doing tremendous things at the school, and people said, "Well, Ken, is the substance really there?" So there was a feeling on the part of some faculty that, "I've been doing great things all along and all of a sudden [the Coalition] is getting a lot of publicity for some things that I've been doing because they're just good teaching and good coaching, and [the Coalition] is out there getting awards and getting articles written." . . . You've got all this ego stuff. . . . Behind the scenes some of it was pretty personal, and I know [the coordinators] took their lumps, and some of the decisions they made, and some of the ways they approached it, and some of the things they did caused that, but some of it was also pretty unkind. And that bothered me. Certainly, participation in the Coalition is less important than having a faculty who has the ability to work together . . . and not be at each other's throats.

PHILOSOPHICAL TENSIONS AND QUESTIONS ABOUT THE NEED FOR CHANGE

From the outset, there was concern about whether faculty had to accept all nine principles, even though the early work of Elliston's Sizer Study Committee deemphasized this issue and stressed only those principles the staff found useful. When faculty initially spoke to the Coalition central staff, some recall being told to pursue what they found useful and not to concern themselves with what was not.[3] After Sizer's letter asserted the fundamental interconnectedness of the common principles, some faculty challenged his stance. One teacher recalled: "I think many of us . . . see the Sizer principles . . . as one piece of something that you

3. Many Elliston faculty noted this, but it became increasingly unacceptable (and inconceivable) to the central staff that schools could view the principles as separable. The central staff's view, which became commonly accepted, was that the common principles are fundamentally interconnected and although schools may determine the most appropriate place to start, they will have to work toward implementing all nine.

do in your classroom: the student-as-worker, providing the students with some questions, and having them go out on their own and find the answers and working with them. It's one method that is valuable, but it's not the end-all. There are other methods. Lecture is another way of getting information in. Again, that's not the end-all, either." Other teachers felt they should pick and choose from various reform ideas: "Mostly the people felt that . . . Sizer has some good things, but . . . there are other methods out there. So . . . why not take the best of each one of them instead of tying ourselves to one—especially when Sizer says that we have to accept all nine principles?"

In addition, faculty voiced reservations about specific principles. The final sentence of the first principle proved particularly contentious: "Schools should not attempt to be 'comprehensive' if such a claim is made at the expense of the school's central intellectual purpose." Teachers worried about what might be eliminated if Elliston were no longer comprehensive.

> I think the biggest philosophical disagreement that people had was a fear that Sizer was talking about a school much different from ours in terms of a comprehensive high school. People generally feel strongly that they want a high school in Elliston that offers physical education, that offers health classes, that offers business classes.
>
> I believe in a comprehensive high school. I believe in a "shopping mall high school." Society has made certain demands on us because of needs in society. . . . I do think also that we need to have options for kids. I think we need to recognize that kids are different . . . and it's okay if kids have different courses . . . if they take other courses—other than the core. . . . There's different information out there that would be more beneficial . . . for certain kids.

Faculty felt so strongly about this issue that, after leaving the Coalition, they voted to reaffirm their commitment to being a comprehensive high school in their mission statement.

A second philosophical tension centered on the concept of teacher-as-generalist and stemmed from the larger issue of professionalism in secondary school teaching. At Elliston High, teachers identified closely with their specialties. As one explained, "Elliston is such a great organization because every teacher thinks their subject is *the* most important subject." Many faculty resented what they perceived as the Coalition asking them to sacrifice their specializations to accept varied tasks within the school, some of which they felt unqualified to handle. One respondent remarked: "The biggest conflict was over the [principle] about teacher-as-generalist. . . . I could teach an AP European history class, but if you put me into AP American [history], I'm not as qualified. . . . Also I think some teachers think that the chemistry teacher all of a sudden will be teaching English, and I don't think the Coalition meant that, but I could be wrong." Elaborating, she stated, "A lot of the teachers didn't want to get involved with counseling." With some skepticism, she added, "Does the Coalition actually think that teachers could do college advisement?"

Throughout the interviews, Elliston faculty presented two dissonant perspectives of what it meant to be a professional. In one view, increased professionalism, self-esteem, and recognition would result from the re-thinking that Coalition philosophy encouraged, including the idea of teacher-as-generalist. In the other view, professionalism derived from one's expertise—one was a chemist or an historian who taught. Ultimately, the faculty concluded that they would retain their specializations and become a large faculty with a comprehensive mission, and such specialized individuals as guidance counselors and drug counselors would handle other facets of school life.

Two additional issues were whether the school should adopt student-as-worker and teacher-as-coach as its dominant metaphors for classroom practice, and whether less-is-more was an appropriate way to structure the school's curricula. One Coalition advocate described the dilemma faced by a colleague:

> [One colleague] may not talk about this, but I think he was an example of the group of faculty who felt they hold other notions about teaching. And "threatened" may be a strong word, but certainly they looked at what was being advocated in terms of the role of the teacher-as-coach, teaching kids to think, and less-is-more, and it was to some degree a contradiction as to how they'd spent their professional career . . . which was essentially teaching [their] courses in a fairly traditional manner, using the lecture, recitation method . . . as the main methodology. And to see things

like group projects and student-as-worker and to make choices about what curriculum to cover, thinking about different assessment devices, was all pretty threatening to . . . how they had been teaching for years.

Teachers also questioned whether the proposed changes would improve anything, whether there was evidence that Coalition practices were more effective. Often they used their own logical starting points—such as issues of coverage—as tools of analysis. For example, one teacher said, "[A colleague] used the Sizer approach in his social studies eleven class—he just plain did not cover, so to speak, the same amount of material that the rest of the department was covering." Faculty also questioned the practicality of such Coalition ideas as interdisciplinary studies that were integrated across the curriculum: "I think Sizer is naive in thinking we can present a curriculum to kids that shows the interrelatedness of all things. I'm not opposed to that, but I'm not so sure that his idea, from the way he described it, [is] possible." This teacher felt if Sizer's ideas were fully implemented, eighty students per teacher would be *too many* students. He concluded, "I don't think his ultimate dream is practical."

COALITION CENTRAL STAFF INVOLVEMENT

When asked about assistance from the Coalition central staff, most Elliston faculty agreed that they received help or clarification in a useful and timely way. One woman said: "I thought it was more than supportive . . . there was never a problem. . . . It felt very comfortable to call or contact if need be. I never thought that there were any communication problems or that there wasn't support there if we needed it." Another said: "We were in constant contact, and we wrote long letters to Ted [Sizer] because we wanted long letters back. And he certainly did that to clarify a lot of the issues. . . . And he did a good job of it, except for a couple of things about which he never quite satisfied our staff because they were never going to be satisfied about those issues anyway. So consequently, we did all we could to have the Coalition sell central headquarters, so to speak."

Ken Wallace also felt the Coalition staff had been responsive and that no further assistance had been needed: "Assistance [as we went] through this process of review was probably not even appropriate . . . because unless somebody wanted to come and live here for six months . . . and try to work as a facilitator to manage the process, the assistance would be almost inappropriate. It was a struggle that had to play itself out."

Elliston staff who attended Coalition-sponsored workshops, conferences, or symposia were enthusiastic about these experiences. They described Coalition staff as knowledgeable and enthusiastic, and they appreciated the opportunity to learn how others were rethinking their teaching, student learning, and school structure. One teacher even described a workshop he attended as "a personal and professional epiphany," after more than twenty years in the classroom. He advocated sending faculty to similar functions before deciding on membership: "I definitely think as many people as possible should get involved in the summer training sessions before they decide anything [about membership]. Get involved. Try to get as much information on it as you can. I know that it is not possible to send a quarter of the faculty to a summer workshop, but certainly people have to get a better understanding of it.

In examining what occurred at Elliston High, we note a few points. Perhaps the most critical is that, from the outset of reform, there was no consensus that fundamental changes in school structure or in individual teaching practices needed to occur. To support this stance, faculty regularly cited the school's history of success. As one teacher remarked, "It always gets turned around to the old idea: 'If it ain't broke, don't fix it.' You know, trying to tell people in a school where 90 percent of the kids get a three or above on an AP exam to change how they're teaching [is not easy]." Given the school's success with AP exams and student acceptance by prestigious universities, it was not enough for Elliston faculty to hear that Coalition reforms might improve student learning; they wanted proof. Otherwise, experimentation might jeopardize student performance in terms of these accepted measures of success and thereby undermine the school's reputation.[4]

4. This point is ironic because many schools visited during Sizer's original study ("A Study of High Schools") were more like Elliston than those that joined the Coalition and Re:Learning. Indeed, the argument of *Horace's Compromise* and *The Shopping Mall High School* was not that schools were failing dismally, but that they were not sufficiently challenging, engaging, or thought-provoking.

Faculty also resisted change because of such perceived constraints as administrative turnover. One pro-Coalition faculty member summarized these concerns: "Well, that's the line from some of the older teachers: 'We've gone through this stuff over and over again, and all you do is get a new superintendent and he changes everything. A new principal comes in, and you're right back where you started from. All this time and effort and you've gotten nowhere. You've got yourself all psyched up and ready to go and then somebody steps in and says, "Sorry. I don't like that."' There's a lot of that around." Another faculty member offered a comparable assessment of faculty cynicism toward change: "We had so many problems with modular scheduling. It was Band-Aid, Band-Aid, Band-Aid. Make it work. Make it work. Make it work. Well, it just wouldn't work. And [after almost twenty years] we finally [have come back] very close to our traditional schedule. The politics at this school says, 'Oh no, not another innovation! . . . New principal. New ideas.' You see, this has nothing to do with the Coalition."

By the time Elliston voted itself out of the Coalition, this lack of consensus was evident. But when the Coalition effort began, it was masked somewhat by agreements about how to begin the project, by the early emphases on involving only those willing to participate, and by Elliston's initial interpretations of the common principles which downplayed those principles that proved most divisive. Since there was no expectation that change had to be schoolwide, faculty adopted a live-and-let-live attitude. However, once Sizer announced that the second step of reform should entail schoolwide reexamination of structure and practice in line with all nine common principles, the situation changed markedly. Increasingly, faculty claimed that they were being force-fed Coalition practices. Pedagogical and philosophical issues that had been problematic from the start—such as whether Elliston should be a comprehensive high school, the concept of teacher-as-generalist, and the pedagogical implications of student-as-worker and less-is-more—and which had been ignored, reemerged. All these tensions were implicated in the decision to leave the Coalition.

In an assessment of that decision, a related observation seems noteworthy. In many respects, Elliston faculty were quite empowered. They demanded a vote that led to the school's leaving the Coalition, indicating that power relations between faculty and administration differed from those at other schools where Coalition membership had not been perceived as negotiable. At other study schools, faculty resistance was not given credence by administrators nor was it discussed at faculty meetings.

Further, unlike the staff at other schools where we worked, Elliston faculty carefully considered the implications of *all* correspondence from the Coalition central staff. In our interviews, these persons frequently referred to the programmatic shift in the Coalition that was highlighted by Ted Sizer's January 1989 letter as one important turning point vis à vis the school's involvement with the Coalition. In part, proponents' statements that this shift exacerbated the problems at Elliston should be given credence, largely because Coalition opponents regularly cited this development as one reason for opposing the Coalition. That is, what was supposed to be local interpretation of reform philosophy was, in their view, slowly becoming directed by the Coalition's central staff.

A final implication concerning the Elliston faculty should be mentioned. Their decision-making process was thoughtful and reflective. Although the strong sense of professional identity (tied in part to subject matter specialization) held by many Elliston faculty was an impediment to accepting Coalition philosophy, Coalition membership did promote facultywide discussion of aspects of school life that typically went undiscussed, including the school's philosophy and the need for change. As one teacher remarked: "I think . . . that [Coalition membership] stimulated an awareness that reform—some reforms—are necessary, that things are not all wonderful here." One active critic of Coalition philosophy made a similar judgment: "I think it did have a positive effect in that it got us talking philosophically about what we're doing and that kind of dialectic is good. It made you examine what you're doing and either junk it or try to justify it. Some people kept some of the ideas and are using them in their classrooms." A science teacher identified how this process influenced his department: "In essence we gained—we pulled out of it what we found we could use. We think we can do our own program still within a traditional schedule, still within the funding that's allowed by the district, but still move much closer to student-as-worker and coaching techniques."

Ken Wallace also viewed the school's involvement positively: "It was successful in terms of transforming a number of individual teachers, and it was successful in helping us to develop a mission statement, to look at an approach to schooling, accept some of it and reject parts, to influence the debate." Many agreed with Wallace that the long-term consequences of Coalition involvement were likely to be a continuing conversation about the school's mission and philosophy. As one noted: "[the issue of change] generated numerous educational discussions and, we've had to challenge some of our basic thoughts and philosophies in education. And I think it's ongoing. I think the work we started is continuing whether we belong to the Coalition or not."

After leaving the Coalition, the school adopted a new mission statement that incorporated ideas all factions recognized as echoing Coalition ideas. The mission statement also reaffirmed the school's commitment to being comprehensive and to reflecting continually on its practices and philosophy. Thus, the ongoing reassessment promoted by the Coalition as an essential part of school life should continue at Elliston, albeit within a framework that does not embrace all of Coalition philosophy.

5

"BUT WE'RE *NOT* FAILING *HERE*"
THE COALITION AT EVANS HILL HIGH SCHOOL

The better the high school, the more skeptical the faculty. . . . The more they have to protect—especially that which they think they do well—the less they have the impetus . . . to look at what they do. If a school faculty thinks it's one of the best, what do they have to [change]?
—MARY ELLEN SMITH, PRINCIPAL

Looking back . . . we learned some important lessons about change. We learned the value of political savvy in times of reform, the need for mutual support and comradeship, . . . and that responsibility for reform must shift from those who lead to those who do.   —A PRO-COALITION TEACHER

When changes require teachers to think and behave differently than what they have been schooled in and experienced at doing, then you need to provide support for them. Teachers need to gain confidence at performing in their new role, and they need a clearly articulated intellectual framework. . . . It is ironic that administrators so often forget that their job is still educating, only it is educating the teachers. Success requires that vision, and the resources of time and money.   —THOMAS SPRINGER, PRINCIPAL

In this chapter we look at a Coalition reform effort in another public high school with a record of academic success. Evans Hill and Elliston (see chapter 4) serve similar populations: affluent, primarily white, suburban students who plan to attend prestigious colleges and universities. Both schools went through similar investigations before joining the Coalition of Essential Schools, yet Evans Hill—unlike Elliston—did implement various Coalition-based reforms. A forceful principal, Dr. Mary Ellen Smith, and a small group of interested teachers, dubbed the "Sizer group," developed an interdisciplinary (English, history, and art) program, an alternative form of governance, and an advisory program. They also received a grant from the Coalition to develop exhibitions for their classes. Apart from this small grant, Coalition activities were largely funded by the Evans Hill public school budget.

At Evans Hill, as at Elliston, Coalition membership was problematic, and faculty resistance—coupled with the unanticipated departure of both the principal and assistant principal—left those committed to Coalition ideas feeling isolated and embattled. Although the school never left the Coalition, its faculty and local community had not wholeheartedly embraced change by the end of our research (June 1991). In effect, Coalition-inspired innovations became a part of Evans Hill's many curricular offerings, and students selected them just as they might take an AP course or join the yearbook committee; they were not efforts to reconceive how best to educate all students. For most Evans Hill teachers and parents, the school already offered its students many outstanding opportunities.

EVANS HILL HIGH SCHOOL

Evans Hill is one of a patchwork of tiny communities in a county adjacent to a large metropolitan area. It is known for its residential desirability and its excellent school system. Mansion-like homes are common. Indeed, homes rarely sell for less than $400,000. The community's public school (a K–12 self-contained district) is housed in a conspicuous, castle-like edifice surrounded by manicured lawns and playing fields. Its parking lots are filled with late-model cars belonging to well-paid faculty and, just as often, to upperclassmen who drive to school. The school building offers an impressive mix of traditional and modern. The turn-of-the-century building has been freshly carpeted and painted, but much of the original woodwork has been carefully preserved. The foyer is filled with displays of student artwork. A walk through the hallways provides a sense of the community's ability to provide for their children: one sees computer labs, small classes (the student-teacher ratio was 15-to-1 and average class size approximately twenty), an expansive library, several auditoriums, and a cafeteria with a short-order menu and a student lounge.

Evans Hill High enjoys a favorable reputation in the community and throughout the county. Most faculty hold multiple degrees, are tenured, and view themselves as specialists in their fields. Graduates frequently attend Ivy League universities and other exclusive colleges. The school's student population is 96 percent white, 3 percent Asian, and less than 1 percent "other." The number of Asian students reflects the fact that in the late 1980s many Asian businessmen relocated their families from overseas to this community. The "less than 1 percent other" are generally the children of live-in servants and service workers. Between 1982 and 1990, because of demographic shifts, the school experienced a 30 percent decline in enrollment (from 440 to less than 300). Coupled with a relatively fixed education budget and a shrinking tax base, this decline meant that per pupil expenditures rose to well over $10,000.

If Robert Coles had visited Evans Hill, he might have included its students in his work on the "privileged ones" (Coles 1980). In general, students are attentive in class, their responses to questions are articulate, and their frequent references to personal experiences that bear on class-room discussions suggest lifestyles and opportunities uncommon to most high school students. However, these students are not trouble-free; substance abuse and other adolescent ills arise frequently. Nevertheless, their upbringing has tended to prepare them to assume that a promising future will follow success in high school and college. To help ensure this success, most work hard. In fact, Evans Hill students reported the most time spent on homework assignments of eleven schools we surveyed in a student questionnaire, significantly higher than any other school.

Parents are actively involved with the school and are often perceived as pressuring their children to participate in more activities and urging the school to offer more electives and extracurricular activities to enhance their children's chances for college admission. In a long-term planning outline prepared for the Coalition central staff in 1987, Evans Hill faculty addressed this concern: "In a college preparatory program the pressure is to offer more rather than less, because more is better both to the community and to the colleges. The more [AP] classes, foreign language classes, and other activities a student participates in, the better the student is able to compete in the college admissions game." In line with this goal, in 1985 Evans Hill introduced an entirely new schedule, based on an eight-day, rotating pattern intended to minimize the loss of elective offerings due to declining enrollment and to allow students to take more courses.

THE COALITION AT EVANS HILL

A teacher-ethnographer summarized the first steps that Evans Hill took toward becoming a member of the Coalition in a report for the 1985–86 school year:[1]

In fall 1984 at the opening day faculty meeting, Dr. [Mary Ellen] Smith [the new principal] invited the faculty to [discuss] recent national reports on high schools published by the National Commission on Excellence in Education, and by individuals such as Goodlad, Adler, Boyer, and by Sizer. In October four teachers and Dr. Smith went to Brown to meet Theodore Sizer. Dr. Smith then invited Theodore Sizer to speak at a faculty meeting. Following his address, interested faculty members formed a study group to discuss the high school curriculum. A dozen teachers met weekly through the winter and spring.

According to participants, these sessions offered teachers a chance to talk about special and routine problems of teaching at Evans Hill. During these often emotional discussions, the teachers shared their frustrations with the status quo and developed a desire for change. The committee became interested in joining the Coalition of Essential Schools. In April, three members of the committee attended a meeting . . . directed by Theodore Sizer. There they learned how the coalition was to be formed and how to apply for membership. The committee recommended that the board of education authorize the district to become a member of

1. As part of our research, we held workshops for teams of CES teachers and students, with the goal of helping them understand ethnographic research and apply this understanding to critical examination of their schools' efforts at change. The teacher quoted was the faculty representative at Evans Hill and a member of the Sizer group. Although her perspective reflects a positive attitude toward the Sizer group, she seemed sensitive to the differing opinions held by other faculty.

the Coalition. The proposal was accepted by the board of education in June.

In spring 1985, after nearly a year of preliminary discussions about curriculum restructuring and meetings with Sizer, Evans Hill joined the Coalition, without a faculty vote but with the full endorsement of the board of education. To build schoolwide support, a summer workshop was offered for interested faculty, as well as planning meetings and professional development activities during the 1985–86 school year. In addition, a voluntary committee, the Sizer group, met during the summer and once a week after school to craft a pilot program proposal for the 1986–87 school year for an interdisciplinary Western civilization elective.

Problems that surfaced during this period forced a partial retrenchment. First, planning was difficult for the Sizer group because other pressing school obligations—many of its members were active in planning a new middle school—made meetings difficult to arrange. Second, existing faculty rivalries coalesced into opposing political factions. Reflecting on the emergence of political tensions, the teacher-ethnographer wrote:

> The Sizer program became entangled in the political life of the school. Historical alliances and rivalries in the faculty mobilized around . . . the work of the Sizer group. In part, the committee became the issue in the struggle between these factions to establish some control over school reform. In part, it became the scapegoat for all the fear, confusion, and frustration that faculty suffered during a year of much change: the new schedule, the establishment of a middle school, curriculum changes . . . and last, but not least, the leadership from Dr. Smith.
>
> The interdisciplinary elective became the focus for the classic struggle between those who wanted to change and those who resisted change. . . . For example, the art and music departments worried that the interdisciplinary elective would conflict with their courses and thus reduce enrollment. In a community where the study of the arts is not considered as important as the study of "academic" subjects, these teachers saw the interdisciplinary elective as another threat to their survival. Reduced enrollments in their courses could mean the loss of jobs. Others were reluctant to

let teachers experiment with the curriculum or with teaching practices because they suspected that eventually, everyone would be forced to teach according to the Coalition's principles. . . . In essence, the committee's work was perceived to touch on the most sensitive of issues in teaching, job security and autonomy in the classroom.

By the end of the year, Sizer group members were disillusioned. They had experienced a lack of support and even personal attacks from colleagues. Parents, too, had objected to creating a "special program" and argued, "If the pilot were good enough for a few, it should be offered to all." The Sizer group's considerable time and energy had appeared to have produced little. As the teacher-ethnographer wrote: "We were frustrated and impatient with the pace of reform, but we had also become wary of the risks and responsibilities of orchestrating an experimental program. Instead of moving forward, we felt that we had succumbed to a powerful resistance to change from faculty, students, and parents."

THE INTERDISCIPLINARY PROGRAM

Despite the apparent scrapping of all plans for the program, a small interdisciplinary program was piloted in fall 1986. In its first year, "Interdisciplinary," as the program came to be known, enrolled fifteen ninth-grade students. During each eight-day cycle of Evans Hill's schedule, Interdisciplinary met jointly five times. The course involved teachers from two departments (history and English) who integrated the first year of a two-year Western civilization sequence with an English course that emphasized myths, legends, and classic works from the same period. For instance, while studying Greek history and philosophy in Western civilization, students read *The Odyssey* in English. To add a third dimension to the course, and to help link history and literature, an art teacher was part of the team. She taught the art of Western civilization, and she helped students develop the art projects that were integral to the course. These projects, for example, a mural depicting Renaissance life, reflected the major themes from their history and English classes. Each major course assignment, then, had three components: the art project, a research paper on some related aspect of history or English literature, and an oral presentation that linked the artistic work to the themes of the period and included an explanation of the creative process used to produce the artwork. During the oral presentation, students addressed the entire class and fielded questions from the three teachers and from other students.

Over the next four years, Interdisciplinary expanded to include grades nine through eleven; it came to incorporate the second half of Western civilization and U.S. history and the sophomore and junior English courses. Two sections of the elective were made available for each grade. Each team of teachers approached Interdisciplinary somewhat differently. For instance, the degree to which the fine arts were integrated varied, and the projects developed in each course ranged from art projects linked to history and literature, to mock trials of historic characters, to classroom debates. And although all teachers were teamed, what constituted team-teaching differed depending on the composition of the teams, the number of scheduled back-to-back periods, and the subject. In some years, because of leaves or scheduling conflicts, teachers teamed with people whose views differed from their own. When this happened, teachers often expressed frustration, and classes reverted to being taught separately, except when specific art or music projects necessitated collaboration. As one teacher commented: "You have to team with people with whom you feel comfortable, who have similar styles, and with whom you can make joint decisions. Otherwise it is so frustrating that it is not worth the effort." Still, the courses shared certain characteristics: the English and history teachers, for example, sought to keep their courses chronologically parallel (reading *The Grapes of Wrath* in English class while studying the Great Depression in U.S. history). Also, all three grades relied on block scheduling and, in some years, had common planning time.

From 1986 to 1990, the number of teachers directly involved in Interdisciplinary increased from three to seven. Some faculty were drawn from the Sizer group, but leaves and retirements in the English and history departments allowed Dr. Smith to hire long-term substitutes and new faculty to bolster the Interdisciplinary faculty. Because Dr. Smith felt that Evans Hill was committed to the Coalition, she hired teachers whose philosophies were compatible with the common principles and who were willing to join Interdisciplinary. During this same period, the number of students in the program increased from 15 to 115, roughly one-third of the school. For the first Interdisciplinary course, students were recruited through parent meetings, and participation was dependent on parental approval. The following year (1986–87), because of well-publicized descriptions of the program and its successes (both to the school board and at parent meetings), recruitment was not an issue. However, when the program expanded to the eleventh grade, recruitment was problematic, in part because some students felt self-imposed and parental pressure to take advanced placement U.S. history.

In Interdisciplinary's fourth year (1989–90), personnel changes and shifts in scheduling priorities had a significant and negative impact. Although all English and history teachers were provided more common planning time, they had fewer back-to-back classes and were no longer assured of being free during the "other" period of Interdisciplinary. The art projects linking history and literature had been possible because of the back-to-back periods and each teacher's voluntarily using his or her free time in the other subject's class, so these changes hurt the ninth-grade program. The tenth grade underwent modifications as well—one teacher was absent and the others were unwilling to team. The eleventh grade's approach was undermined by schedule changes that prevented the two Interdisciplinary teachers, who had worked together closely, from being in the same classroom together. Finally, that fall Evans Hill hired a new principal to replace Smith (who had taken a new job to be closer to her family). He asked participating faculty to reassess Interdisciplinary and to consider such questions as: "What is interdisciplinary about Interdisciplinary?" and "What are the continuities between the three grade level Interdisciplinaries?" With these changes, by January the teachers questioned whether the program could continue and whether—given their current situations—the courses were even remotely interdisciplinary. Although Interdisciplinary continued into 1990–91, administrators, Interdisciplinary faculty, and parents voiced concern about further expansion and scheduling issues as well as about the program's intent.

THE STUDENT-FACULTY LEGISLATURE

In addition to the Interdisciplinary program, Smith attempted to restructure the school's governance by blending the Coalition's common principles with Lawrence Kohlberg's ideas of the "just community" (1980, 1981, 1984, 1985). Smith, a student of Kohlberg's, saw these as compatible philosophies that would promote democracy and moral development. Specifically, she sought to replace Evans Hill's student government, which in her words had been "the group responsible for bake sales and other social activities," with a more representative group that would make decisions for the entire school. Together, students and faculty researched and designed the new government, called the Student-Faculty Legislature (SFL). Smith described it to a group of educators in August 1987:

> It is important to note that we call this a school government rather than a student government. The difference in definition is not just semantic; rather, it goes to the heart of the just community concept. A student government is generally an elected body of students who meet to plan and execute social functions. A school government, however, is far more comprehensive. It includes the various constituencies of a school, students to be sure, but also teachers, secretaries, custodians, and administrators. Because of the variety of points of view and stages of development in such a diverse group, it not only becomes a microcosm of the school as a whole, but is a ripe environment for moral growth.
>
> The Student-Faculty Legislature is the legislative branch of school government and is designed to allow students, faculty, and support staff to decide on the noncurricular issues that govern the life of the school. It rests on the democratic idea that members of the school community ought to have the privilege and responsibility of governing the community. Incorporated into its operating procedures are the following key principles:
>
> 1. Any student, teacher, or member of the support staff (clerical, custodial, civil service) may present a proposal to the legislature.
> 2. All decisions [made] by the legislature will be by majority vote.
> 3. Proposals passed will be sent to the principal for veto or approval. The principal constitutes the executive branch.
> 4. The principal's veto may be overridden by a three-fourths vote of the legislature.

The SFL consists of four officers, four schoolwide representatives, class presidents (grades 9–12), two representatives per grade, representatives of the student publications and athletic council, four at-large representatives, eight teachers, two representatives of the support staff, and the [principal and assistant principal].

During our research, the SFL tackled many issues. First, it created a time block for its meetings. Every Tuesday was designated an X-block day: each period was shortened and an additional period created so SFL and other school activities could meet. Students not involved in an activity were released early. The legislature also held discussions about the athletic pledge for team members and the consequences of violating it, created a policy to deal with multiple tests on the same day, helped to develop sanctions for violating the no smoking policy implemented by the board of education, sponsored a day-long discussion of pressure and cheating at Evans Hill, wrote a new tardy policy, investigated inequities in the school's athletic programs, and drafted a constitution. This final action was completed after Smith had departed and Thomas Springer, the new principal, attempted to modify the frequency of the X-block schedule, because he and some members of the Evans Hill community were concerned about the SFL's structure and decision-making power.

Student participation in SFL was limited to members until 1990, when Springer made attendance twice per quarter a requirement of the Seminar program (described below). Although students often complained about having to attend meetings, faculty and SFL members felt that students benefited from this requirement. Many nonmembers spoke during debates, and almost all participated in straw polls of nonmembers before SFL votes.

THE SEMINAR PROGRAM

The Seminar program, implemented in fall 1987 for the ninth grade, was another part of the Sizer group's reform efforts. Originally a component of Interdisciplinary that provided enrichment activities to the entire grade, its purpose gradually shifted until by 1990 it became a course fulfilling a state-mandated participation-in-government requirement. Before the program's inception, Smith and the freshman Interdisciplinary teachers spent several weeks conceptualizing and planning the program. Smith wanted it to be both advisory and interdisciplinary and to reinforce the work of the SFL. The first year's schedule called for whole class and small group meetings. In the class meetings, students watched films, heard lectures, saw plays, and attended activities designed to complement work undertaken in Western civilization and English courses. The small groups tackled issues related to the transition to high school and student governance. Four-fifths of the faculty recruited to serve as advisers to the small groups were from the Sizer group. On the first day of Seminar, students received this "welcome card," which explained the purposes of the course:

Class of 1991

Welcome to Freshman Seminar!

> Freshman Seminar is a unique class which you will be experiencing throughout your first year as an Evans Hill High School student. It is unique for several reasons: First, it is a class which can change size with great ease. It can be a small group of 15 or a large meeting of the entire ninth grade. For instance, sometimes you may be working in small groups to practice critical thinking skills, or you may be viewing a dramatic presentation with the rest of your grade. Second, it is a class which can easily change teachers. You may find your English teacher leading one session and your math teacher presenting yet another. Third, it is a class that can combine subjects. You may find that a particular science topic is crucial to understanding an event in history. This class can combine these two subjects, as your teachers cooperate in planning for a common time. Finally, this class time can be used to respond to school community events, and to serve as a common forum for building a strong class of 1991.

> The flexibility that has been built into this class can serve you well in allowing for many opportunities for your growth and development as a member of the high school community.

In the first year, many faculty were frustrated with the freshman Seminar because they felt that the course had too many foci. In addition, many students were resistant. They were confused by the structure, by homework assignments ("If I do an assignment about history for my math teacher, where does it count for a grade?" "Where do I put these notes, in my history notebook or my science notebook?"), and about the grades and credit they received. Many students complained to their parents and the guidance office, especially when they realized they had to take the course, for which they would receive no credit, and that they might have to give up a second language or an elective, as Seminar met for three periods a week.[2]

The second year, Seminar expanded to include sophomores. As with Interdisciplinary, each grade evolved its own approach. The freshman Seminar was still tied to Interdisciplinary course work, but its emphasis on student participation in school life grew to include student government and freshman class activities. The sophomore Seminar was not linked to the tenth-grade academic program, in part because only one teacher who served as a Seminar adviser also taught tenth-grade students. This Seminar did some work on film analysis, student governance issues, and moral dilemmas.

When Thomas Springer arrived as principal, he observed the Seminar program for a few months and concluded that it was operating without clear goals, that teachers had not had proper training, and that some natural connections—for example, with the guidance department— had not been incorporated into the original planning. Working with Phil Winston—a member of the Sizer group, but one of the few teachers not identified with any faction at the school—he revamped the program, eliminating its interdisciplinary focus, incorporating leadership and guidance components, and making it a requirement for all grades. Winston coordinated the new program. In Springer's view, the new program served a different purpose for each grade. In ninth grade, students explored affective components of education, in part through discussions about moral dilemmas, to complement work they had done in advisory groups during middle school. The tenth grade focused on individual and institutional decision making, again using moral dilemmas but also looking closely at how organizations and governmental agencies make decisions. Eleventh-grade seminars were devoted to leadership training. The twelfth grade emphasized participation in government through examining such issues in American society as racism and crime. Winston recognized that these changes constituted major shifts

2. Students were required to take Seminar even though they received no credit for the course during the years from 1987 to 1990. Beginning with the 1990–91 academic year, students received academic credit for state-mandated government participation, one component of the course.

in the program, but he saw them as improvements because they reinforced the work of the SFL and now the course fulfilled a state-mandated government requirement, for which students received course credit. In an interview three months after the program began, he said: "We still face a certain amount of student resistance but . . . it has to do with throwing more stuff at them without clear explanations. At this point we're using the Seminar program to meet the state requirement for participation in government. I don't think that's been conveyed to [students] clearly. They still see this course as a burden . . . when they could have taken an elective or had a free period."

The newly constituted Seminar program met for two periods every eight-day cycle, and all students were required to attend two meetings of the SFL each quarter. Winston considered this reasonable: "After all, now they are receiving credit for a course which has that as its only requirement." Springer also arranged for all Seminar teachers to receive instruction in running seminars, since many had never done the types of activities associated with Seminar. Winston appreciated these professional development opportunities: "[Teachers are realizing that they] may be able to establish a situation in their own classrooms that operates like the seminar class, where . . . it is the kids talking about what they are learning, and analyzing, and evaluating." Yet, he also felt that this work competed with planning; seminar teams had only two common planning periods per month, and one of them was devoted to working with a professional consultant. He added that he often reminded himself, "We're only in the . . . third year with the Seminar program. . . . Each year it gets better. We have a better sense of what we want. . . . The kids have a better understanding of that too."

THE EXHIBITIONS COMMITTEE

During fall 1987, the Sizer group applied for and received a grant from the Coalition to develop and implement exhibitions in some classrooms. The exhibitions committee consisted of some teachers from the Sizer group, including four history teachers (all involved with Interdisciplinary), three English teachers (two from Interdisciplinary), two foreign language teachers, the art teacher who worked with Interdisciplinary, and a math teacher, as well as Dr. Smith, and the assistant principal. Throughout the 1987–88 school year, they met regularly to develop exhibitions and criteria for assessing them, to debate the skills exhibitions should draw upon, and to research forms of alternative assessment.

In early December, the group discussed specific class assignments in light of two papers they had recently received from the Coalition, one on standards by Sizer and another on exhibitions by the central staff's director of research. After reading the papers, teachers voiced several concerns. One involved accountability: "How can we get reasonable accountability for students who play more passive roles in group work?" Another related to skill development: "We would like a synthesis of material from [English and history] which is sometimes very difficult." A third concerned having students reflect on their work in terms of the personal meaning it had for them. Some teachers felt this was a promising idea; others feared it would be impossible to grade such work.

To determine what constituted an exhibition, the group often used examples of assignments they had given their classes. At the December meeting the assistant principal offered the following example:

Crime and Punishment

> Among other themes in *Crime and Punishment,* Dostoevsky suggests a redemptive power in suffering. Fortunately, most of us have no personal experience with the kind of pain Raskolnikov and his cohorts endured.
>
> In a clearly organized, documented essay, use one character's experiences to illustrate what Dostoevsky feels about suffering. Then . . . try to come to some conclusions about whether you accept or reject his notion of suffering. Give explanations which explain how you reached your personal conclusion.

Group reactions varied. Some thought schoolwork should contain both a personal and an academic aspect and should combine skills that were usually sought in separate assignments. Others, however, disagreed. One said: "Exhibitions ought to be more grand, more encompassing." Another teacher added, "Perhaps we should focus on the criteria for what makes an exhibition rather than the criteria by which we think we should grade it." A history teacher suggested coming up with a menu of essential skills that could be demonstrated through exhibitions.

In fact, at the January meeting, this teacher described four criteria he had used in a simulation exercise for teaching about Andrew Jackson: that the exhibition require research, that a point of view be presented in a paper summarizing the research, that student work include an oral component, and that students answer (in some form) the following question: Did your opinion change (and how) as a result of this work? At the end of the December and January meetings, each participant agreed to try something exhibition-like in their classes during the next month or two.

The exhibitions committee members continued to design assignments with exhibition-like components throughout the spring of 1988, and in their final meetings they made a series of recommendations. These included making more time for planning, continuing the exhibitions support group, sharing their work with other faculty, recruiting faculty from the science and math departments, bringing in outsiders, visiting other schools, and trying to create a final exhibition for a global studies course. During the 1988–89 school year, the group met occasionally but members felt that the new principal did not support their work. Indeed, Springer discouraged such meetings because he felt they deepened rifts in the faculty. He maintained that all aspects of Coalition membership, including exhibitions, should be discussed by the entire faculty.

ADMINISTRATIVE TURNOVER:
NEW DEFINITIONS OF THE COALITION AT EVANS HILL

Mary Ellen Smith resigned in spring 1988 for personal reasons,[3] and so did the likewise pro-Coalition assistant principal. Although the Sizer group and many in the local community were disappointed by Smith's decision, many teachers welcomed her departure. One faculty member remarked: "[People] either loved her or hated her. No, that doesn't go far enough. They either idolized or loathed her is probably more accurate. She really polarized the school, divided us in half. Very few people crossed the line [i.e., changed their minds about her or her programs]."

3. Her resignation had nothing to do with activities at Evans Hill. After her husband got a new job and her family relocated, she took another job as principal; her new school also joined the Coalition.

The departure of both pro-Coalition administrators could have signaled the demise of the Coalition at Evans Hill. As one teacher put it:
"Despite what the literature said and the number of times Mary Ellen
brought Ted Sizer here, the Coalition at Evans Hill was Mary Ellen's
Coalition. If you liked her, fine. If not, then you did not—could not—
like the Coalition. It was that easy." And another teacher remarked: "I
knew I could wait her out. I've been here more than fifteen years, she's
been here less than five. I figured she'd be gone soon. So much for her pet
programs."

In seeking a new principal, however, the board of education and the
superintendent targeted candidates knowledgeable and enthusiastic
about the Coalition. Nevertheless, the different interpretations of Coalition philosophy by Dr. Smith and Thomas Springer had serious consequences for Coalition programs at Evans Hill. To illustrate, Smith
encouraged meetings of the Sizer group, gave priority to the Interdisciplinary block in scheduling to provide common planning time for
teachers, provided the Sizer group with release time to work on exhibitions and develop the Seminar program, and exempted them from
certain duties (for example, homeroom). In contrast, Springer discouraged private meetings, arguing that if the whole school belonged to the
Coalition, the entire faculty should take part in conversations about
Coalition efforts. He questioned the SFL's power to modify the school's
schedule when only 3 percent of the school participated in SFL meetings.
Moreover, a lack of consensus about Interdisciplinary created tensions
between Springer and these faculty. Teachers saw his attempts to clarify
the interdisciplinary nature of the program as critical of their efforts,
whereas Springer viewed it as a means to ensure consistent expectations.

Springer was aware of divisions within the faculty and the problems
generated by differing interpretations of Coalition philosophy. In an
interview four months after becoming principal, he outlined his objectives for the year: "My first agenda is to get the whole faculty as close
together as they can be, closing whatever divisions and wounds that
exist. . . . If we don't have that, we're not going to go very far at all. The
second objective . . . is to get the faculty all focused and working on the
same task—[defining] what are the essentials that must be mastered
prior to graduation."

To build consensus within the faculty, he reintroduced discussion of
the common principles and Coalition membership at a faculty meeting

in February 1989. As part of his principal's report, Springer listed fourteen issues he felt needed to be addressed, explaining that these issues had emerged from discussions at a meeting of department chairs held to assess the state of the school. When he mentioned the Coalition of Essential Schools, there was little faculty reaction. A buzz began, however, when he mentioned reviewing methods of assessment, talked about the Coalition's idea of exhibitions, and added: "What standards *do* we have? Up to now, none of the reform efforts have dealt with this, but until we do, nothing will be able to prove its effectiveness." Springer then asked what Coalition membership had committed the school to and challenged faculty to define what was essential in their curricula. At this point a vocal opponent of Coalition membership asked Springer what he thought Coalition membership entailed. Springer and the assistant principal both responded that it did not mean that there had to be villains and heroes in the school or that politics had to dominate. Springer added that objections had really been to the *who* with which the Coalition was associated (an indirect but obvious reference to Dr. Smith) rather than the *how* and *what* of the Coalition itself. Then he remarked, "The problem is not with the common principles, but with how the school has tried to approach Coalition reform."

Two members of the Sizer group then offered brief testimonials to how enjoyable their work was now, how their teaching had improved, and how they valued the collegiality that Interdisciplinary had created. Afterward, Springer described what had happened at Evans Hill to date as ironic: "The Coalition's presence here has split the faculty rather than helping it coalesce. There is a lot of confusion about what the Coalition is, who Ted Sizer is, and what the Coalition stands for." He added that despite many waves of reform, "schools have remained remarkably similar." A teacher objected, "But we're *not* failing *here*." After Springer attempted again to explain what Coalition membership might do for the school—even acknowledging that it was an exceptional school—the assistant principal interjected: "Just what is threatening here? Are you viewing this list as a report card? Try not to think of it as a judgment of your work." A Coalition supporter added, "They are threatened by the Coalition, by Sizer's idea of teacher as coach." Ignoring the raised hands in the room, Springer ended the discussion: "The school belongs to the Coalition of Essential Schools. We cannot have a subgroup speaking for the whole faculty. Their work must dissolve and be merged into the work of the whole school. . . . We cannot move forward as a school if decisions are made that are not widely understood or known about. We must move away from the idea that one group of teachers can come up with ideas that threaten other teachers' job security. We must have an open climate—no hidden agendas—and we must put this difficult and divisive episode into the past."

Reopening debate about Coalition affiliation pleased no one. Already considerable tension existed between Springer and the Sizer group, which felt Springer's interpretations of Coalition philosophy were conciliatory rather than thought-provoking and viewed his request that they clarify their work as a lack of confidence in them. Further, they worried that his efforts to disband them would end the school's involvement with the Coalition, rather than lay the groundwork for broader participation. Although it might seem that questioning the Sizer group would garner support from its opponents, this did not occur. The rest of the faculty remained opposed to the Coalition or not interested and seemed unlikely to support Springer without assurances that Coalition affiliation would be ended, a decision Springer was not prepared to make for two reasons. First, he did not feel that the decision was within his jurisdiction. The board of education, not Dr. Smith, had committed the school to the Coalition for four years. Eighteen months of that commitment remained. Second, he personally thought that the Coalition was asking the right questions and working on issues that even exemplary schools needed to address.

Despite controversy, Springer felt that the meeting had been productive. In an interview a few days later he described the Coalition at Evans Hill as "an open wound that needed to be attended to before the school could move on." Although he supported the Coalition's ideals, he said, "doing things differently did not automatically equal doing things better." He also questioned decisions made by Smith. He felt, for example, that department chairs, demoralized during Smith's tenure, needed their leadership affirmed, not questioned. Along these lines, he decided that the Coalition coordinator would no longer attend meetings of department chairs, as the Sizer group requested and as had occurred during Smith's tenure. He also reiterated that the Sizer group would be dissolved so that faculty could address issues of standards and essential curricula on a schoolwide basis. For the good of the school, he concluded, "We must remove [the Sizer group's] halos: they are not the only good guys in the school."

In a very short time, Springer's attempts to assess where the school stood vis-à-vis the common principles created hostility throughout the school. In addition, there was a growing sense that, like Smith, Springer was manipulative.[4] Although some suspicion and anger sprang from the faculty meeting, other events contributed to it. Springer's attempts to modify the X-block schedule and to reduce the frequency of SFL meetings met considerable resistance. The SFL had come to have wide faculty and administrative support and was seldom linked to the Coalition by the time Springer arrived. In fact, the SFL appealed Springer's decision to change the schedule, and even though the superintendent recognized that the X-block created problems in the master schedule and that attendance (to that point) at SFL meetings had not been substantial, he reinstated the X-block schedule. Although disappointed with the outcome, Springer commented: "I'm satisfied that at the present time for me to talk about changing the structure of the SFL would be damaging to the fabric of the school."

Springer had his own vision of what Coalition membership entailed and of how its ideas should be implemented at Evans Hill. His vision of change was moderate, and it certainly acknowledged the traditional strengths of the school. As he noted in "Report on the Coalition of Essential Schools at Evans Hill High School," which he distributed to faculty, administrators, the board of education, and Coalition central staff: "The [Common] Principles of the Coalition, if realized in most high schools, would signal a genuine transformation. It is clear to me, at least, that Sizer was not describing Evans Hill High. . . . Many of the characteristics of good schools were already evident at Evans Hill before Sizer articulated the Common Principles. Therefore, joining the Coalition was never likely to have a revolutionary impact at Evans Hill such as it might have in most other high schools. Like all institutions, however, our school can, has, and should improve, and the Common Principles are one thing which we can embrace as guideposts to that effort."

4. Also, ironically, the Sizer group began to accept that Dr. Smith had been manipulative in her dealings with others, but members of the group continued to perceive her actions as justified, even as they condemned what they perceived as Springer's manipulative efforts.

Though seemingly more conciliatory and consensus-based than Smith in his approach to change, Springer became a focal point of an ongoing debate about the need for change. At the end of the 1990–91 school year he resigned as principal.

That many faculty resisted or ignored both principals' efforts is not surprising. As we saw at Elliston High, teachers in schools with strong reputations felt more would be lost than gained in experimenting with change, and few believed change was necessary when their schools were already achieving their communities' desired ends—universal graduation rates and virtually universal college attendance rates. The attitude toward those who sought change and experimented in their classrooms was laissez-faire, until people perceived that specific innovations or reassessment of the status quo would occur schoolwide.

THE SIZER GROUP

Although the transition from one principal's vision of change to another's was painful for the Sizer group, it was not the only problem Coalition supporters encountered. There were problems in scheduling, particularly articulating Interdisciplinary and the Seminar programs with the rest of the school and expanding the programs each year. According to Dr. Smith, the 1987–88 school year schedule required ninety-nine computer runs to accommodate the block scheduling for two grades of Interdisciplinary.[5] Difficulties also arose because overall declining enrollment coincided with the implementation of the Coalition program, which some faculty viewed as a threat to elective courses. (The enrollment was below two hundred students, grades 9 to 12, by 1990.) Furthermore, program expansion was complicated by the existing well-established AP program. (Evans Hill offers ten AP courses for juniors and seniors.) Finally, senior English teachers were unwilling to restructure their classes around the global studies curriculum, and thus no expansion of Interdisciplinary into the twelfth grade occurred.

From the outset of Coalition involvement, many faculty were skeptical of Coalition philosophy and reluctant to become involved with its

5. Given the school's small size and the number of single course offerings, one cannot attribute these difficulties solely to one program. Nevertheless, block scheduling was an issue.

programs. Since most were tenured, they felt immune to efforts to convince them to embrace Coalition ideas. Also, most had seen administrators come and go, and with them their special programs. Many faculty saw the Coalition in this light. In addition, the Sizer group were perceived as the principal's favorites. Whereas pro-Coalition teachers found Dr. Smith to be visionary and inspirational, other faculty viewed her as manipulative, and accusations of trade-offs (power for allegiance and so forth) lingered long after she left. Dr. Smith was relatively new to the school (having arrived in fall 1984) when she introduced Coalition philosophy to the faculty. The Sizer group, her strongest allies, was composed largely of women teachers, also relatively new to the school—in other words, teachers likely to have limited power in a business-as-usual environment.[6] Moreover, throughout our research, those in the Sizer group frequently reported that they were "burning out," "trying to do too many things," and "feeling stressed"—predictable reactions given their participation in so many activities while trying to negotiate their way through a school divided over change. Nonetheless, the charges of favoritism created divisions within the faculty that endured after Dr. Smith departed. After four months as principal Springer described one of his biggest tasks as: "convinc[ing] the faculty by what I do and what I say that I am going to be very open. We may have fundamental differences on matters of policy, but everyone is going to know what the issues are, what the facts are, and then if we disagree, we disagree. But not that some . . . little group is favored, while another one isn't."

Throughout the two administrators' terms, the Sizer group's isolation from the rest of the school grew. It first emerged during the Coalition planning phase when they met during lunch, free periods, and after school, and it resulted more from the quantity of work than from dissension. As divisions became increasingly evident, it simply became less stressful for the Sizer group to work during their free time rather than to socialize with skeptical colleagues and endure their often cynical comments. This isolation seemed to have several consequences. First, because there was little contact between Sizer group faculty and other

---

6. Interestingly, the two men who taught Interdisciplinary had (or quickly acquired) more power among the faculty than the women with whom they worked. One was the union president; the other was involved with coaching. Likewise, neither described the same sense of isolation that their female counterparts did, nor were they closely identified with the Sizer group.

teachers, the latter were ill-informed about activities within Inter-disciplinary and the Seminar program, at least until Springer's arrival. Second, this lack of information was accompanied by mistrust, which was magnified by the perception of favoritism toward the pro-Coalition faculty and the perceived secrecy about their activities. And finally, added to this was the early belief that Dr. Smith would "foist" the Coalition program onto the entire staff as soon as she thought she "could get away with it." The alliances and collaboration necessary for schoolwide expansion were difficult to initiate once participating teachers were seen (and defined themselves) as isolated from the rest of the school.

As at Elliston High, an additional point of divisiveness was whether Coalition reforms at Evans Hill were really grassroots efforts. In the opinion of those teachers actively involved, they were. Given their au-tonomy and their interaction with Smith's administration during the planning process, this perspective is understandable. For the most part, noninvolved teachers viewed neither the program nor the Coalition as a grassroots initiative. They saw both as "Smith's babies." Many claimed that Coalition membership was forced on a faculty that lacked interest in change. To support their claim, they cited the limited participation of veteran teachers, Smith's manipulations, and Interdisciplinary's mar-ginal place in the life of the school. Both administrations characterized the reform as a grassroots initiative—either because of the new roles teachers adopted or because of the administration's responsiveness to teacher interests. Springer also felt that his efforts to broaden discussion of Coalition practices would promote greater faculty ownership of change.

WHOLE SCHOOL OR SCHOOL-WITHIN-A-SCHOOL COALITION EFFORT?

An important piece of this Evans Hill–Coalition puzzle is that adminis-trators and teachers held very different perceptions of Coalition mem-bership. Neither principal ever labeled the school's participation as a school-within-a-school project. As Smith put it: "The whole school will be undergoing change as a result of our Coalition membership. Inter-disciplinary is only one aspect." Smith considered two other changes she introduced—the Student-Faculty Legislature and the Seminar program—to be part of the school's overall implementation of Coalition ideas. Springer opposed the Sizer group's working separately and advocated a whole school effort. The faculty, however, focused on Interdisciplinary, as they believed it embodied the school's restructuring efforts. Subsequently, many suspected that Interdisciplinary was a pilot program (a SWAS) intended to spread to the entire school and that they would soon be pressured to team and develop interdisciplinary curricula. Despite administration efforts to separate Interdisciplinary from Coalition philosophy, it was still viewed as "the Coalition in this school."

The Coalition at Evans Hill straddled two normally distinct categories of Coalition schools, the school-within-a-school and whole-school effort. These differing views of the school's Coalition status set up different expectations about what change would entail: the administrators, the superintendent, and the board of education viewed Evans Hill as a whole-school member of the Coalition making changes broadly where necessary and appropriate. Most faculty saw Interdisciplinary as a Coalition SWAS. Interestingly, faculty rarely associated Smith's other innovations—the SFL and Seminar program—with the Coalition, and participation in both gradually became widespread.

The initial implementation of Coalition ideas at Evans Hill, particularly the formation of Interdisciplinary, satisfied those who wanted change, but subsequently made it difficult to include others in the change process. This arose partly because of the early emphasis on interdisciplinary work and partly because everyone recalled a turbulent history of accusations and actions that separated rather than united, increasing factionalism and making power relations within the school problematic. Perceived manipulation by the first principal and continued identification of the Coalition with her hampered its general acceptance at Evans Hill. One pro-Coalition teacher felt that the animosity toward Smith articulated after her departure was so strong (emphasizing her allegedly "underhanded actions") that her detractors would not be satisfied until every program she had begun was dismantled.

It is somewhat ironic that the eight-day rotating schedule introduced by Smith served as a symbol of change, particularly a symbol of Coalition change, since its purpose was to preserve a large elective program and allow students to take more courses. These aims might have been seen as preserving elements of the educational tradition of a school threatened by declining enrollment and as in conflict with the Coalition aphorism less-is-more. Nevertheless, throughout our research teachers made comments that essentially supported Springer's conclusion: "The schedule is a visible manifestation—a *daily* visible manifestation—of personalities that at least some of the faculty did not like. It is also a daily manifestation of the whole notion of change, which upset lots of people. [This] faculty . . . was very stable, teachers had been used to their routines. To have everything suddenly get changed . . . created . . . animosity."

As many teachers acknowledged, Evans Hill was committed to several aspects of the common principles (such as personalized education), and this commitment was strengthened by such developments as the Seminar program and the Student-Faculty Legislature. But these programs were not widely recognized as part of the school's involvement with the Coalition, and they became less identified with Smith each time their structure or aims were modified. They have persisted and, most would agree, have flourished in the school, an accomplishment of some note given the initial resistance they encountered.

Teachers at Evans Hill often reminded us that membership in the Sizer group had not been consistent. Some who initially joined found their explorations of educational philosophy and change fascinating but were not willing or able to be part of Interdisciplinary. Other members of the group left after disputes with Smith. By the time Springer arrived, only two members of the original group remained: Smith had recruited all other participants because they possessed a strength or expertise that the program needed, because she perceived them to be philosophically compatible with the group's ideas, or because a faculty member needed to fill out a teaching schedule in a department that was overstaffed given declining enrollment. Many in the Sizer group had joined the Evans Hill faculty to replace teachers on sabbatical or those who had retired. In several senses, then, the Sizer group was a group assembled by Smith, further making the label of "grassroots" reform problematic at the school.

The debate surrounding the Coalition at Evans Hill High School never focused on the philosophical issues associated with the common principles as directly as it had at Elliston High, perhaps because opponents had more concrete targets (specific programs and people associated with them, a new master schedule) and stronger opinions about the source of Evans Hill's Coalition membership (Mary Ellen Smith). Working in two well-regarded high schools with strong faculties, all three principals (Smith, Springer, and Wallace) faced the same dilemma: how to introduce discussions of change without implying that current conditions were deficient? The political issues surrounding the introduction of a reform philosophy at both schools were similar and can be summed up in a phrase heard often at both sites: "If it ain't broke, don't fix it." For students, the effects of each school's membership in the Coalition depended on whether they elected to participate in courses that were experimenting with Coalition ideas, a choice that Evans Hill students often perceived as limiting access to other equally, if not more, desirable opportunities.

6

"I'M NOT IN THIS ALL ALONE"

THE WADE SCHOOL AND COALITION PHILOSOPHY

> I never realized the power I have in the classroom, how much my students watch me. —A TEACHER

> Less-is-more is about less subjects, more learning.
> Less kids, so you can give them more attention.
> Less textbooks, more learning. . . . I mean we're
> not copying, we are learning to *do* it. —STUDENTS'
> COMMENTS

> The point is not our schedule, the point is our owner-ship of the schedule. —A TEACHER

A growing number of new elementary and secondary schools are being designed with the Coalition's common principles as their underlying philosophy. The Wade School, the first and one of the better-known secondary schools, is the subject of our final case study. The school was founded by Helen Markham, an educational innovator with a history of involvement in alternative elementary education.[1] In the 1970s she founded a group of alternative elementary schools in the same district as Wade. Markham decided to open Wade in part because she felt that graduates of the three elementary schools she founded were being ill-

---

1. We rely on Harrington and Cookson's definitions to distinguish between "alternative schools" and "schools of choice": "By definition, an alternative school is not just chosen; more important, it is a nontraditional school in its educational values and teaching methods. It provides an alternative (for teachers, students, and parents) to the 'regular' neighborhood public schools. A school of choice is only chosen. It is not necessarily different in any way from the regular schools—in fact, it usually is a regular school." (1992: 183)

served by the secondary schools they attended. In particular, she was distressed by the boredom, anonymity, and lack of challenge that the students reported after moving into the city's public secondary schools, even some of its well-known schools. Markham and her small, hand-picked staff spent one year planning and designing Wade.

Wade is located in a large urban system. Within this system a number of alternative and magnet programs have been founded to meet the needs of differing student populations. Although an area of poverty, violence, and joblessness, the district where Wade is situated is acknowl-edged to favor innovation. District administrators, for instance, have provided political support and fund-raising assistance for the fledgling school.

Wade requires students to apply for admission and to visit the school with their parents before enrolling, but Markham has sought to balance several factors in selecting students: "We made an early decision that we should be designing a program for every kind of kid. . . . And that the school ought to be mixed: we didn't want all high achievers or all low achievers. The next criterion was that any kid coming out of our elemen-tary schools ought to be allowed to come here because we wanted that continuity. Next, we have a strong focus on families, so we ought to give first preference to the siblings of kids who are already here. . . . Then we have some decisions to make because . . . we want [the school] to be representative of the [city's] population, ethnically, economically, and so forth, but we also want to make sure we have enough kids [from this neighborhood]." In 1985 the school opened with about 80 seventh graders, and added one grade per year for six years until it reached its present size of approximately 450 students. Wade graduated its first class in 1991.

Throughout our research, Wade enrolled approximately 40 percent African-American students, 35 percent Hispanic, 9 percent white, 6 percent Asian, and 10 percent biracial.[2] The administration and staff are also committed to building a multicultural faculty: nearly one-third of the faculty are African-American, and Hispanic teachers represent a growing presence in the school. Because of the school's reputation,

2. Students self-reported "biracial" in the "other" category on a survey we ad-ministered, often adding other relevant details—e.g., "mother, Hispanic; father, black."

many local college students seek to be student teachers or interns at Wade, and faculty members are often recruited from their ranks.

In characterizing the school community, teachers, administrators, and students frequently use family metaphors, stressing the caring and sense of common purpose shared by staff and students. Further, both staff and students seem comfortable with Coalition rhetoric. Students described themselves as "workers," prepared "exhibitions," and discussed topics that derived from "essential questions" they were studying.[3]

CREATING A STRUCTURE AND CURRICULUM TO REFLECT COALITION PHILOSOPHY

In many respects, the school's structure, curriculum, and dominant pedagogical techniques embody Coalition philosophy. For instance, five essential questions guide inquiry in the classroom and throughout the school: How do we know what we know? What's the evidence? Whose viewpoint is represented? How else might it be viewed, seen, considered? and What difference does it make? Rather than strict age-grading, classes contain two grades. Wade is divided into three administrative divisions: what are typically seventh and eighth grades comprise Division One, ninth and tenth grades form Division Two, and the final two years of school are the Senior Institute. Each division's curriculum is structured by essential questions.

In Divisions One and Two, students have three classes per day: a two-hour humanities class, a two-hour period of math-science (sometimes instruction was interdisciplinary but most often each subject was taught for one hour during the block), and a one-hour advisory period during which students and their advisers discuss schoolwide issues as a group or students work individually. Since students must demonstrate foreign language competency before graduating, many attend optional Spanish classes before the school day officially begins.[4] Once each week students in Divisions One and Two perform community service in a three-hour

3. "Essential questions" are a curricular framework promoted by the Coalition (see Wiggins 1987a). In contrast to the common curricular focus on coverage, essential questions are intended to focus curriculum on a specific topic in depth.

4. During our research, these classes became required for students until they passed a state-mandated competency test.

time block. A one-hour lunch break during which students can eat and play intramural sports (which fulfills the school's physical education requirement) rounds out the formal school day. Parents and community members are encouraged to become involved with the school, and the building is open daily for such after-school options as karate and dance classes.

The Wade School emphasizes the concept of personalization. For example, no teacher is responsible for more than eighty students, and each student is part of an advisory group of ten to fifteen students that meets daily. In addition, advisers schedule at least two parent-student-teacher conferences per year. To promote continuity in this relationship, students keep the same adviser throughout their stay in a division. Further, each division includes two "houses," each with eighty students and a team of teachers—one math, one science, and at least two humanities teachers. The teachers meet regularly as a team to discuss student progress. These teachers see students daily in classes that are rarely larger than twenty. Because teams have the same students for two years and encounter only forty new students each year, teachers have an uncharacteristic amount of time to come to know their students.

Another Coalition aphorism, less-is-more, plays a prominent role in the school's philosophy. In the thematic, pared-down curriculum, students take only a handful of subjects, each organized around essential questions. Students do not study all of American history. Instead, they examine such topics as revolutions, immigration, and the nature of American society. In the Senior Institute, students may specialize in such aspects of American history as the labor movement or Puerto Rican history.

Teacher-as-generalist is another Coalition belief that informs Wade School policies. Although the school offers psychological and social services, classroom teachers fill many guidance roles. To help students resolve problems among themselves, most teachers have studied conflict mediation.[5] So that student-teacher ratios remain low, all administrators have advisories and sometimes teach. The generalist principle is also evident in the Senior Institute, where teachers help students find

---

5. Many students also participate in the school's conflict resolution program and then serve as mediators.

internships that accord with their post–secondary school plans and help them select appropriate colleges or technical schools.

Exhibitions, the performance-based assessment technique promoted by the Coalition, are common at Wade. For each subject or unit, students prepare oral and written exhibitions, individually or in groups. For their end-of-the-year exhibitions, students often present original research to teachers, parents, and other adults. And, in many ways, the Senior Institute is a two-year-long exhibition, where students must define their topics of study, conduct relevant research, and present their findings to a panel of evaluators. Designed from its inception with Coalition principles in mind, Wade is quite different from our other study schools. A closer look at some key features of school life make the differences even more apparent.

ADVISORY

Advisory periods, during which groups of students meet daily with an adviser, have been part of Wade since its founding. Individual teachers have considerable autonomy in structuring their advisory, and the content depends, to a large extent, on their inclinations. For example, several teachers use advisory time to explore affective dimensions of learning by discussing students' lives and schoolwork. Other teachers may first try to promote trust within the group and later discuss such sensitive issues as teen pregnancy, city politics, racism, or homophobia. Others use advisory to build group participation and leadership skills by having students take turns leading discussions on topics of their choice—from the Olympics to date rape to salsa dance competitions. With still other teachers, advisory is more like a typical homeroom period—announcements are made, the school newsletter discussed, and students talk among themselves, do homework, or plan trips for their advisory classes.

A short excerpt from a Division One advisory we observed in fall 1988 offers some insight into what occurs. This teacher used current events and issues raised by students to reinforce skills being taught in humanities classes—how to lead discussions, ask good questions, and respect others' opinions, for instance. In a conversation about the Olympics, the topic turned to doing one's best and whether recognition was needed to judge one's performance. After a student moderator led a discussion on winning and losing in athletic competition, the teacher introduced a twist:

ALLEN [TEACHER-ADVISER]: Many of you have said, "As long as I tried my best [at the Olympics], it would be enough." What about school work? Do you get a sense of accomplishment when you do well in school?

SUSANNA: Yes, when I write a good summary.

ALLEN: Tad, how about you? [No answer.] Leita?

LEITA: What, you mean with school work? If the teacher gives me a good grade, I show my mother, and we are both happy.

ALLEN: Are you saying that you need me to tell you that you are doing a good job?

MATT: Yes.

LEITA: Not necessarily.

[At this point the student moderator again took over directing the class.] SUSANNA: Matt, what do you mean?

MATT: If I do all that work and don't get no compliment, it's like it was a waste. It's like going to an amusement park on a scary ride by yourself. It's not as much fun. It's like watching a movie by yourself. It's boring.

SUSANNA: What if only one person said it was good?

MATT: It's better than no one.

SUSANNA: Lisa?

LISA: It's like Jane [one of their teachers] checking our homework. She does not check it, [so] it's like she doesn't care. Someone else has to care. I care.

SUSANNA: Yeah, that's like if Allen forgot to check our reading journal. Would you do that?

ALLEN: No, because it motivates you.

Allen's students regularly led discussions in class and in advisory. He spent much of each fall modeling good leader and participant behavior for new students, in part by using his students from the previous year as role models. Students selected their discussion topics, budgeted time, and directed the flow of class. During advisory, Allen tried to be another participant, not the authority. Success, he admitted, was intermittent: "Some days are better than others, some kids can handle this approach more easily than others. . . . But I like it when it works. The kids have fun and we all learn a lot."

Each year, every advisory makes a two- or three-day trip to a site with academic relevance that also offers the opportunity to visit a college or university. For example, advisories regularly visit Brown University to allow students to sample college life and to encourage them to feel comfortable in those settings. During these trips, Wade students stay with Brown undergraduates, attend classes, talk with students and professors, and generally participate in the life of the college. They also visit local historical monuments and museums.

Throughout our fieldwork at Wade, student-student and student-teacher interactions seemed most relaxed and revealing in advisories. In debating such issues as abortion, Supreme Court confirmation hearings, the World Series, and how to alleviate homelessness, students expressed a range of opinions, knowledge, and understanding of these issues. Occasionally, students assigned each other reading homework (or television watching) so as to bring more issues into a discussion. In interviews students did not always say they liked the advisory period; but they were nearly unanimous in saying they liked having an adviser, enjoyed and learned from advisory trips, and appreciated the concern and respect that teachers and students tried to create in this setting.[6]

COMMUNITY SERVICE

As with everything at Wade, the Community Service program has evolved as the school has grown and as its relationship with the local community has deepened. The first year of Community Service, seventh-graders either worked within the school (doing cleanup, repair, and beautification work) or served as classroom aides at one of Wade's associated elementary schools. Community Service was a two-hour obligation one day a week, eighty students were divided into two groups, and their service allowed teachers time to plan together.

Since the first year, the number of Community Service placements

6. That advisory is an integral part of education at Wade was brought home to us when we asked student ethnographers (see appendix) to videotape what they thought best represented their school: most of the tape focused on advisory discussions. Further, when student guides conducted tours of the school, they often stressed their appreciation for their advisers and for the advisory program.

needed has grown steadily. To meet this need, placements have been made outside the Wade-associated schools. As students have generally proven reliable, many organizations that joined tentatively now have several student volunteers working with them. Community Service became a three-hour weekly commitment, allowing subject matter teachers in each division more time for team planning. To prepare students, in seventh grade they receive a semester-long orientation to the responsibilities associated with community service work.

Wade students work in pairs or larger groups at local hospitals, newspapers, museums, theater groups, senior citizen centers, and day-care centers, to name a few options. When possible, placements reflect student preferences, but this is often a challenge. As the Community Service director remarked: "One . . . problem is that [students] would like an office job, but they don't have any office skills. So, we are in a sense presenting them with a reality that they will hit later on." Although the program gives students opportunities to explore potential career paths, it is not designed to teach them specific skills, such as computing or bookkeeping, and placements are not usually available for more skilled work. The director feels that the program provides students many, varied experiences during their years at Wade. To ensure this, students are usually placed twice a year. Yet, if it seemed appropriate and beneficial for a student, the school tried to be flexible. As the assistant director explained: "Usually the kids change once [during] a year. They'll work until January and then change. [But] some kids stay on all year, if it is a good match. . . . We have one student who is working at the Institute for the Blind. She was there all last year and she's there now. And she has formed a really special relationship with the woman she's working with. We feel it's really important for her to maintain that. . . . So she's there." Interested students are encouraged to seek part-time work (for pay) at volunteer sites.

Before students are placed at a site, they must arrange interviews with the persons with whom they will be working. As the director explained: "We . . . talk to [the students] about what they can expect on an interview. We talk about . . . career readiness, job preparedness. We encourage. We follow up with kids who have to make appointments. . . . We go through a lot of rehearsing and role playing. . . . We do help out, but we want people to make their own arrangements. . . . So we coach them through those sorts of things." To assess community service experiences, on-site supervisors write up evaluations of students' activities and students report on their experiences. Students also evaluate the site and discuss their work. Such feedback is used to assess a site's appropriateness. Reports about a student's placement become part of his or her record or portfolio.

Summarizing the goals of the program, the assistant director said: "Through [Community Service] students experience the world of work, they get to go out and [work] in a variety of places, they have an opportunity to be in decision-making roles and to see the consequences of their decisions. They help [other people]. And it shows them that they can contribute now. I also think that for the majority of them, it makes them feel good about who they are and what they can do to help. . . . It's part of empowering the kids to be thinking on their own and to be doing things on their own. They are student-as-workers, I suppose, if you want to take it literally." Emphasizing this sense of empowerment, the director noted: "I want our kids, as a result of Community Service, to feel that, and to act upon the belief that, there is no institution in [this city] that they may not have access to and use." As the school grew and the Senior Institute was formed, the Community Service program's assistant director helped develop an internship program to fulfill some of the same functions, and it was tied directly to the older students' future work plans.

THE SENIOR INSTITUTE

The Senior Institute, which corresponds roughly to the junior and senior years, is designed to provide Wade students with opportunities to explore their academic interests and plan their futures. The Senior Institute's director spent two years planning and determining criteria for graduation.[7] To her, the Senior Institute was "to be a transition to the world of work or going off to college. It is not to make kids feel happy or feel at ease or feel secure. It is really to help kids to make changes . . . to see things differently; to help kids to function in the world differently. To look at the world and see how they fit in."

During their last two years, students may spend their school day at

7. One must complete course requirements satisfactorily to complete the year(s) at the Senior Institute, but one graduates from Wade.

Wade, at city colleges and universities, or wherever their internships lead—for example, an automotive technical school or a law office. To complete the Senior Institute students must prepare and defend a set of portfolios, which are compilations of work demonstrating competence at required tasks, skills, and abilities. Topics that are included range from math, foreign language, writing, and literature to an autobiographical narrative and an internship in an area of potential employment. Students continue to have an advisory period in the Senior Institute, but the adviser's role shifts somewhat to focus on helping students plan how to fulfill Senior Institute requirements, as well as how to prepare for post-secondary education or work.

As the first class of Wade students completed their second year in Division Two, the institute's director began preparing them for the Senior Institute. She remarked:

> The beginning of [this] first year was really positive. The kids came in and they were extremely excited. . . . We had done some prepping with the kids last year [when they were still in Division Two] . . . small group meetings . . . [describing] the program, how they fit in, and how they could work within it. . . . We [even] had an overnight retreat with them.
>
> The week before school started I must have gotten phone calls from every kid [wanting] to know who their adviser was and who was in their advisory. So that's an indication of how excited they were to come back . . . and . . . be in [the] new situation . . . of choosing classes rather than having . . . a core curriculum. . . .
>
> At the same time that they were very excited about starting the Senior Institute, there was a lot of uncertainty about it and that made them . . . really nervous too. . . . They think the standards are very high in the Senior Institute. . . . They're very nervous about interacting with a whole new staff. . . . They are aware that they have more choices and they fought for these choices for a long time. [Students had been requesting open campus privileges and electives, which they would now have in the Senior Institute.] But having to make decisions that they're not accustomed to making makes it nerve-racking for them. . . . They're having a hard time with the whole concept of working more independently. They have fought for more independence; but given the leeway, they are

nervous about their ability to do it—like any other kid their age would be. Adults have a difficult time with that. And so here they are trying to formulate their own academic program within . . . the Senior Institute and they are feeling nervous about that. But at the same time, they feel very good about their new stature as young adults.

Framing the Senior Institute in terms of the common principles and the Wade School philosophy, she elaborated:

Coalition philosophy and the philosophy of Wade School throughout the years have been to provide a personalized, individualized approach to education—to be respectful of kids and to look at the child as a whole and to integrate that child into the world. Those things haven't changed [in the Senior Institute]. But when you look at who that kid is when he's sixteen or seventeen years old . . . [and] has already been [at Wade] for three to four years, . . . it's no longer a question of orienting kids to a personalized education. Or orienting kids to understand habits of mind, questions, and thoughtfulness. It really is a question of how [the student is] going to take all those things . . . and apply them to the world. . . . How can they take what they already know and apply it to [their] aims? . . . Here, they have the advantage of thinking through these things very early on in life so that school means something to them. Some of the things that I only picked up in graduate school, they are grappling with right now. But they have support to do this. . . . They are doing it in an environment of support. They are not adults. . . . We are asking them to think like adults . . . but with the same support [that they have had in the earlier divisions].

Other aspects of Coalition philosophy are also stressed in the Senior Institute. For one, knowledge and competence are demonstrated through exhibitions of mastery, not tested in more traditional manners. For another, age-grading and expectations that the program must be completed in two years are deemphasized. Convincing students of the merit of this has been challenging. The director noted: "One challenge . . . is to get the kids to understand that they have time to work, . . . that this isn't a program that they should finish in two years. It is a program that they should consider taking their time getting through so they can get where they want to go successfully. If it takes two and a half years . . . [or] three years, they should take the time. That's the biggest challenge: getting them to see there is no time expectation . . . only that they demonstrate knowledge through the portfolios."

Students were nervous about the transition to the Senior Institute and about graduation requirements. In a focus-group interview in April of their first year in the institute, one girl remarked: "Sure, they say we shouldn't worry if it takes longer than two years to finish all the requirements, but my mother will kill me if that happens. And I don't want to be in high school the rest of my life. Why can't we graduate like everyone else, you know, after two years? I mean, come on. I've been a good student—mostly distinguisheds and only a few satisfactories [the Wade system includes D for distinguished, S (satisfactory), U (unsatisfactory), and I (incomplete)]. How can it be that I might not graduate on time? I can't get my head around that."

Other students echoed her comments and spoke of the amount of work they were doing and the time it was taking to adjust to having more teachers than they had had in the lower divisions. (Wade students had three or four teachers—their house team—for two years in lower divisions. In the Senior Institute they took more classes [at the school or elsewhere] and had five, six, or more teachers each year.) They also questioned whether they would be prepared for college. As one student remarked: "Yeah, we are really famous here in the city. But when we start applying to colleges everywhere else, how [are] they going to make sense of our grades and all this portfolio stuff? And that list [of activities and subjects available to high school students—part of a form that accompanied a standardized test the students had recently taken]: we don't have any of that stuff here. We don't have astronomy, we haven't studied most of the science on that list, we don't have a student council, we don't have any clubs. How are we going to compete with students who do?" Other students said they hoped colleges would be intrigued by their transcripts and that the autobiographical essay in their portfolio would help colleges understand what they and the school were all about. A student commented: "We have a lot of freedom here and, if you plan it right, you can combine portfolio items together so it won't be as much work. We are getting to take courses at college now—that must be an advantage, don't you think?"

When the traditional graduation date for the first group of students approached, some fifteen or so students had not completed their portfolios and so did not graduate "on schedule." Nevertheless, all eventually graduated, and all but one has pursued higher education.

During the institute's first year, some teachers in other divisions and administrators were concerned that the program was too radically different from the rest of the school. To address this, schoolwide meetings by discipline were held, and the faculty was asked to consider how they might make the transition to the Senior Institute smoother and what preparation students might need. Articulating the Senior Institute with the rest of the school, when its structure and goals were seen by many as quite different, was difficult, and tensions among the divisions ran high, particularly during the first year when most institute faculty were new to the school. The dialogue that resulted is acknowledged by most faculty to have pushed the entire school to think more clearly about how best to assess students' work and their understanding of complicated ideas. Further, once they were acknowledged publicly, concerns about how well the Senior Institute meshed with the rest of Wade led to concerted efforts to create a coherent educational climate from seventh through twelfth grade. Like other aspects of Wade, the Senior Institute is viewed as in process, not as a finished product: regular reflection on purpose, design, and standards is undertaken, not just by the institute faculty, but by Wade's entire staff.

A FLEXIBLE SCHEDULE

The schedule for Divisions One and Two at Wade is simple—two two-hour classes, an hour-long advisory, and an hour for lunch and recreation. Initially the schedule was: one two-hour time block (9–11); advisory (11–12); lunch and recreation (12–1); and the second two-hour time block (1–3). In January 1988, three years after the schedule had been devised, teachers complained that afternoon classes were less productive than morning classes. After considering several options, the faculty moved both two-hour classes to the morning, scheduling lunch later, and advisory during the final hour of the day. The entire school shifted to the new schedule the day after the decision was made.

Because Wade's schedule is so simple, it can accommodate varied student and faculty interests. For instance, time has been created so that students can work with writers- or poets-in-residence, serve as interns at local museums, and participate in experimental curricula developed in conjunction with educators from nearby colleges and universities. This flexibility is facilitated by Wade's organizational simplicity. Institutional structures—the arts, vocational programs, elective offerings, and AP courses—that made change, as well as schedule modifications, more difficult at other study schools were not considered compatible with Wade's purpose and were never established. The few that were defended in early faculty meetings—community service, the library, and Spanish—were viewed as integral to the school's goals, and all remain part of life at Wade. To create such a simple institutional structure, Wade needed to maneuver through the labyrinth of state, city, and district bureaucracies. The elaborate local and state requirements seemed antithetical to the school's focused set of objectives. Negotiations with district and state administrators resulted in the waiving of some requirements that were viewed as contrary to the school's goals (particularly credits awarded per course and required subject areas).

In many ways, Wade's schedule is a fundamental element of its identity. It reflects the school's priorities: students can explore topics in depth; advisories provide a means to help address the affective dimensions of school life; and student and faculty interests that do not fit within normal time constraints can be accommodated.

COMMUNICATION WITH FAMILIES

Wade faculty and administrators regularly communicate with students' families and interested community members. A weekly newsletter, which includes a column by Markham as well as notices about schoolwide events, advisory activities, upcoming deadlines, and sports scores, is distributed to all students to share with their families. The newsletter also serves as a forum for students, teachers, and administrators to express their views about such issues as education, reform, and community politics. Markham, for example, has provided parents with information on how to watch television interactively with children, how to help students develop effective study habits, the school's philosophy, and where and when local school board elections were to be held. Announcements of citywide activities or opportunities of interest might also appear. Occasionally, articles are written in both Spanish and English. Students discuss the articles in advisory before taking the newsletter home. As the school has become increasingly well known, the newsletter has become a more formal publication and is widely distributed in the educational, as well as local, community.

The teams and division teachers also regularly communicate with families about classroom activities. In one letter the humanities teachers describe activities planned for Division One classes:

Dear Students and Families,

In our study of American history this year, we are focusing on the concept of power and the nature of political change: who has power and how it changes hands. We'll start by looking at the elections, and then investigate political change in the United States from the time of the American Revolution (the 1700s) to today. In addition to learning . . . general history, each student will follow one sector of the American population (Blacks, Hispanics, Native Americans, women, labor) in its quest for power, for a greater say in America's decisions.

For each unit, the class will try to answer some essential questions. As we study the elections, for example, the students will keep in mind seven questions: What is political power? How is it achieved? How does one get the majority of the country to agree? Does your vote count? Is this the best way to choose a leader? How do the media influence the elections? Are "voting blocks" really blocks? The students will have texts providing them with overviews of each historical period, as well as newspapers . . . other media (magazines, films . . . and television), and journals.

The literature studied this year will relate to the issues and language of power and to the individual groups striving for control over their lives. But beyond those issues, with novels, journals, short stories and plays the classes will study literary analysis—style, content, grammar—and apply it to their own writings and readings. We will work together on several aspects of writing: from sentence structure to those things which make a piece of writing interesting and engaging.

To draw things together each day, the students will write a brief summary of the main ideas they have explored individually and as a class. A file of daily summaries will be kept in the classroom for students to review. These summaries will include the homework assignments. Students will have homework every night. Some of it will be due the next day; other assignments will be ongoing— reading to be done continually, writing and re-writing; revising earlier work.

We will be tackling some interesting and important ideas this year and urge you to discuss your views and knowledge of these topics with your family. We look forward to a stimulating and hard-working year.

—The Humanities Teachers

Similar letters were distributed by math and science teachers.

In addition, Wade teachers schedule parent meetings to explain schedules, curricula, or assessment practices. Advisers meet with each student and his or her parent or guardian at least twice a year to discuss the student's performance and areas where school and home might work together to reinforce academic growth. The following vignette describes one such meeting held in early fall 1989.

The student, Jeremy, began the meeting by saying, "I like science." His adviser replied, "We don't just want to know what you like, but we really want to know what you would like to tell us in this meeting." Jeremy said, "My attention wanders sometimes and [pause] I don't like to admit that I don't understand something." His mother said: "Can I ask him something? What about some of the things you have told me about the groups [group work]?" Jeremy responded: "Oh, yeah. The group I'm in fights all the time. The group leader [another student] is cranky."

After acknowledging that he, too, felt that group dynamics had been difficult, the teacher asked, "What would you like to come out of this meeting?" Jeremy responded: "That you and I are better friends. That you tell me what you think of me. Am I a good kid or a troublemaker?" Jeremy's mother added: "What can I do to help Jeremy? I would also like to give him a sense of the three of us as a team, particularly concerning homework." Jeremy added a few more of his expectations, then the teacher said: "What I'd like to get out of this is a better understanding between the two of us and more trust about homework between you and your mom. What can you tell her about homework?" Jeremy talked a bit about homework assignments, then the teacher added: "Can your mom trust you to tell her about homework? She has had to call me to find out what you are supposed to be doing." Jeremy responded: "I didn't understand it [that homework is not always formal assignments, but that students are expected to do work each night]. I thought this would be like my old school. [My mother] doesn't like my resentfulness. Some things are hard for me. She gets angry. She's not like a teacher." The teacher responded, "Both parents and teachers get angry." His mother added, "You get angry too." The teacher then asked: "Do you want your mom to help you? Is she helping you?" Jeremy answered: "She should stay out of it for a while. I'll ask her or others for help." His mother answered, "But he hasn't done too much homework so far."

After discussing possible scenarios for how and when Jeremy would do homework, the three talked about Jeremy's apparent unwillingness to follow directions from his mother and in class. They next considered the teacher's perceptions of Jeremy, who sometimes would not listen to others in class. Toward the end of the meeting, the teacher asked Jeremy to summarize what had been said. Jeremy said: "First, kids in the class have their own points of view, and I need to listen to them too; second, you think I'm bright; and third, you don't want me to just get up and leave class." The teacher encouraged Jeremy to sum up his mother's perspective as well, which he attempted. Then the teacher acknowledged that there had been problems with the small groups, thanked Jeremy and his mother for bringing it to his attention, and said: "That is a problem and we will work on it." The meeting lasted approximately forty-five minutes.

From our observations of other parent meetings and talks with teachers and students, this description is fairly typical. This vignette also highlights several aspects of communication between Wade faculty and students' families. First, many teachers and parents interact regularly, in person and by phone. This parent had spoken with her son's adviser several times about homework before the meeting. Second, the student was expected to participate actively—voicing his concerns as well as reflecting on his behavior. Third, students and parents were encouraged to talk about the student's program. In this case, both student and parent were concerned about small-group work. The teacher acknowledged the difficulties and said that the class would continue to address this issue. Finally, this excerpt reveals some of the difficulties students have adjusting to Wade's educational approach. Jeremy had trouble listening to others when working in groups, and he was somewhat confused by the lack of formal homework assignments.

Parental involvement was a condition of admittance to Wade, and it was reinforced by administrators and teachers. Teachers sometimes called students' homes until well into the evening if parents or guardians were unavailable during the day. Parents interested in Coalition reform sometimes represented Wade at ces-sponsored conferences to learn more about the reform effort.

LEADERSHIP AND SHARED DECISION MAKING

As most anyone associated with the Wade School would agree, the school owes much to the leadership of its founder, Helen Markham. Her reputation as an educator and her ability to build strategic coalitions are widely acknowledged. She is highly regarded nationally, and she writes and speaks regularly about educational reform, school choice, and her experiences with alternative education and small schools. As previously noted, she founded a group of alternative elementary schools before starting the Wade School. In what many who know Markham might consider typical fashion, after receiving a substantial cash award for her work in education, Markham used some of the funds to help create a center at Wade for communication, professional development, and fund-raising for like-minded experimental schools in the city.

Shared decision making is one tenet of Markham's leadership style. According to many at Wade, the staff and administration have allocated tasks so top-down administrative decision making is balanced with more grassroots faculty decision making. For example, curriculum, pedagogy, and assessment are discussed at all levels of the school, by teachers and administrators. Although Markham hand-picked the original Wade staff, hiring decisions have since been made by the team of teachers who will work with the new teacher. During interviews, Markham sometimes remarked to us that she was not the most appropriate person to question about certain topics—for example, hiring, curriculum decisions, and admissions procedures—and directed us to the appropriate teacher or administrator. Markham's leadership also entailed protecting her staff from the whims of city and state educational bureaucracies, and teachers were grateful for her efforts to protect the school. As one teacher remarked, "She really goes to bat for us downtown, she'll push as hard as she needs to get us what we want." Many at Wade also appreciated Markham's success at raising additional funds for the school.

As the school grew in size, Markham began meeting with the heads of divisions and teams in addition to attending faculty meetings. Some teachers worried that this was a prelude to increased hierarchy at Wade. Others feared that important voices would be lost if decisions were routinely made by the smaller group without consulting the entire faculty. Although the meetings have continued, efforts have been made to keep all faculty involved in decisions that would affect their class work and planning. In 1990 Markham hired a codirector to share the duties of running Wade so that she might participate more actively in other aspects of school reform.[8] Relative to Markham's influence in the broader educational arena, faculty commented that their collective work was at times made difficult by Markham's commitments outside Wade.

The presence of a strong leader with much at stake professionally in a school committed to collaboration created a tension between the ideal of shared decision making and the weight of Markham's personality and style, which appears autocratic to some. Most teachers who remained at Wade throughout our research thought the faculty and administration were steering a careful and, for the most part, workable course of compromise and consensus building, with the education of Wade students their shared goal. Nonetheless, others felt intimidated by Markham and remarked that decisions were made collectively only when she agreed with the popular opinion. Still, even those who said they felt stifled by Markham's forcefulness, including some who left the school, recognized her commitment, political savvy, and intellect.

THE COALITION CENTRAL STAFF AND THE WADE SCHOOL

Since the Coalition's inception, the central staff and the Wade School have had a great deal of contact. Wade was the first school designed according to Coalition philosophy, and the staff regularly requested assistance from the Coalition. Wade staff attended many CES-sponsored

---

8. Many viewed hiring a codirector as an important step in Wade's transition from being Markham's dream to becoming a viable institution in its own right.

professional development activities, including working parties at Brown, meetings of the original Coalition principals, conferences, and workshops. Moreover, Wade staff were willing to discuss with the central staff their frustrations as well as their accomplishments in their experiments with Coalition ideas. The central staff valued the honesty of Wade's faculty and wanted to keep close track of what happened there. Finally, Wade was an urban school located in an area of poverty, and it was apparently making significant gains with its students: it had national visibility and public relations value.

Central staff involvement with the Wade School has taken many forms. Wade was chosen to participate in the Coalition's Five Schools Project, which made extra funding and central staff resources available to promising Coalition schools. Wade teachers and administrators frequently make presentations at CES and other conferences, and the school's new codirector was a Thomson fellow. Most of the school's science and math teachers attended a weeklong Coalition workshop at Brown to explore student-as-worker pedagogy in interdisciplinary approaches to their fields. The central staff has also assisted Wade's fund-raising efforts. Together, Helen Markham and Ted Sizer are a formidable and persuasive combination when meeting with educators or potential funders.

When a Coalition-sponsored region that included Wade was formed, the school received additional support, and the regional center was later housed at the school. The networks of elementary schools that Markham founded and of alternative schools in the city also belong to a center housed at Wade. Together, CES regional staff and the city-based, alternative schools staff work to promote and support educational ideas that are consistent with Coalition philosophy and that Wade-affiliated schools practice from kindergarten through twelfth grade.[9]

CONTINUOUS PROFESSIONAL GROWTH

Most aspects of Wade's structure provide opportunities for teachers' professional growth. Two or three times a year there are two-day, all-

9. The Coalition of Essential Schools is not the only reform organization with which Wade is affiliated. Several people have done research at Wade or work collab-

faculty retreats; house teams meet for three hours of curriculum development per week; and pedagogical and curricular issues dominate the weekly faculty meetings. Wade faculty generally plan and conduct their own professional development activities. Professional interactions with colleagues is continuous as staff members plan schedules, develop curriculum, assess priorities, and evaluate student work collaboratively. This planning, decision making, and reflection influences teachers' professional self-perceptions and how they work with students.

TEAM PLANNING

Each faculty member in Divisions One and Two belongs to at least two teams, a house team and a cross-house (sometimes cross-division) subject matter team. The house team—a house is half a division with about eighty students and at least four teachers—meets to discuss individual students, student and teacher workloads, advisory trips, and such housewide activities as trips to the park and to local points of interest. Since there is little time during the day when all members of the house are free, these meetings are often held during lunch or before or after school.

Each subject matter team (math-science and humanities) in the two divisions has three hours per week of collaborative planning time. (Faculty have no teaching responsibilities during this time because students are at Community Service placements.) In many ways, these meetings are at the heart of Wade's approach to education: curricula and assessment strategies are designed collectively by and negotiated among all those doing the teaching; appropriate pedagogies for specific topics and units are discussed and debated; and interns and new teachers are socialized to Wade's approach to schooling through their participation. Further, team planning meetings mirror the collaborative work that Wade teachers expect from students: individuals are responsible for researching topics and presenting them to the group. The group decides whether to incorporate the material or teaching strategy into their

---

oratively with Wade faculty or Markham. Further, Markham serves on numerous national commissions, and her views, like Sizer's, inform the national discourse on educational reform. She frequently invites members of these commissions to visit the school.

work, but individual teachers determine how to use the group's work in the classroom. Excerpts from a November 1989 planning meeting illustrate the nature of this collaboration.

Six teachers and a student intern attended this Division One humanities meeting. Humanities classes were studying "Identity and the Peopling of America," and the meeting began with discussion of two upcoming trips, one to a Jewish museum and the other to a museum featuring an exhibit on Woodland Indians. The intern had prepared the following information sheet for students going to the Jewish museum:

> You have been specially selected to go to the Jewish museum with other students . . . a number of times this year. . . . We will be going for two reasons:
>
> 1. We will learn about how museum exhibitions are put together, [asking and answering] questions like: Where did the museum get this stuff? Who decided to put these things here? Why was the exhibition put together this way? Their exhibitions are not too different from our exhibitions so . . . we can ask ourselves the same habits of mind questions that we ask . . . at Wade: What's the evidence? How do we know what we know? Who cares? What if . . . ? What's the viewpoint? What difference does it make? How does this "fit in"? Can we imagine alternatives?
>
> 2. We will learn from a specific exhibit called "Gardens and Ghettos: The Art of Jewish Life in Italy." How in the world (you might ask) is this connected to what we are doing in humanities . . . the Peopling of America? Well, the Jews are *an example* of a small group that lives in a country where the culture is different from their own. For over 2,000 years, the Jews maintained their culture, while absorbing bits and pieces of . . . Italian culture. This is very similar to what . . . groups who have come to America have done. OH! So—we can ask ourselves our humanities essential questions in this exhibit: How does an individual define his or her identity? What changes "they" to "we"? Does the nation change the group or does the group change the nation? What is a Jew? An Italian?

Your role: You will be expected to bring back to your humanities class what you have learned at the Jewish Museum. . . . The "Gardens and Ghettos" exhibit will be at the Jewish Museum until the end of January. We'd like to take humanities field trips over there where you will act as *museum guides* for your fellow students, showing them what you have learned about museums and cultures at the museum.

After talking over plans for these trips, the group brainstormed other local resources they might use to gather information for upcoming units.

The topic then shifted to the substitute teacher policy. According to the group's facilitator (one of Wade's original faculty who was serving as division mentor that year): "When we go to speak some place [that is, represent Wade at a conference or at another school], we 'sub' for each other. But when someone is out—on an advisory trip or sick—substitutes will be hired. The problem is that we need to socialize the subs to the way we do things, and we need to . . . leave them things to do."

The team returned to discussing upcoming units and assessing the Woodland Indian materials. Team members related how they were helping students organize and relate the somewhat disparate information they were getting about these Indian groups and discussed note-taking techniques used in their classes. One teacher stressed organizing information by the essential question it addressed. Another posed some intermediate questions to help students organize information: How does geography affect culture? What roles did men and women have in the group? What makes up your identity?

In addition to the historical material, these classes were reading *The Light in the Forest* and *Sing Down the Moon,* two novels for adolescents about Native American experiences. The different approaches teachers had taken were also discussed. One teacher asked students to list characteristics that seemed important to the main characters. Another teacher had students devise their own questions and pursue them in class. She noted that the students' first question was why the author of *The Light in the Forest* called Indians "savages" in the book's acknowledgments. Overall, this discussion focused on how the books reflected issues central to the school's essential questions and whether these materials engaged student interest.

In the midst of this discussion, a first-year teacher asked: "Is it assumed that we are connecting everything to every essential question? Because I have been connecting things to one question at a time. With *The Light in the Forest*, it was the identity question. With *Sing Down the Moon . . .* " He was quickly interrupted by colleagues, who explained why questions about identity should be part of the discussion of all course materials.

After a break, the team turned to planning and evaluation issues related to the next two units—"the Conquistadors" and "African Forced Migration." The facilitator (who had taught in Division Two the previous year) described the form used by that division to evaluate students and said that the team had reached consensus about its structure and had used it for three trimesters—a record at the school, she thought. She went on to explain her goals about assessment: "My goals are to communicate to . . . students first—parents second—where they are, what the next step is, what they are doing very well, and what I would like to help them with. And the second part is: some understanding . . . a general sense of what their strengths and weaknesses are. . . . So there are two kinds of standards—the kid compared to himself and the kid compared to some sense of students in general." The previous year, Division One had had long debates about grading and evaluation. Team members outlined some of those issues (including how often to evaluate and whether all team members had to use the same criteria and form) and their stances, and then they discussed the facilitator's distinction between evaluating students against themselves and against students in general. Team members talked at length about the many assessments they make—those made daily (about work accomplished, attention to classwork, and participation) and those intended to determine mastery of course material, skills, and ideas.

The topic then switched to grading oral presentations. One teacher had devised an experimental form and shared it with the group, explaining: "We need to demystify our expectations. . . . Students don't know what they are being graded on. How can they aspire to the next step? 'Evaluation' means 'what do we value?'" Another related his more subjective approach to evaluating oral presentations: "What happens with Leslie, for example, is that she has a grade when she stands up to do her oral presentation [based on my perceptions of her preparation]. And now she's either going to verify—solidify—it or undo it. Based on everything that's gone on before these fifteen minutes, my impression is that she has learned what she could. . . . Another kid will be different. Leo [for instance]. He's been wasting time. . . . Listening to him will be important for other reasons." Group members expressed strong opinions about grading, about whether "incompletes" should be given in place of "unsatisfactories" until missing work was completed. When discussion exceeded the allotted time, the facilitator suggested a partial agenda for the next meeting: incompletes, evaluation in general, and the standards for oral presentations.

The group then turned its attention to upcoming units on Conquistadors and African slavery and discussed possible resources. As the meeting ended, the facilitator asked what materials teachers needed, even though little money was available. One teacher responded, "Time. Is time on that list?" Others laughingly agreed.

In our research at Wade, we observed teams reach a working consensus about their academic goals, then renegotiate those agreements regularly. Sometimes renegotiation occurred during subsequent meetings; other times it was ad hoc, such as when problems arose between meetings or unscheduled trips or student reactions slowed classwork or caused teachers to question its appropriateness. When consensus seemed unlikely, teachers agreed to disagree and pursued their individual goals for a portion of a unit. Although Wade teachers required group work from their students, they were sympathetic to the difficulties of working by committee. Division and house team meetings were often contentious, and decisions were sometimes made simply because, as numerous teachers remarked, "We've got to do something with the kids on Monday and this arguing could go on forever." Teaming sometimes proved difficult, but one teacher articulated the general sentiment about its benefits: "The fact that we have the teams allows us to say, 'We have backups in school . . . we have support in school.' This creates a sense that, 'Okay, I can relax for a little bit, I don't have to get crazy. I'm not in this all alone. People are going to help me.' That helps you and your classroom."

Team membership, particularly the multiple team memberships at Wade, offered a layered socializing experience for faculty. Additionally, faculty recognized that they had substantial responsibility and authority, not only in their own classrooms, but also in terms of decisions that affected their division and house. Teachers felt closely linked—some said "too closely linked"—with colleagues and, unlike at our other study sites, no one complained about feeling isolated.[10]

RACISM AT WADE: A FACULTY RETREAT ABOUT AN ONGOING ISSUE

In an urban environment filled with overt and subtle racial confrontation and innuendo, racial tensions among faculty and between faculty and students at Wade seemed ever present and occasionally led to angry exchanges. Consequently, an early faculty retreat was devoted to confronting issues of race and ethnicity, which were causing difficulties at Wade. Markham explained:

> Last spring we had a retreat in which we tried to . . . discuss the racial tensions among the staff members. We brought in someone to serve as a moderator. We wanted to discuss resentments and feelings people had about whether white teachers could really teach black kids and other unspoken questions among the faculty. . . . I just felt with the secondary school you absolutely have to [address these often unspoken concerns]. The kids themselves are going to face it in the world they're going into and dealing with colleges and jobs. If we can't talk to kids about race, we're leaving out too large a dimension [of real life]. If teachers can't talk to each other about it, how are they going to talk to the kids about it? If white teachers don't know what black teachers feel about things, then they're missing a lot. How do we talk about what black parents feel? What's happening when they're having a conference if they're not discussing how that parent is feeling about them as a white teacher? It was important. We had an extraordinarily explosive meeting. [Yet,] it broke the ice. There was enough desire of people in the school to make this school succeed so that it wasn't a disaster. If we had done this two years earlier, it could have ended the school.

10. During our research only one teacher, a recent college graduate, said he would like more mentoring, as he felt ill prepared in terms of classroom management and interdisciplinary instruction. While at Wade he sought assistance not only from his team but also from faculty in the associated elementary schools.

Well, we followed it up . . . by taking a step back and approaching [the issue of racism] a different way. We decided to approach it by bringing a conflict resolution program into the school for students, parents, and faculty, to talk more about how you talk about conflict, how you deal with things that are hard to talk about . . . hoping to then move back into racism. For the first . . . series of meetings with the staff it was just about conflict and how to position yourself in a conversation when it's difficult. How to talk about things that are difficult. The last two meetings have been on race. So we are coming into it the back way, and I hope we will be able to get back to the conversation we had last spring.

The retreat was student-centered, responsive, and daring. Tensions ran high as people of varied backgrounds discussed feelings and reactions related to race that they had experienced both at Wade and in the rest of their lives. Faculty disagreed about what incidents between teachers and students implied about a teacher's racial beliefs. Despite the stress and occasional animosity, most agreed that open discussions were a necessary prelude to more genuine and responsive interactions with students and to addressing race and ethnicity more effectively in the curriculum. During informal discussions at the retreat and in interviews afterward, various white teachers described the experience as "incredible" and "unforgettable." Many added that they had never fully understood their subtle yet discriminatory actions toward people of color. In contrast, faculty of color generally felt that many of their white colleagues were naive about the importance of race and somewhat oblivious to the subtle distinctions they made as members of the majority group in U.S. society. Although tensions among individual faculty members have persisted and racism has remained a topic of concern at Wade, most felt the administration took an enormous risk—one that paid off—in trying to face the issue directly and respectfully. Many teachers felt that there would be immediate benefits in their classrooms as they dealt with race and ethnic difference more sensitively.

PROMOTING PROFESSIONAL SELF-REFLECTION IN FACULTY MEETINGS

Faculty meetings might seem an unlikely source of professional development at many schools, but almost from its inception the Wade faculty has tried to reserve some portion of these weekly two-hour meetings for discussing educational philosophy, pedagogy, and curriculum.[11] Faculty have considered such issues as the implications of using student-as-worker and teacher-as-coach pedagogies in their classrooms, how to increase student engagement with their work, potential assessment techniques for the Senior Institute, and training in conflict resolution. Although announcements and committee work have not disappeared from Wade faculty meetings, the goal has been to limit "administrivia," so there will be time during the school day for work that will further the professional education of staff members.

BUILDING ON SUCCESS AND COPING WITH CRITICISM

Wade is viewed by many as the most successful Coalition school. Although dropout rates in the city are high, there are very few dropouts at Wade.[12] In addition, all but one member of the first graduating class pursued higher education. Some fifteen students did not graduate "on schedule," but all eventually completed their degrees. Further, since its inception Wade has enjoyed a highly favorable reputation, in part as a consequence of Markham's successful elementary school network. Staff members have discussed their philosophy and program highlights in various public forums. They have made presentations and have written articles describing their work. Wade also allows researchers and those interested in educational change to visit, even providing a visitors' orientation (staffed by teachers and students).[13]

Unlike our other study sites, Wade had few problems with preferential treatment or job security. Job security issues, like many problems Wade faces, result from budget deficits in the citywide system. They

11. This began in fall 1987 and was initiated by two teachers who had attended a CES workshop on student-as-worker the previous summer. They used this time to share what they had learned.

12. Wade keeps track of the students who leave its program, and according to its records, students who leave Wade continue at other schools. Markham hired a researcher to track former Wade students through their high school years and into college.

13. Feedback from researchers and other visitors is reviewed and sometimes incorporated into the school's ongoing discussion of its work and mission. For instance, we shared summaries of Wade students' responses to a survey we conducted. Later, in two issues of the school's newsletter, Markham summarized these findings and suggested links between them and some issues facing the school and its philosophy.

never seemed to threaten people's loyalty to Wade; rather, the problems often seemed to increase faculty commitment to the school.

Nevertheless, the school does face some difficult issues. Feelings of exclusion from decision making or that shared decision making is inauthentic have at times created discontent. And the workload has taken a toll on the faculty: turnover has been a concern from the start. Some faculty suggest that these problems (particularly high turnover) are the consequences of working so closely together and working to achieve consensus at many levels simultaneously.

Not everyone in the education world is enamored of the school's approach. Critics have questioned its applicability as a model for school reform because of its admission requirements (most notably, that students and parents agree to be active participants in the life of the school) and because of the additional funds that Markham and the Coalition have raised for the school.

Faculty and administration readily admit that the school struggles with some difficulties. But one difference at Wade is that problems usually become the object of reflection by the whole staff, not by a chosen few. Further, schoolwide commitment to ongoing reflection contributes to making Wade's overall evolution everyone's concern. The careful articulation of Coalition philosophy with the school's design and approach to curriculum, instruction, and assessment has yielded a continual focus on students, a personalized environment, and a structure designed to focus on the few subjects the school's staff wants students to take seriously. Issues of power and control are not absent from Wade, but in an environment where professional and self-reflection permeate school life and where teams spend substantial in-school time discussing how best to get students to engage with curriculum, one senses that everyone—administrators, teachers, students, and parents—is pulling together to help each other so Wade's students can realize their fullest potential.

7

A COMPARATIVE LOOK AT SCHOOLWIDE CHANGE

Central Park East Manhattan Debra Meyer

The preceding case studies describe what happened in five secondary schools that joined the Coalition. In this chapter we consider several dimensions of these reform efforts. For instance, we contrast what happened at schools with strong reputations with what happened at those with more troubled histories. We also compare schools that opted for a school-within-a-school approach and those that attempted to make reform a schoolwide effort. In considering how making the reform process more inclusive at the school site contributed to sustaining and deepening change, we look at the three study schools identified by the Coalition central staff as having taken the second step toward schoolwide reform and detail the characteristics they shared that seem to have been pivotal in their reform efforts. We then discuss four issues that cut across all school sites—lack of consensus about the need for reform, political strains generated by change efforts, time constraints, and tension between deepening understanding and sophistication of reform and broadening participation in these efforts. Finally, we discuss the increased reflection on philosophy and practice among faculty and administrators that occurred at all our study sites.

REPUTATION AND HISTORY

Among our study schools, those with relatively poor histories before CES membership—including Lewis, Russell, Wade,[1] and Green Valley (to be discussed in chapter 13)—experienced improvements in dropout

---

1. As Wade was a new school created grade-by-grade, it had no reputation at first. Nonetheless, we feel that our generalizations are accurate for Wade because it is part of a system with a poor reputation.

rates, daily attendance rates, and discipline referrals.[2] These relative successes helped the schools promote and expand their Coalition programs because they offered district and school administrators, parents, teachers, and students evidence of the programs' effectiveness. Also, faculty at these schools often changed aspects of their classroom teaching, commonly increasing students' active participation in classes and incorporating research papers, essay exams, and oral reports into their courses—tasks usually associated with higher academic expectations. In addition, these schools increased graduation requirements, which made them look more like college preparatory programs since students had to take additional courses in science, math, and social studies. These changes often enhanced the reputation of Coalition efforts at these schools.

Another significant development was that many students' post–high school plans changed. In each of these schools, college attendance among CES-program participants has been relatively high. Increased college attendance was not a stated goal of these programs, but most aspired to make more options—including college—available to students. Through visits to colleges, assistance preparing for PSATs and SATs, and advisory discussions about future plans, further education became a common expectation for many students who admitted that they had previously given it little, if any, thought.

Although three of these troubled schools (Wade, Lewis, and Green Valley) were designated as exemplars of Coalition practice,[3] their change efforts were facilitated by two factors unrelated to CES. First, as organizations they had simple structures.[4] Special programs, such as advanced placement classes, magnets, or extensive elective offerings, were largely absent. And second, compared with those at the other study sites, the principals in these schools had more power to replace personnel reluctant to change, either by transferring them to other schools or dismissing

2. This was particularly true in terms of their previous performance or similar measures for their larger school counterparts (in the case of SWAS programs).

3. Although they served as exemplars, neither the schools nor the Coalition central staff considered these schools to have fully implemented Coalition ideas. All involved with these schools' efforts continue to pursue reform agendas.

4. The structures were simple, but in other ways the organizations were complex (in dynamics, leadership, and decision-making processes).

them. It seems noteworthy that Russell High—a troubled school where these factors were not present—improved all of the above-mentioned dimensions but remained split over Coalition membership and is not considered an exemplar school by the central staff.

In contrast, at those more traditionally successful schools that served affluent communities, convincing faculty members (as well as students and parents) to adopt Coalition philosophy and practices and determining the effectiveness of Coalition reforms proved more problematic. These schools already had good student attendance rates, high SAT scores, many successful graduates, and virtually no dropouts. Essay tests, research papers, and oral reports were commonplace. Improving college attendance was not an issue. Faculty at these schools often questioned the need for Coalition-based reform with three assertions. Many claimed, "We already do it. So what do we need to change?" Somewhat paradoxically, others maintained, "This can't be done" and cited institutional constraints that would make aspects of Coalition-related change practically impossible. And teachers felt confident saying, "This, too, will pass," implying that they had seen change efforts come and go and expected the same for the Coalition. Such reactions were evident at all of our study schools, but they had the greatest impact on Coalition-based efforts at schools with reputations for excellence.

In many ways, however, Coalition membership provoked faculties to reconsider their commitment to existing philosophy and practices—something most faculty found to be a positive aspect of Coalition association. Yet, this increased professional reflection often highlighted differences among faculty concerning the school's mission, in effect disrupting the unquestioned assumption of shared purposes, values, and beliefs. For instance, once Elliston High faculty began debating the school's mission, so many philosophical divisions emerged that it voted to reaffirm its commitment to being a comprehensive high school and left the Coalition.[5] Reflecting some of the tension that emerged when Coalition-related changes began to affect her school's curriculum, a teacher at Silas Ridge (another of our study schools with a reputation for excellence; see chapter 11) stated: "Who came in and said there was

5. Hart's study (1990) of the effects of redesigning teacher work on school life also found increased contentiousness once aspects of leadership and decision making became problematic.

something wrong with [our] curriculum? Ted Sizer never came in and said there was something wrong. . . . It is a sequential curriculum . . . American, English, and World literature—sophomore, junior, and senior year. . . . Who said that [it would be better to have] the sophomore English curriculum a 'topic-based' curriculum? . . . We were changing, I thought, what was good about Silas Ridge—its strong academic curriculum. [We had] high standards and kids getting into the top colleges in the country. What was wrong?"

As had happened at Elliston High, Silas Ridge faculty grew so divided that their SWAS program was terminated by a vote of the school's Coalition steering committee and their Coalition affiliation jeopardized. In each of the traditionally more successful schools, after reexamining their existing values and practices as well as planning and implementing Coalition philosophy, teachers reaffirmed their commitment to existing practices, structures, and values rather than adopting the reform philosophy. None of these schools have served as exemplars of Coalition practice. In part, the changes implemented at schools with relatively poor previous reputations were accepted by faculties and the local community because there were signs of improvement in students' performance associated with Coalition membership and because these changes fit with existing ideas about what constituted "real" school.[6] For the "good" high schools, establishing success proved more difficult, and faculties questioned both the need for change and the value of Coalition philosophy.

PROGRAM IMPLEMENTATION: SWAS AND WHOLE-SCHOOL REFORM

Since the Coalition's inception, the central staff has encouraged a variety of approaches to school reform among its members. A number of member schools created SWAS programs. This was not novel to the Coalition; in fact some study schools had SWAS programs in place when they joined the Coalition. Four factors made this structure appealing. (1) Because of a school's responsibility to society, public schools find it

6. For a discussion of the notion of "real" school and its consequences for reform see, e.g., Meier (1992) and Metz (1990).

difficult to implement unproven, broadly encompassing reforms. The SWAS structure allowed schools to start small and build. (2) Many administrators, both at the building and district level, considered it most appropriate to approach change cautiously, in order to balance concerns and reactions among their various constituencies (students, teachers, administrators, parents, coaches, and so on). (3) School departments seldom have the funding to support large-scale change. Each of our SWAS case study schools relied on supplementary funds from private and state-sponsored sources to support their programs. (4) The SWAS ostensibly offered schools an opportunity to involve those faculty members willing to experiment with change without compelling others to join.

To varying degrees the SWAS approach affected the educational impact of the reforms as well as the peace of the schools. In particular, five issues proved troublesome: allegations of favored treatment for participating teachers; the isolation of SWAS faculty from non-SWAS faculty; questions of SWAS success; difficulties expanding SWAS programs when there was no consensus about the need for Coalition reforms; and challenges to expansion from scheduling and space constraints. Some of these issues also arose in schools that attempted whole-school change. Accusations of preferential treatment, for example, existed in each site, even at Elliston where no formal Coalition program was implemented. But with SWAS programs, faculty divisiveness was heightened by structural manifestations that served as symbolic divisions between the involved and uninvolved. In contrast, where reform was a schoolwide effort, differences often emerged but were not reinforced by structural factors.

Further, planned expansions of SWAS programs over time led to difficulties articulating the program with the rest of the school. Because SWAS efforts located reform work within a limited context, when schools sought to build on this structure and make change and restructuring schoolwide priorities, they often encountered problems. (This was the case for all four of our SWAS study schools, although Lewis's SWAS has grown consistently since its inception.) Over time, the constraints that the programs faced contributed to hardening differences between SWAS proponents and those not involved with the program. In three of the four SWAS efforts we studied—Russell, Evans Hill, and Silas

Ridge—the reforms ended up as specialty shops within shopping mall high schools, not as pilot programs for schoolwide change.

Whole-school efforts at Coalition reform also proved difficult and sometimes for similar reasons (issues of communication and preferential treatment), but these schools generally avoided the pilot program difficulties encountered by the SWAS cases. There were three schools in our study that attempted whole-school change: Wade (already discussed); Barrett (an urban private school that is the subject of chapter 8); and Green Valley (the only rural school in our study; it is described in chapter 11). The schools shared certain features that shed light on why they chose a schoolwide implementation strategy. First, the schools were small, and SWAS programs would likely not have been feasible.[7] Second, each school had a new principal who was forceful, committed to CES philosophy, and had the power to hire new staff and replace those unwilling to explore CES philosophy. And finally, each school was seeking a new identity. Being associated with the Coalition and Brown University—a national reform movement and an Ivy League school— was viewed as beneficial to this identity building.

What of Elliston? Betwixt and between the categories of whole school and SWAS program, the Elliston case illustrates what can occur when reform is attempted and there is no consensus that change (and, more specifically, Coalition-proposed changes) is necessary. Initially, CES membership led individual faculty at Elliston to experiment with Coalition philosophy at the classroom level; there was no formal program and no required involvement. A proposal to create a SWAS program led to debates at which the concerns elaborated in the four SWAS cases were laid out as potential problems. Ultimately, the faculty, unconvinced that change was needed, rejected the idea that Coalition philosophies and practices, if implemented comprehensively, would improve the school. This conclusion, coupled with the distinction we made earlier between troubled and good schools, is interesting. The opposite occurred at the troubled schools, where expanding the reform effort was felt to create a deeper and more enduring change, which many in those schools viewed as a real improvement.

---

7. Indeed, some argued that it was not really feasible at Evans Hill, which, with a population of around three hundred, was larger than any of these schools.

INCLUSIVENESS OF REFORM WORK AT
SECOND-STEP OR EXEMPLAR SCHOOLS

In looking at reform from a schoolwide perspective it becomes apparent that the more inclusive such an effort became, the more likely it was to endure and deepen. By "inclusive," we mean involving multiple levels of the educational system (the classroom, individual departments, the school, the district) and multiple actors in that system (teachers, students, administrators). When the Coalition central staff sought to promote and nurture the work of those schools they considered exemplars of Coalition practices, and which had taken the second step toward schoolwide reform, schools that had made their efforts broadly inclusive were selected. The Wade School, for example, made it a priority to involve all faculty in the change process; it created many forums through which to promote teacher input, from planning and implementing change to assessing its effects. Although the school relied somewhat on teachers' good will and commitment, these efforts were not wholly volunteer—administrators made planning and reflecting on school change a normal part of teachers' routine.

Such broad participation often helped create a common purpose within schools about the nature of and need for change. In particular, an inclusive process allowed such schools as Wade, Lewis, and Green Valley to address a critical tension faced by all our study schools: balancing top-down, administrative direction and decision making with grassroots commitment and support. These schools had administrators committed to change who worked to promote Coalition-based reforms. In addition, there was substantial grassroots support. This simultaneously top-down and grassroots approach to change helped the schools work collectively toward a common goal. In addition, it provided continuity for dealing with students, less reform-minded others, and the local community. In contrast, at Evans Hill and Elliston, administrators supported the schools' change efforts and assisted those teachers most actively involved with reform. For various reasons, however, they alienated many faculty members. Some teachers were suspicious of their principals' motives for implementing Coalition reforms, believing that a preset agenda would be foisted on the school. At Lewis and Russell, teachers maintained that administrators favored those faculty members most involved with restructuring—assigning them lighter teaching

loads and extra nonteaching periods. Others felt that principals restricted faculty involvement by making participation in reform voluntary. And still others, because of feuds with administrators, refused to
contribute to any effort that might improve the principal's stature in the
community.[8] Lacking adequate grassroots support, these schools'
change efforts foundered.

Again, it should be noted that the relative lack of organizational
complexity may have made it easier for some schools to be more inclusive than others. That is, schools with extensive AP offerings and magnet
programs found it more difficult to interweave these various programs,
which often had differing interests and competing priorities, and to
generate a shared vision based on Coalition philosophy. Further, many
of these schools' reputations were tied to the array of courses and programs they offered, a perceived strength that many teachers felt was
threatened by the Coalition's emphasis on an intellectual focus.

Students, too, represented an important component in comprehensive change. Where student participation was encouraged and nurtured,
classroom and schoolwide changes were more likely to be sustained and
to deepen. At most schools where students were a part of the reform
effort, it was usually through membership in advisory groups or new
governance systems introduced to allow their input into the process.
Moreover, in those schools students often became proponents of
change—a reaction that seemed to reflect the increased sense of personalization that many in Coalition schools experienced.

Professional development was often an important factor in continuing to make school reform inclusive, in part by helping school personnel
assess current practices and develop needed skills. When these activities
were articulated with the school's goals and the teachers' sense of what
they needed next, and when they were made a part of the life of the
school itself, they contributed to deepening schoolwide reform efforts.

In addition to sending faculty to Coalition-sponsored workshops,
some schools conducted their own professional development activities,
occasionally sponsoring activities for other schools. For some schools,
like Lewis and Wade, these included weeklong summer workshops or
weekend retreats, which allowed teachers to delve into an issue at

8. For discussions of the tensions between teachers and administrators, see Lortie
(1975) and Hargreaves (1980).

length. Other schools, for example, Barrett, Evans Hill, and Silas Ridge, organized schoolwide in-service days.[9] Whereas self-initiated professional development activities were not common at any of our study schools before Coalition membership, six of the eight experimented with them during the research period. Moreover, the schools the Coalition central staff designated as second-step exemplars of Coalition practice all offered their own professional development activities—regular opportunities (in a variety of forms) for staff to reflect on their work, address problems, and consider new directions.[10]

The three second-step schools share all of the features of inclusiveness that we have described. They shared other features that were not as apparent at our other sites, but that seemed to help sustain their reform efforts and make them more inclusive. For instance, each school had a leader who actively supported restructuring efforts, who was respected by most faculty members, and who was committed to change before affiliation with the Coalition. In many ways, the Coalition provided each of these leaders an avenue to realize preexisting ideas about school restructuring. In addition, these principals were at their schools throughout the research period. The five other study schools all experienced some administrative turnover—of principal or Coalition coordinator.

These principals also supported teachers directly involved in restructuring efforts by creating common planning time for involved faculty and by securing funds so participants could attend Coalition-sponsored workshops. Further, the principals took advantage of many opportunities—faculty meetings, professional development activities, and team meetings—to forge and promote a shared vision among the staff and other members of the school community.

All three schools raised monies from foundations and received Coali-

9. Discussing the literature on professional development, Smith and O'Day (1991) observed that professional development funds are often limited and highly susceptible to budget cuts. See also Guskey (1986), Little et al. (1987), and McLaughlin (1990). Smith and O'Day add that teachers who select their own such activities report a more positive experience, and they cite a study by Purkey and Smith (1983) that suggests a positive effect on student achievement. Barth (1990) discusses the importance of schools using professional development to build consensus for change and to work toward improvement. There has been little research on the efforts of schools to initiate their own professional development.

10. Teachers at these three schools reported that such activities prepared them to assist other faculties in rethinking their school practices or philosophy.

tion funds for school-based change efforts and for working with like-minded personnel at other schools. Further, each school used the mounting evidence of success to build support for its work. The central staff invested more time and money in these three schools than in most member schools—possibly because these schools reported regularly on their efforts and requested assistance. In supporting these schools, the central staff did not direct the schools' work; rather, they did whatever they could to support the schools' self-initiated efforts, one of the central staff's ways of demonstrating respect for local autonomy. Because the central staff regarded the reform work at these schools as more ambitious, they were often showcased in CES symposia, workshops, and public relations efforts. Faculty from these schools also attended many Coalition-sponsored professional development activities and made presentations about their work. As a result of these interactions, teachers at these schools generally viewed central staff members as having something to offer and as encouraging their efforts. All these characteristics were present at each of the second-step schools, but our other study sites shared only some of them.

In sum, each of the second-step schools apparently acknowledged the importance of three factors that contribute to systemic change. First, the schools created structures to support school reform, that is, the *actions* supportive of change. Second, they focused on discussing and defining the philosophical and pedagogical assumptions that undergird these actions, that is, the *beliefs* that underlie change. And third, they created opportunities, often in conjunction with the Coalition staff, to help faculty and administrators develop the *skills* to implement their philosophy. These skills related not only to pedagogy and curriculum development, but to improving collaboration with colleagues, making parental interactions more productive, and coping with teachers' expanded role as student advisers. By simultaneously moving on three fronts (action, belief, and skills), schools both created structures to facilitate change and helped equip faculty to implement change, and they also involved more persons at the school site in the change process.

CROSS-CUTTING ISSUES

Comprehensive change efforts at Coalition schools were more likely to take root and endure than those that were more limited. This generalization is also broadly applicable to school change efforts.[11] Common sense suggests that a widespread commitment to reform and shared understandings about change would make reform more effective. Nonetheless, comprehensive change is not a simple, straightforward process. As we discuss below, a lack of consensus about the need for change, political issues, time constraints, and concerns about balancing program expansion with deepening of reform work all were crucial in the change process at our study sites.

LACK OF CONSENSUS ABOUT THE NEED FOR CHANGE

Perhaps the most widespread and problematic tension we observed (at least from the perspective of a need for change) was that in each of our study schools—with the exception of Wade—there was no consensus that fundamental changes in school structure or teaching practices needed to occur. In spite of claims that U.S. schools are shortchanging students and American society, and calls for change that have for years filled the popular media and education journals, many teachers and administrators did not think their school or their teaching needed to change. Rather, some felt that society needed to change, since present conditions (single-parent families, drug abuse, students' lack of respect for authority, and so on) made it difficult for teaching to succeed. As one teacher said: "People assume that traditional teaching practices haven't worked, and they see the school as the effective vehicle for change, and it's not. It's the society that has to be changed. . . . School is a reflection of our society, and education has been overwhelmed by society."

Others who were unconvinced that fundamental change was necessary often noted the performance of their more successful students—citing SAT scores and the selective colleges they attended. Still others questioned the need to change because in their experience, change seldom lasted longer than the tenure of the latest principal or superintendent. Teachers who held these views were often willing for others to experiment with change, but they felt strongly that their own involvement should not be required.[12] This view predominated in schools with

---

11. See, e.g., Cuban (1990), Lieberman et al. (1991), Fullan and Miles (1992), and Sarason (1990).

12. See also Muncey and McQuillan (1993a, 1992a, 1992b) and McQuillan and Muncey (1994).

good reputations, but staff at the more troubled schools also shared this perspective.

As with all aspects of school life, reform efforts are political. Reform rhetoric may stress pedagogical, curricular, and assessment priorities, but none of these can be negotiated in a political vacuum. All school reforms involve shifts in power, prestige, and responsibility and therefore have political consequences. The Coalition's central staff at first assumed that school reform could be effected by focusing on academic concerns—specifically, the triangle of learning (the relationship between the student, teacher, and subject matter). Coalition supporters in member schools adopted a similar orientation and concentrated on program structure, curriculum, and pedagogy while giving limited attention to the political consequences of exerting influence within the school. As was evident at all of our study schools, however, Coalition proponents may have focused on the triangle of learning, but their activities had schoolwide ramifications.

As the effects of reform began to be experienced, various political issues emerged at these schools—the most common and contentious being whether Coalition-related changes were equitable. Questions of equity generally centered on *who* participated in the reform and *how* they were treated. In each of the schools we have described so far (except Wade) a volunteer core of faculty became actively involved in the change effort. Administrators supported them, believing that these teachers would demonstrate the effectiveness of Coalition philosophy and thereby promote change throughout the school. Rather than viewing Coalition proponents as positive innovators, noninvolved faculty often considered them the principal's favorites. This perceived preferential treatment often hampered the spread of Coalition reforms to the entire school because it distanced Coalition supporters from the rest of the faculty, many of whom also dismissed any signs of Coalition success on the basis of these favored conditions.

Equity also became an issue as teachers not directly involved experienced the unanticipated effects of Coalition-related changes and came to realize what little input they had had. For instance, at Russell and at Lewis, some faculty thought that they lost many of the better students to Coalition classrooms. At Evans Hill, Russell, and Lewis teachers were upset with the scheduled special time blocks for Coalition courses, which disrupted the daily routine. And some teachers in all the study schools thought that curricular changes instituted by Coalition faculty were inappropriate. Moreover, since volunteers directed most of the reform efforts, some faculty felt unfairly excluded from the restructuring process. If Coalition reforms were affecting everyone in the schools, albeit indirectly in some cases, why didn't everyone have a say in the process?

The political tensions that emerged also reflected a concern among noninvolved faculty that implementing Coalition programs would adversely affect elective or magnet programs. Coalition programs often had different emphases than the rest of the school. This included more required core courses—English, history, math, and science—and a concurrent decrease in time available for electives and special programs. Some schools experienced immediate reductions in the scheduling of noncore courses. In many instances, teachers who felt that their disciplines or programs were being discredited or that their jobs were being jeopardized came to oppose Coalition-based reforms. In addition, as many study schools experienced declining enrollments coincident with implementing Coalition ideas, there were fears of job loss. In some cases, positions were lost, and the cause was perceived to be Coalition reforms. This often heightened tensions within a faculty.

Political tensions were often exacerbated by the perceptions that different factions had about each other. Coalition supporters tended to be skeptical of those who questioned or opposed their efforts. Conversely, by advocating change, Coalition proponents were perceived as implicitly critical of existing practices (for example, lecturing). Further, some faculty felt that those with increased power and influence were being portrayed in a very positive light, as the persons doing the most exciting and innovative work at their schools.

By focusing on the academic aspects of reform and not its political dimensions, many Coalition advocates were unprepared for political disruptions when they emerged. On top of all the other challenges these teachers faced—developing curricula, organizing schedules, and dealing with the uncertainties associated with something new and ambitious—political opposition was an unpleasant surprise for which few faculty had time or energy. Yet such developments had specific consequences for the reform efforts.[13] For example, political divisiveness restricted communication between Coalition program participants and their noninvolved colleagues. As one Coalition teacher remarked, "We really neglected to communicate enough with the rest of the staff. And I think that a lot of really crazy ideas got circulated about what we were doing—or not doing."

A second consequence of paying little attention to politics was that Coalition supporters at first defined those not involved in reform (and not openly opposed or skeptical) as probable supporters, instead of viewing them as equally liable to oppose their efforts. Given the time demanded by school restructuring, convincing noninvolved colleagues of the program's merits was not a priority for those attempting to implement Coalition reforms. Yet, as some who were initially unconcerned about reform, or who even supported the ideas *in theory,* realized the ramifications of these changes *in practice,* what seemed like a good idea or, at worst, a harmless experiment could generate substantial controversy.

A final consequence of political tensions was that many schools eventually had to address issues not directly related to Coalition philosophy. At Elliston High, for instance, faculty shifted their attention from interpreting Coalition philosophy to deciding whether they wanted to remain a comprehensive high school. The philosophical and political often became so entwined that it was difficult to determine which generated greater tension. Specific concerns differed from school to school, but addressing these issues proved divisive and dismaying for many faculty members and ultimately undermined the schools' restructuring efforts.

TIME CONSTRAINTS

At all steps of the school change process, time was a major constraint—in developing a program, charting future directions, and assessing program effectiveness. At each of our study sites time was a scarce commodity. Schools often relied on teachers and administrators who were willing to volunteer their time to design and implement Coalition pro-

13. Although Wade was not immune to political tension, factionalism and opposition to CES ideas were much less evident there than at other schools.

grams. After programs were in place, teachers needed time to assess and refine their teaching techniques and program structure. But in many schools experienced Coalition teachers had little time to enhance their understanding of Coalition philosophy. At Silas Ridge and Evans Hill, two schools that relied on faculty voluntarism to initiate their programs, several Coalition proponents grew fatigued from the additional work they accepted (such as writing grants or submitting the application for Coalition membership to school boards and the Coalition central staff). Since much time and effort were directed elsewhere, teachers commonly felt dissatisfied with their classroom efforts, as well as disillusioned when political tensions arose. In certain instances, such as with Russell's policy on incompletes, teachers initially took pride in what they and their students had accomplished, but some wondered about maintaining the pace and feared burnout. In contrast, at Green Valley and Lewis, one reason why the programs have been widely embraced may well have been their principals' ability to secure foundation support and to commit time during the normal school day and during the summer so faculty could work on program and personal development.

DEPTH VERSUS BREADTH

The tension between depth and breadth runs throughout the Coalition movement. For reform-minded individuals in schools and for the reform movement as a whole there was agreement that program expansion and deepening of reform ideas (through practice and reflection) were both necessary. The CES staff and those in our study schools found expansion less problematic than developing or enhancing their understanding and use of CES ideas. At the school level, depth versus breadth caused tensions about how best to socialize teachers to Coalition philosophy. Original team members at most of our study sites were given release time to design their program structure. Often they were also allowed time to develop curricula, attend Coalition conferences, and familiarize themselves with Coalition philosophy. At Russell High, for example, the first SWAS team was freed for an entire semester to do this work. Teachers who joined the programs later were never provided release time to explore Coalition philosophy. And the introductions they received were often less comprehensive than those given their veteran colleagues. The assumption seemed to be that once a faculty had accepted a reform program, there was little need for ongoing reflection. In effect, planning for change became defined as part of the start-up for change rather than part of an ongoing process.

Other socialization-related issues also favored expansion over deepening. As Coalition programs evolved, so did the day-to-day logistics of running a special program. At two schools this became so pressing that new faculty orientations emphasized the logistics of operating an Essential School and gave less attention to the philosophical or pedagogical components. At some study schools, teachers looking for a job knew that they improved their chances if they were willing to participate in the Coalition program. Some teachers might therefore agree to team or teach collaboratively when they actually had little experience with or interest in this approach. In other instances, teachers already at a school perceived that it was in their best interest to affiliate themselves with a Coalition program; otherwise they might be transferred. We are not suggesting that these persons were poor teachers, only that their understanding of and receptivity to Coalition philosophy often differed from those of people who joined a program because of a philosophical affinity. In other schools, staff turnover impeded efforts to deepen Coalition ideas. As one teacher said: "The turnover in teachers is a problem. We must keep our teachers. . . . The strength of the program will depend on the same teachers coming back year after year, getting to know the [philosophy], making use of [it], and getting cooperation from within their departments to experiment with the ideas."

The impediments to deepening reform efforts at individual schools seem myriad, and the advantages of expansion all too apparent. Still, many schools cited program expansion or scheduling changes as evidence that the program was taking root. These structural developments represented signs of change, but they did not necessarily reflect a deepening of Coalition ideas in practice.[14]

Although change proved difficult at these schools, there was one notable and consistent effect: regardless of a school's reputation, Coalition membership increased the entire school community's reflectiveness about their work and the school's mission. No matter how contentious

14. Newmann (1993) explored in some detail the dangers of assuming that fundamental restructuring will occur without concomitant changes in practice, beliefs, and commitments.

school change issues became, teachers and administrators (both Coalition advocates and opponents) acknowledged that involvement with the Coalition of Essential Schools made the faculty as a whole more reflective about their work. Many teachers reported that they were reexamining their approaches to classroom learning and that they welcomed the opportunities that shared decision making, for example, offered them. Some mentioned that they had joined committees to investigate new governance structures; others were examining possible budget reallocations or alternative ways to assess student learning. As a teacher from Elliston High explained: "I think [discussions about our Coalition affiliation] made a lot of teachers look at what they were doing in the classroom and how they were presenting their material. . . . The Coalition got us talking about what we want out of education and what direction we should be going in. . . . That was extremely healthy." Another teacher's comments are also revealing: "We have had the best discussions—the best arguments, the best rethinking. . . . People never used to talk about what they were doing in the classroom."

III

MORE FOCUSED LOOKS AT SCHOOL REFORM

8

"IF ONLY I HAD THE TIME"
A TEACHER IN THE MIDST OF CHANGE

> Everybody becomes a new teacher when they come into a new teaching situation that demands new kinds of teaching skills. . . . Without support, the experiment—the change—ends up defeating itself. You put yourself into a situation where the frustrations build so much that rather than looking for a place to lay blame, you lay blame on the change as opposed to on the lack of support. —NEIL ALLEN, a Barrett Preparatory School teacher

> It is one thing to embrace a doctrine of instruction and quite another to weave it deeply into one's practice. —DAVID K. COHEN, "Revolution in One Classroom (Or, Then Again, Was It?)"

Neil Allen's experiences as a teacher at Barrett Preparatory School, the only private school in our study, are the subject of this chapter. Allen is typical of the teachers who embraced Coalition philosophy and practice, and his reflectiveness provided substantial insight into how teachers internalized Coalition changes. Although he was initially resistant to and skeptical of change, Allen became a Coalition supporter after experimenting with its ideas in his classroom. As his commitment to reform grew, he assumed more of a leadership role at Barrett while continuing to innovate in his classes, until he began to feel overextended. To regain a sense of control, he began, in his words, to "backslide a bit." After seven years of experimenting with change, Neil Allen remained committed to Coalition ideas and to change, but he continued to ask where the time to support the process was to come from and how to resolve the philosophical differences within his school.

Barrett Preparatory School is a small K–12 private school located in a multiethnic neighborhood in a large eastern city. Students from a wide range of backgrounds attend the school, and for many Barrett students, English is not the only (or even the primary) language spoken at home. The administration's strong commitment to recruiting students of color has resulted in increasing numbers of African-American students. The student body is heterogeneous in ability as well. Students' need for personal attention is often cited as a primary reason for attending Barrett. Some attend the school as an alternative to a heavily criticized public system; others attend on merit scholarships. Some have had problems at other schools. Most graduates go on to college.

Neil Allen returned to teach at Barrett—his alma mater—in 1983, a year after the arrival of a new headmaster, Dr. Winters. Winters encouraged the entire faculty to read *The Paideia Proposal* (Adler 1982), *Horace's Compromise* (Sizer 1984), and other books about educational philosophy and school change. Winters also established a committee, consisting of most of the upper-school faculty, to consider the possible implications of this research for reform at Barrett. On the basis of these discussions, the headmaster prepared the Barrett Educational Plan, a statement of the school's philosophy, which was discussed among the faculty and formally accepted by the school's board of trustees. Because the Barrett plan was similar in intent to the Coalition's common principles, Winters approached Ted Sizer at a national independent schools conference about joining the soon-to-be-formed Coalition. Barrett became one of the earliest member schools (in 1984).

After a year of reflection, the school adopted a modified version of the common principles and a new schedule based on the Paideia arrangement of lectures, Socratic seminars, and tutorials. This design was later modified in two ways: first, increasing emphasis was placed on interdisciplinary work, such as pairing English and history; second, there was a continued effort to increase the time students spent in seminars and to decrease the time they spent in lecture classes. By the 1988–89 school year, the schedule was completely transformed: English and history were taught as one subject for a double period daily and for two additional single periods each week. The double-period blocks were for seminar classes; the single-period blocks were for teacher-centered presentations, testing, or questions and answers. In addition the school operated on a trimester system rather than the quarter or semester systems of the public schools we studied.

As Neil Allen's case study reveals, Barrett teachers were very much involved in the change process. All the teachers there were favorably impressed with the students' work in seminar and were favorably disposed toward student-as-worker ideas. At the same time, they had mixed reactions to teaming and supported changes that gave them more autonomy in the classroom.

ALLEN'S INITIAL REACTIONS TO THE COALITION

Allen was initially skeptical of the school's implementation of Coalition ideas. Although he endorsed the general philosophy, he and other faculty disliked many changes implemented during the first year of reform. Allen remarked:

> The students hated it, particularly the seniors. . . . Students saw it correctly as more work for them. They had been trained to accept a certain kind of teaching and the role of passive learners and memorizers. . . . The ones who had been successful at it found that the new way was more difficult and called for a kind of retraining that they didn't feel was justified in their [last] year of high school. . . . The eleventh grade resisted it somewhat less and the tenth grade somewhat less. . . . [But even] the ninth grade resisted it in their own way.
>
> Before coming back to Barrett, I had been a department chairman in a small school, and I was a successful teacher. . . . I knew where all the signposts were so that if something was going badly, I could see the signposts and I could improve it. And if something was going well, I could foster that. Under the first year of the Barrett plan I taught seminars for everybody—the eighth, ninth, tenth, eleventh, and twelfth grades. . . . As a seminar teacher, I felt I had been told by the administration that there was just one kind of teaching that I was to be doing—that is, what Adler and Sizer

recommended. . . . As a teacher who had been successful, I had a full arsenal of things I could do—Socratic questioning being just one part. . . .

Suddenly, everything that I knew I could do was cut down to a few things I was supposed to do, and I didn't have any of those signposts that would reinforce that I was doing a good job. . . . If I were teaching seminars with a teacher who could go through an entire Shakespeare play in a week of lectures, I had only two seminars to discuss the play with the students. I was teaching at that speed as opposed to letting the lesson take its speed from seminar discussions. . . . Without my usual forms of self-assessment in the classroom and with teaching to other people's rhythms, I was just a nervous wreck by the end of my first year, so I was really violently opposed to the scheduling that went along with the ideology. Now, the ideology I basically agreed with, but the scheduling made the ideology impossible for me to achieve. . . . The lack of any sort of reinforcement—particularly assessment—made it even more difficult to achieve because there was no way to know whether what I was doing was as good for the kids as what I had done before. . . . I felt as if I had just walked in and been told that everyone must work this way.

In the first year of the Barrett plan, teachers' schedules resulted in their being responsible for five or six different class preparations. Because seminars and tutorials were scheduled simultaneously, some teachers led seminar or tutorial sessions for classes whose lectures they could not attend. Allen's schedule and his negative reactions were common that first year. Teachers felt overwhelmed by the reading they had to do to prepare for seminar discussions and by the lack of connection between the various components of each course resulting from the number of faculty involved. Allen talked about the need for time to plan and reflect collaboratively and individually: "What would have helped me was simply getting together with other people teaching seminars and having time, and having someone say, 'We know this is going to be frustrating. Here is a session for those of you who are teaching seminars to talk about what happens in them; to work out some of those frustrations.' What we ended up doing was having those things develop of their own, but they were informal and almost illicit. . . . It was like you were meeting outside, plotting the overthrow of the czars—saying, 'It isn't working for me.' 'Well, it isn't working for me, either. Let's get together and talk about this because it's supposed to be working.'"

During our fieldwork, Allen was primarily responsible for three courses—English/History 8 (The World We Live In and Where Do I Fit In?), English/History 10 (European Origins and the Western World and Life, Love, and Being), and English/History 12 (The Modern Age and Contemporary Society and Identity, Purpose, and the Future). In 1987–88 Allen was paired with a history teacher for his upper-school classes and taught one of two sections of a combined English and history double-period for eighth graders. He found teaming difficult. He felt restricted by the chronological orientation of the history teacher; he preferred to discuss literature thematically. Whether teaming with a different subject-matter specialist or with the other eighth-grade teacher, he found it difficult to coordinate efforts because the schedule provided no time for team planning. He remarked: "To work with other teachers, I slice time. . . . I meet with one teacher over lunch when we can catch each other, or I try to stop by his office. It is almost always done during free periods and off moments, sometimes between classes."

Even though insufficient planning time was a problem, reviewing the effectiveness of the 1987–88 schedules for the middle and senior high school led the faculty to adopt the daily double-period of interdisciplinary course work for all grades, seven through twelve. Each English and history teacher would teach both subjects instead of being paired with another subject-matter specialist. Teaming would exist only to cover multiple sections of the same course. According to Allen, the faculty felt they had received two clear messages—that both student-centered seminar learning and interdisciplinary courses were more effective ways to engage students in the work teachers thought they should be doing. In spring 1988, Allen remarked:

> The new schedule will move even further away from teacher-centered teaching and move even more along the lines of student-centered learning. . . . They will have ten periods a week of English and history seminar and two single periods a week of English and history lessons. . . . By doing this, we're really trying to "force" the kind of coordination in curriculum and in teaching that we have found, thus far, very difficult. Now if I get bogged

down in World War I, I'll be the one bogged down. It won't be another teacher in history who is bogging me down, and I'll know where the problem is and either find material from each discipline to support it or find a way to cut through it faster.

Allen was enthusiastic about the proposed changes because he viewed them as "attempts to keep the school's message straight, to be interdisciplinary in the English and history department, to really combine the curricula."

ALLEN'S EXPERIMENT WITH TENTH-GRADE
ENGLISH AND HISTORY

In 1988–89, following the faculty's decision to pair English and history in the upper school, Allen attempted to merge the two subjects in his tenth-grade class.[1] The first day of class Allen and his teamed teacher (Dr. Winters, the school's headmaster) explained the structure of the class and the ideas to be discussed during the year and fielded questions from confused and skeptical students.

> NA: English and history will be taught as one subject.
> A STUDENT: What about grades?
> NA: I'll come to that. Let me continue: works of literature are reflective of social times. Literature and history were not (and really are not) separate disciplines. The distinction, the separation, is a modern one.

Allen continued to describe connections between literature and history for some time, then turned to the course organization.

> NA: The essential questions we will address for each time period we study this year are: (1) What happened—at least, what is our best guess about what happened? (2) How did it happen? (3) Why did it happen? (4) When did it happen? (5) How did people live

1. Although we focus on one classroom, it is important to remember that Allen's sense of being overwhelmed resulted from trying to do similar work in three or more classes while rethinking schoolwide practices and undertaking more of a role in schoolwide and departmental decision making. This contributed to his later decision to backslide in his experimentation and take stock in order to plan his next steps.

during that period? (6) What did it feel like to be alive then? (7) How did what happened influence how people lived?

A STUDENT: Will there be one or two finals?

NA: One, and you will receive one grade for English and history. . . . Again, we will think about the history we study from the perspective of literature. How did the authors feel about the periods of time we are studying? . . .

There are two single-lesson periods. These will be shared: Dr. Winters will teach the one on Tuesday, and I will be responsible for the one on Thursday. These are enrichment. We will talk about some issues and general themes that encompass what we are talking about. The seminars are the heart and soul of the course.

A STUDENT: Then what is going to happen in seminar?

NA: Two double periods each week will be text analysis and two double periods will be for you to work on projects that will help establish what life was like. We will start with the Fall of Rome.

Here's your first question: "What did the Fall of Rome sound and feel like? Try to describe it. And why did it feel that way?" . . . The course covers the period between the Fall of Rome and the start of World War I. We aren't going to look at everything, but what are we going to look at?"

A STUDENT: The most important things.

NA: How do we determine what is important?

ANOTHER STUDENT: It is an event that changed our lives from how it was then to how it is now.

NA: Yes, we will be exploring all this and revising our definitions of "important" as we go. Today we will start thinking about projects. . . . One project this trimester will be to design and build a cathedral. You will have to think about the answer to many questions about the cathedral in terms of its design, its contents. To build a medieval cathedral you will need to find out many things about medieval life.

Toward the end of the class period, Allen reminded the students that they were expected to keep journals about their reading for the course and added that the journal should also serve as a notebook and would be collected each week. An essay would be required every other week and three short research papers each trimester. He ended, saying: "My personal goal is for each of you to do and make history using the processes of historians and writers. . . . Remember I asked you to think about the Fall of Rome. (1) What were the problems people faced? (2) What solutions would you have proposed? (3) What solutions did the people of the time propose? Talk a little bit about why 2 and 3 are different." He then dismissed the class.

This tenth-grade class consisted of seventeen heterogeneously grouped students, only three of whom were reading at grade level. The students seemed confused about the interdisciplinary approach, even after Allen had answered several questions. But most were not too worried because "Mr. Allen has a reputation for being fair."

In an early fall interview, Allen talked about his goals for the year, the organizing motifs he planned to use with the class, and his timetable:

Our question is: "How did people live?" The idea is to understand the problems people had and to work in groups to do it. . . . What I've been trying to do is to get each of the groups in the tenth grade to form their own medieval village, then to grow: village to town to city. Then each city will build its own cathedral. . . . The literature we do contributes to their immersion in the Middle Ages. Following the Middle Ages, we'll do the Renaissance and the literature of that era will lead into an immersion in the Renaissance. . . . But we are always focusing on how people lived: What were the necessities? What were the problems? How did they solve their problems? My goal is to get them to "make" history rather than to "study" history, to give them some sort of basis from which to understand who they are and to foster in them a desire to look at the details of living, because it is details that make history what it is. I would like them to look at the details that underlie the great events so that they begin to understand what living means.

But it's very difficult. . . . I'm having a hard time. . . . It's not a traditional approach and as a result I'm a bit at sea with it right now—partly because this period of history and this period of literature are not my areas of expertise. . . . So I don't always know what the right thing for them to be doing is. . . . I'm constantly revising and reevaluating and reestimating things. . . . For example, today I'm going to give them an assignment. I'll say:

"We've talked about the impossibilities of large groups of people existing together effectively, but were there any attempts to have large groups of people live under one ruler between 464 and 1100? Were there any big kings?" . . . I'm hoping we can use the library so that they can find out about Charlemagne, what Charlemagne did, the reforms of Charlemagne, the nature of his court, and all that. But I want them to find it themselves rather than my giving them a lecture.

By October 1988, Allen had undertaken changes in all his classes—including group work, a project-based curriculum, increased use of Socratic questioning, and peer-editing of essays—while also trying to give his students a more interdisciplinary focus. By his own account, these classroom-based efforts and collaboration with his colleagues had energized him professionally. But when asked to assess the changes, Allen said it was too early to know. He saw promising signs, particularly when students took responsibility for getting their work done, working in groups, and asking thoughtful and challenging questions of one another and him. But he was frustrated by how slowly they were moving through the course material and how difficult it was to have discussions if not everyone was prepared, as sometimes happened.

Repeated observations of this class during the first trimester confirmed that students frequently posed and addressed provocative questions about the Middle Ages. For instance, in one class during late October, Allen began with an overview of how decisions were made during Charlemagne's time. Students were interested in questions of inheritance, and when one asked about the health of members of the apparently large medieval families, a lively give and take ensued—What was the relationship between marriage and love in medieval society? What were the prevailing attitudes about sex? Was sex "officially" restricted to marriage partners? Was premarital sex common or accepted? What happened to a marriage if the wife couldn't bear children? How did people deal with retarded children? After about fifteen minutes' discussion, Allen asked students to break into role-specific groups—lords, priests, craftsmen/merchants, farmers, and doctors—and to continue building an understanding of what daily existence would have been like for occupants of that role, incorporating the questions just raised where relevant.

Before taking a break, Allen told students there would be a test the following week. It would consist of four questions that he would use regularly throughout the year to assess their work:

1. What were the elements that went against human survival at this particular time? How were they surmounted?
2. How did the literature describe or embellish and fantasize about the life people led?
3. If you had to divide society into three groups, what would they be and why?
4. What was the influence of the Church at this time?

While lectures dominated during the first time block, most of the second period involved student group work focused on the questions raised during the previous period. Allen's role was to clarify and provoke the groups to further elaborate their understanding of medieval life. He was also asked to clarify what he meant by the questions he had written on the board.

Throughout the fall, students kept journals and wrote several compositions, including one comparing the life of a peasant in the Middle Ages with the life of a homeless person in New York City today. They also prepared questions for an interview with "Charlemagne" (played by another Barrett teacher) and wrote up their interviews for a newspaper, *The Medieval Times*. Their group project was to construct a model of a medieval cathedral and show through their work the place such a building had in a city of that time period.

In early December, Allen discussed his goals for the trimester and the successes and failures he felt the class had experienced.

> My goals this trimester, from the standpoint of content, were to cover the Middle Ages and the Renaissance. I know that the word "cover" sends little tremors through everybody. . . . We weren't going to go over *everything* in both entire periods but we were going to touch on both periods. . . . So far, we have not reached the Renaissance. In that respect we have covered less ground than I had anticipated.
>
> Insofar as their skills were concerned, it was a trimester to focus on research skills, on oral skills, on writing skills, and on seminar skills—particularly question-asking and -answering skills. . . . I

think their research skills on the whole improved, but they are still below what I would consider grade level. They're still encyclopedia-bound. They have begun to learn that there is material to be found. And when I say "they" I should add that the best students are beyond this and have begun to find that there are sources other than encyclopedias that they could use. All of the students are more library-aware now than they had been. . . . It's just not moving as fast as I think it might or it ought to move.

For most of them, their oral skills are improving. They're talking up. They can now stand in front of the class and give a report—most of them—without dying of nerves. But they still have problems with seminar skills. By "seminar skills" I mean group dynamics and interaction skills: one person talking at a time, listening skills, either nonevaluative or evaluative commenting, rational support of material, reference to text. . . . They still respond like little children in a group discussion situation. I have to keep saying, "Talk one at a time. Talk to each other, not to me." But their ability to ask questions is really improving. As I think of all the skills I was going after this trimester (and that I constantly go after with my students), the question-asking and question-answering skills are really starting to improve. It's the one area I'm very positive about.

There are some attitude things that I'm also very positive about. One of the reasons I'm trying this approach with them is that I've seen enough history classes and English classes dealing with this period where the kids have become just deadly bored by the material, bored with themselves, bored with the teacher. They become unresponsive and uninvolved. But I think my students' attitudes for the most part have improved—they are far more involved now and are enjoying themselves since they are directing much of what happens during class. Hopefully I can structure next trimester based on what I learned this trimester and make it even a little more active for them—really get them involved in the Renaissance. . . . We haven't finished the Middle Ages by any stretch of my or anyone else's imagination, but we're going to leave them.

The thing I'm most disappointed about is that one of my goals was that they understand what life was like in the Middle Ages. And I think we failed. I think the failure has to do with the research problems. The research is not yet alive for them. The history doesn't come as alive for them as what they read that's literary. And I haven't yet helped them fully make the connection between what they're reading about in "The Miller's Tale" and life in the Middle Ages.

Allen also discussed two other changes, the use of ungraded assignments and peer-editing with extensive rewriting:

Another thing I've added this year is that I'm now grading either an "excellent [E]," "satisfactory [S]," or "needs improvement [NI]" for their writing and quizzes, borrowing from the middle school evaluation form [see figure 8.1]. . . . I don't want them to think of themselves as failing, so I tell them "If you continue to need improvement and you don't do something about it, you will fail, but we're involved in a process. If your work needs improvement and suddenly it becomes excellent, then the 'excellent' is where you're going to be rather than the 'needs improvement.'"

Their writing is improving. . . . They peer-edited most of their assignments and then handed me the peer-edit and a rewrite. I read it, corrected it, and then they wrote it again. . . . The third rewrite was the one on which I put a letter grade. . . . I have insisted that before receiving their letter grade, they have a conference with me about the paper, so we can talk about the process and about improving the grade. It's time-consuming, but they're actually writing more than they did last year.

In general, I find their writing skills to be like their reading skills: still tied in a fairly childish way to their interest level. When they are interested in an assignment and challenged, their work is generally better. For example, when we finished Dante they loved writing their own "circles of hell." On the other side, they hated writing "four influences on the Middle Ages." . . . When they can be excited about an assignment they will do more and their writing is better.

Generally, Allen was satisfied with his students' responses to his innovations. However, he described resistance to his project-based curriculum and to the number of assignments he gave. At one point, frustrated in his efforts to reorganize the curriculum and experiment with group learning, projects, and an interdisciplinary approach, he asked

Student's name _____   Department/Subject Area(s) _____
Grade level _____   Period from _____ to _____

Key: E = Excellent, G = Good, N = Needs Improvement. (Skills not marked were not emphasized this period.)

Group Skills
_____ sharing information
_____ giving/accepting criticism
_____ cooperating with teachers
_____ cooperating with peers

Writing Skills
_____ originating developing idea
_____ organizing/outlining
_____ applying grammar skills
_____ shaping sentence structure
        and paragraph structure
_____ editing for effectiveness

Oral Expression
_____ listening
_____ asking informed questions
_____ engaging in discussion
_____ articulating ideas

In-School Social Behavior
_____ respecting self/others in
        action, language, attitude
_____ accepting responsibility
_____ practicing self-control

Study Skills
_____ following directions
_____ setting priorities
_____ planning
_____ researching
_____ note taking
_____ homework

Problem-Solving
_____ abstract reasoning
_____ conceptual understanding
_____ computation
_____ computer skills

Figure 8.1. Barrett Middle School Student Evaluation Form

students to write self-evaluations. From them, Allen determined that the students were struggling with the new approaches, overestimating (in his opinion) their success in the class, and still measuring that success in standard ways, such as by taking lots of notes or turning in work on time. He was somewhat demoralized by these self-evaluations, sensing that students' resistance and their traditional views of school were impeding his efforts to involve them more actively in their own learning.

In early February 1989, we asked half of the class to participate in a group interview about their English-history course. The students gave the class fairly consistent praise, stressing the additional work they were doing and how much they enjoyed the interdisciplinary approach and why. Their primary objection was that they were uncomfortable having to be responsible to their peers and having to depend on them to get group work done.

GIRL: There's much more work. . . .

BOY: More writing.

GIRL: Reading and writing. . . .

INTERVIEWER: Is it possible or are you interested in separating out what's the history part of your work from what's the English part of your work?

GIRL: Yes, we want to but we can't, there's no difference between the two.

BOY: It's easier like this, I think.

GIRL: People are learning. It's kind of fun. It's not as boring as it was last year. . . .

GIRL: Yeah, I like it better this way.

INTERVIEWER: Why is that?

SAME GIRL: Because I usually don't want to go to history class. And now I just go and I don't even realize I'm doing history. . . .

INTERVIEWER: Last fall when I was here you were planning to build a cathedral. [Laughter.] How did that turn out?

BOY: Not too good.

GIRL: We learned something from that. We learned that you can't start it the day before. It really needed to be started at least two weeks before.

ANOTHER GIRL: You really have to have the full cooperation of the whole group, not just two or three people.

INTERVIEWER: Do you like working with other people? Do you like the idea of working with other students.

GIRL: NO!

BOY: I like working alone.

INTERVIEWER: Why? . . .

GIRL: Because in groups you end up with so many different views and it just makes chaos.

BOY: And if someone doesn't do the homework . . .

ANOTHER BOY: . . . and you depend on them, it hurts the group. Say there's seven people in the group, and five don't do the work . . . then those other two are hurt.

ANOTHER GIRL: If *you* don't do something . . . *you* don't get away with it in your group. It's not that your friends are yelling at you for not doing your homework. No one yells. That's not what I mean.

BOY: But you're kind of feeling it though because see, now you face the group. Like you usually get away with it with a teacher, but all your friends in the group know.

Throughout the remainder of the school year, Allen continued experimenting with group work and interdisciplinary assignments, including an essay in which students interpreted *Macbeth* in terms of Machiavelli's philosophy; a research project involving replication of a significant experiment or invention from the Renaissance; a simulation that created the conditions for the plague, and a second one in which four family groups competed to conquer, then rule, Florence; and a series of oral reports summarizing some important changes that occurred during the period of industrialization. For their final project, students considered how the changes they had researched were portrayed in Dickens' *Hard Times*.

ALLEN'S INCREASING INVOLVEMENT WITH THE CHANGE PROCESS

Between 1986 and 1989, Allen became quite committed to Coalition philosophy and practices as he saw them working in his classes and through faculty involvement with schoolwide decision making. In addition to the reforms he introduced in his classroom, Allen participated in such schoolwide innovations as a final exhibition project for juniors, a "recreational" reading class, and an experimental advisory-like period, which Barrett faculty called "dialogue period." All were add-ons to his existing schedule, but Allen felt they were important because they underscored the school's priorities—reading, personalized attention, and demonstrated mastery of subject matter—for students and parents. Further, Allen became more involved in planning professional development activities for the school. This involvement continued into his summer vacation, when he served as a member of a committee that created a middle school at Barrett and an alternative system of evaluation. He also made a presentation about his work with the tenth grade to the entire faculty. In addition, he sought to address ongoing tensions at the school, such as how best to incorporate foreign languages into the core curricuım, and he met regularly, if informally, with a group of faculty to discuss proposed changes.

Hoping to help his department move toward a fuller realization of Coalition philosophy, Allen agreed to a further add-on in spring 1989: he became department chair of English and history. He found that his new position involved a lot of extra work, very little of it satisfying. In addition to substantial paperwork, negotiating for change in an opinionated department of proud professionals proved trying.

> The English and history department is a collection of strong individuals. The problem is that we're a group of individuals as opposed to a group . . . so it becomes impossible for us to reach any kind of consensus collectively. We think we do, but that's only because we reach what I call "semantic consensus" as opposed to . . . an actual consensus. We don't agree on anything. We may say, "Yes, we are going to teach process writing," but that's because I think I know what process writing is, Laura thinks she knows what it is, James thinks he knows, and Robert thinks he knows. But then George doesn't think he knows, and so he asks everybody and finds out there are five different ideas. We've each thought we had agreed to the same idea when we actually agreed to five different things. If you try to find some sort of agreement, you end up running into collective and individual egos. I'm not blaming my colleagues because I'm really a part of the problem too. I firmly believe that one should leave a teacher alone in the classroom and let the teacher teach. But that then leads to problems when things need to be dealt with or created collectively. . . .
>
> This year we are being a "department by consensus." Nothing will be done by the department unless everyone agrees that it is to be done, which means that there may be incredibly little that we do but whatever we do, we *will* do! . . . We're going to get frustrated. We're going to yell and scream. . . . But I want to end up knowing that the yelling and screaming were worthwhile: that the product or the process or both were worth the time.

Allen became chairperson just as the school faced several challenges: the search for a new headmaster, a disruptive construction project, and rumors that the school was overcommitted financially and might close. That same fall he was teamed with new teachers, and reiterated that

teaming required "more organization and more planning" than working alone. In part because of his ambivalence about teaming—he felt
that individual teachers should be left alone to teach, but he enjoyed
team-teaching—he was reluctant as chairperson to force others to team
beyond the rather loose collaborations that evolved when multiple sections of a single grade were scheduled. He did not push for teaming in
the department, citing serious philosophical differences among faculty
members. As he explained at the end of his first year as chair: "I know
it's a good department and so one doesn't try to fix something that's not
broken. . . . I would like to see us share with each other more. But we
don't. It's tough because I have a hard time with it myself."

Allen also reflected on his belief in the efficacy of Coalition ideas:

I have put an awful lot of work into it [reform efforts] because I like
what the Coalition is trying to do. I'm a convert. To be honest with
you, when it started I thought, "Well, you know, I'm a good
teacher. I was a good teacher before the Barrett Plan and I'll remain a reasonably good teacher after the Barrett Plan." . . . But
now I think that the Barrett Plan, if applied, and the Coalition, if
applied, create an environment in which both teachers and students can operate successfully. . . . At its best, the Coalition gives
value to the best things that both groups do. And it recognizes that
it's not only what we say but what we do that communicates and
teaches. . . .

I agree with what Sizer says about reform being an all-
encompassing thing. You don't just change one thing, everything
is interrelated. For example, changing curriculum requires schedule changes. Changing the schedule requires curricular changes.
And this requires evaluative changes. All of those things are tied
together. I think it is important to recognize that.

Allen felt that the changes Barrett had undergone were positive, yet
he recognized there were still problems. He felt that insufficient trust
between the board and school administrators, on the one hand, and the
faculty, on the other, pitted the administration against the faculty and
impeded reform efforts. "One problem that has recurred is that the
administration and the board have for years blamed everything that
went wrong at the school on the faculty. More often than not the faculty
places the blame for the selfsame problems in the lap of the headmaster.

And I think the truth of the matter is that it's everyone's responsibility. We all bear a part of the burden. And if we were working together, the problems would become at least possibly solvable. But if everybody's blaming everybody else, what you spend your time doing is finger-pointing rather than problem solving." Moreover, he felt that the English and history department needed to push change efforts further in order to implement Coalition philosophy more fully, yet he worried that there was insufficient cooperation and ability to achieve consensus within the department to do so. With a new headmaster, he was concerned that a major shift in the school's priorities might occur. Echoing the thoughts of most of his colleagues, he said: "The new headmaster is going to find a faculty who, on the whole, is going to resist another radical change."

REFLECTING ON SEVEN YEARS OF COALITION MEMBERSHIP

In July 1991 we did a final interview with Allen. He discussed the first year with the new headmaster and some backsliding that had occurred in his teaching. With a mixture of regret and enthusiasm, he wondered if it might be easier to teach "the old way" rather than try to maintain the hectic pace that had characterized his life since the school became involved with the Coalition.

> One of the things I've learned is how much time change takes. I guess I wasn't aware of how much time it took me to become the teacher I was before I started at Barrett. Nobody required me to stop and think about time then; for example, no one asked how did I learn to teach the way I used to teach and how much time it took to hone those skills. . . . As I tried to change the way I taught, to change the kind of material I was teaching, I had to reinvest time. It was and still is a massive reinvestment of time. I'm covering ground that I previously covered but in a new way. I find myself not having the time in the school day to do the things I need to do. If I were to write a book about last year, the title would be *If Only I Had the Time.* . . .
>
> For example, last year when I was directing the school play, I would get home at about 7:00 P.M., eat, and then many days be up until 2:00 A.M. preparing to teach the next day. And I would teach

the next day, direct, get home at 6:00 or 7:00 P.M., have dinner, and stay up until 2:00 A.M. again either grading papers or doing reading or getting material ready for the next day. As a result of this schedule, I ended up going back to the ways I had taught . . . before these past six years at Barrett. *Because when I get tired or pushed I go back to old habits,* old habits that . . . I thought were successful. It's not as if the kids this year learned less than the kids in the past few years, but they certainly did less group work, less cooperative learning, and less student-as-worker in my class.

In addition to acknowledging that time constraints had led him to abandon some classroom-based changes, Neil Allen wondered whether the school as a whole would be able to avoid backsliding.

Certainly the jargon here has changed. The way in which we talk about what we do has changed. I think that teachers have been changed. Teachers have been infected by this virus—this Coalition virus—and so their teaching has changed. But whether or not there are institutional changes that will last, I don't know. I'd like to think the attempted integration of disciplines is something that will last. I'd like to think that the seminar-based pedagogy as central to what we do will last. I'd like to think in science that problem-solving-based teaching is something that will last. Because they seem to me to be things that work. I know they'll last with me, at least in my thinking. They may not always last in my actions, as last year proved.

Allen also discussed the effects on students of the school's seven years of Coalition membership.

In the classrooms, it's five hundred little things. For instance, we've got more classrooms with tables in them than we used to have. When the kids walk into a classroom, they will arrange the chairs in a semicircle. They are used to participating in class and to having their input taken seriously. The kids know what the school thinks is important. They may not think it's important, but they know, for instance, that writing is important, that arguing by the presentation of evidence is important, and that there's good and bad evidence. And I think they know that they count. But I don't know how much of that is Coalition and how much of that has been part of Barrett's identity. The fact that the kids know that their teachers care is part and parcel of the seminar thing. But Barrett kids have traditionally known that the teachers care about them. So in the case of personalization Barrett's following the Coalition made more apparent what was already here.

In his reflections, he struck one sour note about Coalition involvement, commenting ironically:

The other thing I would say, looking back on the seven years in the Coalition is it's wonderful to be deserted by them [central staff]. When we first were involved with the Coalition it was with people with faces, people who would come to our school, people who would call. Those people who came had interests that seemed to be our interests; they seemed to share our expectations, our trials and our failures. I sound like my mother: "Now they never call." I know those central staff members have gone their own ways and left the Coalition staff. But I don't even know the new people on the Coalition staff. Maybe the Barrett administrators know them, but I surely don't. . . .

I understand that for people who are involved in nationwide reform the issues are very large and very political. And they have to deal with mobilizing constituencies and developing constituencies and developing audiences. . . . But for the people who are day-in and day-out in a classroom, the people in the trenches, we need to hear once in a while that you're listening to what we say. We need to hear once in a while that you're thinking about what we do because that's what feeds me.[2]

Allen's final observations about Coalition membership echo a number of common reactions of teachers struggling with Coalition ideas—

2. We heard similar comments from other teachers during our research and it was the case that as the number of Coalition member schools increased, the central staff made fewer school visits. At the start of our research, each of the twelve original member schools was visited at least twice per year. As noted in chapter 7, over time Coalition staff had more regular contact with second-step schools than with other schools; and Barrett was not designated a second-step school. We also note that not all teachers felt abandoned by the central staff. For example, the Elliston staff was quite satisfied with the Coalition staff's level of involvement at the school.

guilt about their inability to do more for their students and about the compromises they make so that the job is doable; anger about society's unwillingness to fund education and reform at levels appropriate to the magnitude of the task; and frustration about the overwhelming problems students face outside the classroom.

> Coalition membership has made me feel guilty, because I more clearly see what I could be—or perhaps should be—as opposed to what I am. It's made me feel envious of people whose formal education emphasized what the Coalition talks about. . . . I have come more and more to understand how we as teachers model for our students in a classroom when we're honest, respectful, and caring. It's a long-term, subtle influence.
>
> I believe in students. And I believe in the power of the enlightened mind. But it has become more and more apparent to me how totally frustrating the task that we set for ourselves is. The more I come to see and to know, the more aware I am of how out of step I am with the world that moves around me. We are told, on the one hand, how important education is and, on the other hand, how important the B-1 bomber is. . . . I see much of the problem that we have in crime and drugs and a lost generation of young men and women—in both the ghettos and the suburbs—as a failure of the educational system. And yet, we are told that we now have to do more with less. It's true you don't solve problems by throwing money at them, but you certainly don't solve them by taking money away from them. It's not that I'm less optimistic about education; I'm more pessimistic about what the kids have to deal with daily and the challenges that confront us all.

ANALYSIS

In this section we discuss six themes that emerge from Neil Allen's experience: the time-consuming nature of pedagogical change; the need for accommodation among teachers, between administrators and teachers, and with students in negotiations about what should change; how misunderstandings between faculty and administrators about decision-making domains made it difficult for faculty to create change; students as the central focus of Allen's reform efforts; the danger of backsliding in classroom practices when support is insufficient and teachers are overextended; and the difficulty of assessing the success of experiments in an uncertain environment and without clear standards.

Perhaps the topic that arose most often in discussions with Allen was the lack of time to plan with other teachers, to devote to a topic in class, to envision change, and to do class preparations. Sometimes the conversations about the lack of time were personal. For instance, to do all that he needed or felt obligated to do, Allen often made sacrifices in his personal life—grading papers and planning lessons late at night after teaching a full day and directing rehearsals for a school play. Each night, as he put it, he had to deal with the question: "How do I want to spend the rest of this evening? I've got reading to do for school. . . . Do I want to do some organizing? Do I want to sit and grade papers? Or do I want to do some reading that's important to me personally?" At other times his concerns involved change more generally.

> Everything takes longer than you think it will. And even given the fact that I knew from last year how long things would take, they are still taking even more time. . . . I guess one of the things the Coalition has taught me is the value of time. For example, planning for change takes time, and anything you rush you pay for ten to twenty times in the end. . . . The first year we ended up doing an awful lot of running just to stay in place because we didn't spend time planning before we started.
>
> It takes time for teachers to change, and it takes time for students to change. I recognize more clearly than before that students bring their habits with them into the classroom, and what I'm looking to change is habitual behavior more often than not. That takes time. You might quit smoking cold turkey for a day. The second day you want to smoke. And you have to fight that habit again and again and again. I think the same is true with students.

Allen specifically complained about inadequate time for teamed teachers to plan together; yet teachers were expected to be involved in myriad aspects of reforming and running Barrett. At each step in Allen's involvement and growing commitment to Coalition philosophy and practices, insufficient time made his work and reflecting about his experiments more stressful. Further, it was directly implicated in his return to previous practices during the 1990–91 school year.[3]

A second theme that emerged from Allen's case study was that negotiating change is a difficult process of trying to accommodate multiple viewpoints while still achieving consensus when necessary. This process and its consequences were perhaps most apparent in Allen's discussion of the independence of English and history department members and their tendency to define reforms idiosyncratically. Allen often felt that trying to accommodate so many views threatened to make proposed changes superficial or inconsistent and that reaching consensus was impossible. At times he felt it was a no-win situation.

The presence of seemingly dual outcomes to the negotiation process—accommodation and consensus—yielded much inconsistency in the practice of teaming and in opinions about the benefits of teaming. In general, teaming was viewed as a mixed blessing, and Barrett teachers expressed relief and satisfaction whenever their teaming responsibilities were reduced. Allen often said he enjoyed teaming, but he frequently complained about the difficulties. For example, articulating content-coverage in two classes meant that each teacher had less flexibility in his or her own class. Allen balanced this lack of flexibility with two perceived advantages: first, students were exposed to multiple perspectives about the topics under study and, second, he enjoyed sharing the responsibility of preparing for class.

Allen also recognized that the success of teaming depended on the ability of the teachers to work together. Consequently he did not push for closer cooperation among teachers. Instead, he made his own accommodations to teaming and allowed other teachers to do the same rather than forcing a showdown or encouraging discussion about what teaming meant. Negotiation and decision making tended to proceed

---

3. Insufficient time was a concern shared by almost every teacher involved with reform at our study schools; it was also a concern of the teachers in Sizer's *Horace's Compromise*. In this respect, Coalition reform does not appear to have fundamentally changed the quality of teachers' lives; rather, it has refocused their use of time into different but sometimes more time-consuming aspects of school life. Sizer discusses this in *Horace's School*, saying that teachers continue to have to compromise to do their work, but his hope is that these compromises are having a less detrimental effect on students.

this way at Barrett in part because of the tensions between faculty and administration over decision making and the change process.

Although not emphasized in Allen's case study, tensions existed at Barrett regarding the role of the administration and the faculty over who made what decisions for the school and over the limits on faculty authority in the change process. At times Allen distinguished between his philosophical agreement with Coalition ideas and his practical concerns about their implementation at Barrett. For him, Coalition ideas and practices writ large and as implemented at Barrett were not always the same thing. Allen felt that most Barrett faculty members had few problems with Coalition ideas but that they often opposed the way the administration expected the ideas to be implemented. For example, discussing whether Socratic questioning should be the dominant pedagogical technique used in seminars—the source of much of his early resistance to the Coalition—Allen later said: "I don't know that *the Coalition* was saying there was one way to teach. I know that [the Barrett administrators] were."

This distinction raises questions about faculty participation in the change process at Barrett. In a moment of cynicism, Allen asserted that changes desired by faculty and students were approved as long as they did not interfere with what the administration wanted.[4] The perception that the administration sought to determine the appropriate implementation of Coalition ideas created the impression that, as Allen once said: "More often than not, responsibility is delegated and authority is not. There is little chance for anyone other than the administrators to move things forward on a scale larger than that of personal change."

This concern may have been reflected in Allen's unwillingness to speculate on whether any of the changes made at Barrett would survive a change of administration. He remarked, "Teachers have been infected by this virus—this Coalition virus—and so their teaching has changed. But whether or not there are institutional changes that will last, I don't know." This distinction between individual change (whether through

4. See the discussion of Barrett's "bell" policy in Muncey and McQuillan (1991). A debate erupted at the school over whether to have bells ring to signal the end of class periods or whether students and teachers could take responsibility for moving from class to class. Many teachers, including Allen, felt the involvement of students in the decision-making process was a direct result of their sharing an opinion with the administration—an opinion that differed from most teachers' views.

infection, conversion, or some other process)[5] and institutional change is crucial, for it signals that the Barrett faculty viewed themselves as participating in the change process, but they doubted whether they could create lasting change. This concern lay behind their worries about what a change in leadership might mean for their Coalition-inspired reforms.

Allen consistently maintained that students were the central focus of the school's reform efforts. He began almost every interview and conversation about what had occurred and how reforms were proceeding with a discussion of the impact these changes were having on students. He espoused an increasingly strong belief in the ideas of student-as-worker, personalization, and less-is-more as he saw their positive consequences for students. He said he drew energy and strength from watching students respond well to his change efforts.

While Allen stressed that personalization, one of the Coalition's key tenets, had existed at Barrett before the school joined the Coalition, he also made changes that he felt enhanced the personalized environment —adding a "needs improvement" category to his student evaluations, responding positively to students' comments that they enjoyed less traditional writing assignments (such as writing their own "circles of hell"), using peer-editing, and having frequent personal conferences. This emphasis on students was common among teachers in our study schools. In Allen's case it added to his stress about his reform efforts. He worried when he felt that students overestimated their understanding or resisted his efforts to make them more active learners and when he was uncertain that his efforts to restructure his classrooms were having the desired result. Sometimes he was tempted to go back to his old ways.

As mentioned in the school case studies (chapters 2 to 6) teachers frequently said they felt overextended and committed to doing too many things. Throughout Allen's efforts to change both his own practice and Barrett's structure and philosophy, there were indications that burnout and backsliding loomed as distinct possibilities. He described his eventual backsliding in the classroom as the result of insufficient time and feeling pushed to do too much. Yet it is interesting that this occurred during the transition to a new administration and in an atmosphere that

5. These distinctions were described and discussed by Robert Hampel in a presentation to the Coalition central staff, spring 1989.

seemed indifferent to Coalition philosophy or Barrett's Coalition membership. Allen frequently remarked that he needed support for his and the school's efforts. In his final interview he said: "For me, it's not so much about teacher empowerment as about attention. I know that I'm one small fish in a small pond, but it's the pond I'm in." This seemed all the more poignant because he felt little supported by Barrett's new administration and unknown to the Coalition staff.

Backsliding was often a temporary reaction of our study school teachers to feeling stressed or burned out, but sometimes it signaled a slow, if deliberate, return to previous practice. Allen said in his final interview that he remained committed to Coalition ideas and practices, but he now advocated approaching change more slowly and taking more time to reflect on and evaluate the effects.

Throughout his classroom experiments, Allen struggled with how to assess whether his efforts were successful. For example, he sometimes evaluated success on the basis of traditional measures, such as coverage, even though he recognized that this was inconsistent with Coalition philosophy. Nevertheless, using these measures made him uneasy about his innovating. At one point he admitted: "I've been tempted to give this whole thing up because, frankly, I'm a successful teacher in the old-fashioned way. . . . Without help or stroking or whatever input coming from outside, my temptation is always to go back to old habits. To go back to things that I know work, where I know how to read the success and failure signs—because then I feel like I'm really doing a better job for the kids. Because the bottom line in all of this is my feeling that I may have wasted their tenth-grade year. Have I, because of my desire to try something different, really denied them important educational stuff?"

Nevertheless, he stuck with his reform efforts because he felt that students found them exciting and he believed that the skills he was teaching were useful for his students. As he began to accept Coalition ideas, he tried to incorporate the implications of learning as a process into his teaching, through his pedagogical approach, his classroom structure, and his methods of evaluating students. Yet he found that taking that idea seriously made it more difficult to measure and assess progress in his students' work and the efficacy of his experiments, particularly when he had no standards for comparison, little collaboration from peers, and an increasing sense of isolation from the central staff.

The changes Allen went through as part of his school's membership in the Coalition do not fit neatly into stages, nor were they as distinct as presented in this chapter. Increasing involvement with schoolwide decisions about change and increasing experimentation with Coalition ideas in his classes occurred simultaneously. Further, Allen attempted changes in at least three grade levels each year, and because of the size of the school and variations in class size, he was teamed with from two to six people each year. While Allen's actions and reactions were his own and were personal responses to conditions and decisions at Barrett, the challenges he faced and his responses to them were similar to those of many teachers we studied who were attempting to incorporate change in their classrooms.

9

"BUT WE HAVE ORAL HISTORY PROJECTS, TIME LINES, AND TESTS. WE DON'T EVEN KNOW WHERE TO START"
NEGOTIATION AND RESISTANCE IN A COALITION CLASSROOM

At the start of the year, we had to do so much in a little time—the oral history projects and time lines at the same time. And we were told that we were going to have tests at the end of the year. I thought that I wouldn't be finished. *I had never had that much information at once before.* . . . They were just piling it up and piling it up. . . . It was too much. —A STUDENT FROM THE COURSE

After dealing with the tensions and problems generated in this class, I'd be happy if students just listed ten events on their time lines and did brief essays, using only the text as their source. —A TEACHER FROM THE COURSE

Although many students in Coalition schools appreciated the curricular and pedagogical changes they experienced as a consequence of their school's affiliation with CES, not all students responded enthusiastically to change. At times students resisted teachers' efforts to make them active learners and to have them assume greater responsibility for their learning. As Neil Allen acknowledged, students questioned his initial efforts to change what they had come to expect in their English (later English/history) classes, and in chapter 3 we discussed Russell High's incomplete policy and how students reacted when teachers asked them to redo their work. This chapter examines students' reactions to a performance-based U.S. history class implemented at Russell High in which a team of three teachers sought to have students become their own historians—to research and write oral histories, to define historical periods in their own terms, and to locate their place in American history. In addition to their pedagogical and curricular experimentation, the teachers introduced a new form of assessment: rather than standard exams, students were required to complete a series of seven projects that involved extensive individual research.

Several interrelated reasons appeared to contribute to students' resistance: first, the course was very different from what students were accustomed to. As with most American high schools, Russell classes typically focused on "coverage,"[1] and they were not usually performance-based. Second, students were confused about what they were being asked to do in the course. Third, students considered their teachers' expectations unfair, especially when compared with the amount and type of work in more typical Russell classes—within the Essential School program as well as within the larger school. Fourth, many students felt that they lacked the skills necessary to succeed in the course.

In effect, this case study demonstrates the difficulties of making students active learners in a school where such expectations differed markedly from those held in other classes—specifically, introducing inquiry-based learning into classrooms. As David Cohen noted: "Inquiry-oriented learning. . . . requires that students tolerate considerable uncertainty . . . about what the answers are, and about how implausible answers can be detected and plausible answers defended. . . . Many students find it difficult to accept that knowledge entails the acceptance of uncertainty. They find it risky but also contrary to their conception of knowing. . . . They prefer the certainties of mechanical learning to the risks of more adventurous work" (1991a: 255). Indeed, as Stephen Ball (citing Doyle [1979]) noted, students may respond by challenging their teachers: "Pupils who were confronted with potentially high risk, high ambiguity, learning situations adopted various strategies to resist or reformulate these 'task structures.' In other words the pupils attempted to resist or renegotiate aspects of their teachers' definition of the situation. . . . So what actually comes to pass in the classroom may be seen to

---

1. See, e.g., Boyer (1983), Goodlad (1984), Sizer (1984, 1992), and Wiggins (1987a, 1989, 1991).

be the outcome of the relative capacity of the different actors to establish their definitions of the situation over and against the definitions held by others" (1980: 155).

All these points are evident in the ethnographic vignettes we include in this case study, and all were integral to one key outcome of the experimental class: over the course of the school year, students' reactions to the curriculum, pedagogy, and methods of assessment led the teachers to modify their goals and pedagogical and curricular strategies in favor of less demanding and more traditional conceptions of schoolwork. Given the nature and pervasiveness of students' resistance to teachers' expectations, we should note that these reactions, though not atypical of Coalition classrooms, were extreme—in our view, because of the degree to which teachers' goals deviated from what students had come to expect at Russell. In most classrooms we studied, "change" was much closer to normal school practices.

THE PERFORMANCE-BASED U.S. HISTORY CLASS

The history course was taught by a team of three teachers: the Essential School's coordinator; a university professor who worked to promote change at Russell; and a student teacher who was supervised by the coordinator and professor.

Initially, twenty-six tenth-graders were enrolled in the class. None were repeating the course. For two-thirds of the students, this was their second year in the Essential School. The other third of the class had transferred to Russell and had chosen to enroll in the Essential School. Roughly 40 percent of the students were African-American, 40 percent were white, and 20 percent were Hispanic. Recall that Russell, an urban high school, serves about one thousand students, most of whom are persons of color. Russell's Essential School is a school-within-a-school program that was intended, in part, to improve the school's image city-wide and to attract more quality students through its affiliation with the Coalition of Essential Schools.

One unique aspect of this course (and one that students found especially discomforting) was that it was entirely performance-based. Drawing on Coalition philosophy, the team planned the course curriculum backward (McDonald 1991a; Wiggins 1987b). Rather than organizing the class around the coverage of textbook material, the team identified the skills and the knowledge they considered fundamental to the course and then designed seven projects, which they felt would lead students to master these skills and knowledge. The teachers' role was to help students acquire them. As the course syllabus explained:

> One of the basic ideas of the Essential School is that what counts is not how much time you spend in class, but what you actually learn. Therefore, we are going to tell you now, at the beginning of your high school study of U.S. history, exactly what it is we will expect you to know and be able to do by the time you complete this course. How much time it takes you to master the material and to learn the new skills is not what's most important. What is most important is that by the time you finish U.S. history you will have new knowledge, understanding, and skills. That's what counts. You will show your teachers that you have this new knowledge, understanding, and skills by successfully completing seven projects. . . . When you finish the seven projects you will have completed the course (and not before!). All the work that we will do in class will be designed to teach you what you need to know in order to do a good job on each of the seven projects.

Then the syllabus outlined the three main areas of study: (1) what history is, (2) chronology and periodization in U.S. history, and (3) finding and facing your place in U.S. history. The seven projects were related to these themes: an oral history study, a time line that "charts the major periods in U.S. history," a written and oral test on chronology and periodization, a formal history research paper, and two other projects that would allow students to explore issues of personal interest.

As noted in the syllabus, one of the team's guiding assumptions was that shifting the focus of the curriculum from the traditional emphasis on "laws and wars" to the "intrinsically fascinating" richness of everyday American life would make the study of history captivating to "students from diverse backgrounds and with varied interests." They also expected that students would welcome the opportunity to be their own historians. These assumptions paralleled those of Coalition philosophy: Given the right structure, intellectual work is inherently stimulating; all students can enjoy "learning to use their minds well" (Coalition of Essential Schools 1985).

Besides its curriculum, this course differed from most Russell classes in three significant ways. Homework, at least initially, was not required. The teachers felt that both in-class work and suggested out-of-class work were necessary to complete the projects successfully. Students, therefore, would have to do the suggested homework, whether or not it was formally assigned and graded. The other differences stemmed from the class being part of Russell's SWAS Coalition program: the course met for a double-period every other day, and students received no failing grades because the Essential School program restricted its grading scale to A, B, C (no lower than 75), and incomplete. Work receiving a grade below 75 was returned to be redone. The intention of this policy was to force students to earn at least a 75 on all course work without penalizing them if it took some longer than others to complete the assignments.

As a consequence of the policy on incompletes, some students took more than a year to finish their courses. In fact, roughly one-third of the students enrolled in this U.S. history class were making up work from the previous year's Western civilization course. The expectation was that they would join the U.S. history class when they completed Western civilization. (Eventually three students did.) During class, these students sometimes worked in the same room as the U.S. history class. At other times, they went with the coordinator to a separate room.

The course offered students many unique opportunities—to critically assess their place in the expanse of American history, to define history for themselves, and to explore the world of life-as-lived—but most students did not react enthusiastically. Rather, students continually negotiated with the teachers,[2] often with the apparent intent of limiting the amount of work teachers expected or of getting teachers to modify assignments so that students felt more capable of completing them. The most common form of student negotiation was resistance.

2. Rather than assuming that schools and classrooms have set procedures and expectations, the interactionist perspective stresses how procedures and expectations can be influenced by student-teacher negotiations (see, e.g., Ball 1980; Waller 1932; and Woods 1978, 1980). Even schoolwork is a negotiated commodity. As Woods explained: "What the standard lesson consists of, then, is a number of checks and balances, prompts and concessions, motivations, punishments, jollyings, breaks and so forth, as the teacher displays his professional expertise in getting the most out of his pupils. While the pupils, seeking basically the comfort of their own perspective and reality, will tend to react according to how the teacher's techniques mesh with that reality" (1983: 134).

Students came to class late. They probed for inconsistencies among the team. They disrupted class. They ignored their teachers. And they did not complete (or, in some cases, even start) their work.

For most of the school year, negotiation was commonplace—teachers sought to have students accept the performance-based curriculum and its attendant responsibilities while students contested these ideas and clung to their own view of appropriate schoolwork. By the fourth quarter, there was much less negotiation, suggesting some agreement about the course's structure and requirements. In the teachers' view, this occurred because students now had a greater say in defining homework and because the homework was designed to allow students to work incrementally toward completing the seven projects, whereas before students had felt overwhelmed by the projects and were uncertain how to organize their work into manageable tasks. However, two other factors also helped create a less contentious classroom environment. The teachers began accepting work that students submitted, although much of it fell short of their original expectations, and they stopped pressing students who clearly would not pass the course. At this point, students either submitted work more regularly (and felt better about the course, since teachers were accepting much of their work) or they opted out altogether. Both decisions contributed to reducing student negotiation.

CLASSROOM VIGNETTES

An October class, in which students raised many questions about a time line, provides a sense of the student resistance that occurred during much of the school year. As the course syllabus noted, this assignment asked students to create "a time line that charts the major periods in U.S. history. It will be up to you to decide what the major periods in U.S. history are. But you will have to justify your choices and convince your teacher that your choices are valid. Each period will include significant events and dates that are typical of that period." In addition, students were to label their time periods in ways that seemed logical to them and to defend their choice of specific events and dates in an accompanying essay.

The time line assignment had been due the previous week, but no student had completed one. Addressing their questions to the student teacher who directed class that day, students asked: "Do I need to have a map with this time line?" "What kind of map do I need?" "How many essays are we supposed to have with our time lines?" After answering these and other questions, the student teacher began working with a girl who thought she had completed her time line. The student teacher, however, told her, "This isn't appropriate. You've only listed events without explaining why you've included them with the time line." The student, somewhat upset, insisted that no one had told her that she had been doing anything wrong.

After working with a few other students who had questions about the time line and finding their work inadequate, the student teacher realized that many students were frustrated and confused by the assignment. To discuss this concern, the student teacher and the professor met briefly in the hall. When they returned, the professor addressed the class: "I think we need to talk about this subject [time lines] again. Sometimes things that are new and different need to be done over and over before they are fully understood—for example, a corner kick in soccer. If you did it wrong, it would be absurd for the coach to say, 'I've already shown you. Why do we need to do it again?' For the time lines, you need to realize that it covers an historical period. It's a way to organize things over time. If you made a time line from your birth to now, you'd list the events in your life that are key."

He then asked for suggestions on how they might structure a time line for their lives. The first three students he asked for ideas said that they could think of no key events. The fourth student explained that a key event in his life was, "when I got my braces." A girl who couldn't hear him well said, "Why don't you speak up?" Insulted, he retorted, "At least I wash my hair." Rising from her seat, she fired back, "Your haircut makes you look like a fag and you know it!" The professor quickly defused the argument but the analogy was pursued no further.

The student teacher then said that many students did not seem to understand the essay component of the assignment and had had problems explaining *why* they defined their time period as they had, as well as explaining *how* the events they listed supported their themes for the period. Almost in unison the students replied, "Yeah, it's wrong!" The student teacher responded, "It's not *wrong*. There are things that you did that are *inadequate*." The professor offered another way to think of the project: "Historians can show the passage of time any way that they want. What you need is not just a list of dates. What's important is that you look at those dates as a historian and label the periods in a way that makes sense to you." After these remarks, he discussed the components of the time line project again—particularly the theme for the time period, appropriate events, and the essay that related them.

Giving the students a sense of the teachers' perspective, the student teacher outlined how the Essential School's policy on incompletes fit with the performance-based curriculum: "The advantage to doing the project this way [students having a chance to correct aspects of their work that teachers identify as deficient] is that you're not penalized if something is inadequate. You should look at each time period that you do as a trial run. The final project is not due until April 29. That's what will be graded. We don't expect you to get it completely right the first time."

Yet not all students agreed. The girl who had been told that she needed to redo her work responded, "Why not tell us this at the beginning of the course? Your paperwork is confusing. After we do it one way, you tell us it's wrong." The professor replied, "Honestly, it's so different from other things that you've done in history classes that you need . . . to experiment and then get feedback. It doesn't make sense until you try it. It's like with sports or playing the piano." She replied, "Well I'm saying that when you assigned the time line, you said we could do it like this and then when we did it, we got confused." The professor responded: "I'm sorry to confuse you, but it's not a waste of time because you learned something." Upset, the girl said: "But it makes us mad, and we're so confused that we just might not do it." The professor then addressed the entire class: "How many people think that being confused is part of learning?" Only he and the student teacher raised their hands.

After the professor explained the time line assignment once more, another girl said: "You told me all I had to do was write an essay for the 'Age of Discovery' [the theme for one of that student's time lines] and list ten events and that's all." The professor replied, "That's all for the 'Age of Discovery.' You have to do one for each other period, too." The professor then explained the project again. When he was through, the student teacher remarked: "Let me add one thing: You're not doing work over. You just have to add to the core structure that you've already created. What you've done is not a waste." The professor added, "In writing your essay, prove to us that the titles you have chosen are appropriate." In response, the girl who had had her work returned said, "But you called it wrong." The student teacher replied, "It's not *wrong*. It's *inadequate*." The student responded, "But it's not *right*." The student teacher then spoke generally to the class, "All you need to do is expand on what you did." Various students reacted: "That's a lot of work." "The teachers don't explain it enough." "I'm not doing it." "How come it's not clear?"

The girl whose work was returned then asked, "So how *will* we be graded?" The professor explained: "You will not receive an incomplete unless you don't work. As long as you make progress, you won't be penalized for learning, even if it takes a long time. But, to finish U.S. history, you *have* to finish all seven projects." The student asked: "And we have to do an oral history too? We have to finish *all* of this?" The professor responded, "To do this, you need to do the [optional] home-work and ask questions in class and work in class." The student replied, "But I do the homework, and then I bring it in and you tell me it's wrong." In response, the student teacher again elaborated on the teachers' perspective: "I'm trying to give [in-class] assignments to pre-pare people for larger assignments." The bell then rang, ending class. The student who had had her work returned left class complaining to a friend about the work she still had to do. The professor met with two students who had been late returning from their break and explained why he felt they needed to come to class on time.

This summary of one class reflects what occurred in the course throughout much of the year. Students often did little work during class, in part because teachers were explaining the rationale for the course structure and telling students how they could complete their projects appropriately. Meanwhile, students contested and questioned these ex-planations, supporting and building upon one another's arguments but completing little work. Furthermore, although the strengths of the performance-based curriculum were clear to the teachers, students held a different opinion—it was more work and it was confusing. At times, students seemed insulted by the feedback and teachers' requests to do work over, and this heightened their frustration.

There were also signs that students had little idea how to approach their work—the most obvious example being their inability to define the time periods that they had created. Most students merely listed a series of events and tacked a title onto the period. As the student teacher told the class: "[Your time lines aren't] appropriate. You've only listed events without explaining why you've included them with the time line."

The relation between the performance-based curriculum and the Essential School's policy on incompletes also seemed unclear to students. A telling instance of this confusion occurred when two teachers and a student debated whether work was "wrong" or "inadequate." Finally, the verbal altercation that arose when one student attempted to delineate his personal time line, while perhaps signaling animosity between the combatants, also suggested something of the students' frustration and how it could disrupt classroom learning. In this instance, the prior line of questioning—having a student create a time line of his own life as a model for understanding the teachers' expectations—was not taken up again.

A November class taught by the student teacher and university professor revealed many of the same tendencies, in particular, that students were still uncertain how to complete their work, how their work was being evaluated, and why they were asked to produce multiple drafts. These incidents also show how students could avoid work by continually asking teachers to clarify their expectations. Early in the class, the student teacher outlined her plans: "Today, I'll do examples of time lines on the themes of the 'Age of Colonization' and the 'Age of Discovery.' This is not the only right way to do it, but it should provide you with an idea for how to do a time line. You'll need to keep track of how this was done so that you can use it to do your own time lines. So make sure you save these [examples of time lines and essays]."

Picking up on the need to organize notes and course materials, a student asked, "Can we chuck these papers?" The student teacher replied, "What papers?" Raising a fistful of crumpled handouts, the student responded, "All of them." Somewhat surprised to discover he was holding course materials, the student teacher said: "You'll need to learn to save and order these papers so you can use them later on. You need to see why these papers are important. If you haven't kept track of what you're doing in class, you'll be lost later on. I'll help you organize the materials if you need it." To further clarify their expectations for this assignment, the teachers had developed a handout entitled "Criteria for Evaluation of the Time Line." When students were asked whether they had theirs, few did.

Since the teachers considered most student time lines inadequate, later in this class period the student teacher provided an example of an appropriate time line essay and asked students to rewrite theirs. When they were asked to turn in their work, one student proclaimed to no one in particular, "I didn't do it." Somewhat exasperated, the student teacher directed her attention toward this student and reminded the class: "You'll have an incomplete if your time line isn't in tomorrow. We have been giving you [optional] homework assignments designed to help you do the time lines. . . . If there's any other way that you think you can do the time line, please tell me." One student asked, "Can we work on our time lines without taking notes?" She replied: "You are going to need to take notes in order to do the time lines. The problem with the time lines so far is that you haven't understood what's in the book. Is the book the problem?" A student remarked, "Maybe we could see a movie on the period and that would help us understand the pe- riod." Another student suggested a different tack: "Why don't we all write down the problems we've had with the time lines and compare them. You're saying people aren't doing the homework and we all have reasons." A student volunteered, "I don't do [the homework] because I'm lazy." Another student said, "I keep putting it off and putting it off, then it's too late." As the student teacher once more described her expectations for the time lines, the student who suggested that they review everyone's reasons for not completing the work began talking with a friend. When the student teacher reprimanded him, he retorted, "I'm trying to *help* Steve."

During the second half of class, the teachers directed students to work on their time lines while they both assisted students individually. In one revealing interaction, the professor explained to one of the few students who had turned in the assignment why she had to redo it. Although the professor told her why she received an incomplete, she kept insisting, "But I turned it in on time." To address this point directly, the professor attempted an analogy: "Say, [the principal] ordered desks and chairs from a company and they arrived on time, but some had the tops break when students leaned on them and the seats of others broke when people sat on them. Yet the manufacturer kept saying, 'But I delivered them on time.' Would you expect [the principal] to pay for them?" The student replied, "no." The professor continued, "Would it be appropriate to ask the manufacturer to repair them?" She answered,

"Yes." Concluding, he asked, "So now do you understand what we're trying to say about your time line?" The student responded, "Yes, I know, *but I turned it in on time.*"

Looking at this class suggests that students were still uncertain how to approach their work. One student, for instance, was unclear about whether he needed to take notes, and few students had kept their copies of the criteria for the evaluation of the time line, although the teachers had hoped that these handouts would guide students' efforts. And, at least for one student, the reason for re-doing unsatisfactory work remained unclear. As with the previous vignette, students again completed little work—during class, as optional homework, or on the performance-based projects. Moreover, through incessant questioning, during which students often built on one another's ideas, students once more limited the amount of work they did, at least in the short term, since the teachers devoted so much class time to answering their questions. This negotiation also began to influence the teachers. Although the student teacher had developed two sample time lines for students, because of their reactions to the first one, she never shared the second with them.

By December, the team had changed the course so that it appeared more like typical Russell classes. For one thing, homework was now mandatory. Also, rather than being so performance-based, many assignments involved questions and answers tied directly to the text. Yet as the following vignette makes clear, frustration for students as well as teachers was still high.

The program coordinator began a class in mid-December by outlining work students had not yet done. He then said, "Take out your homework. . . . Who has the homework?" Many students tried to avoid eye contact as the coordinator again asked for their work. Some admitted to not having done it. Two students offered excuses: "I left it at home." "I was absent." At this point, the coordinator addressed the entire class: "I need your attention one more time." The coordinator and the professor then engaged students in a discussion about their failure to complete the work.

COORDINATOR: We have a problem. Do you know what it is?
STUDENT 1: Homework.
STUDENT 2: Yeah, we get too much of it.

COORDINATOR: There's not much happening in terms of getting work done in this class. If you've got so much work to do, where is it?

STUDENT 1: I didn't say that. I'm just not working. That's my problem.

STUDENT 2: It's so confusing in this class that you don't know *what* to do.

COORDINATOR: But if you have to read some pages and answer a few questions, why can't you do that?

STUDENT 3: But we have oral history projects, time lines, and tests. We don't even know where to start.

STUDENT 4: And we have other classes.

COORDINATOR: But everyone has other classes. That's what being a student is.

PROFESSOR: It is confusing, but at least you can always do the questions in the text.

COORDINATOR: Even if it is confusing, what can you always do?

STUDENT 5: Get out of this class, like I've been trying to do all year?

COORDINATOR: What if you're stuck in this class?

STUDENT 5: I'll leave the school.

COORDINATOR: What if you decide that that's not a solution and you want to go ahead and try to make it in this class?

STUDENT 6: Ask for help?

COORDINATOR: Do you wait?

STUDENT 6: No.

STUDENT 7: Sometimes we *have* to wait, because the teacher can't always answer your question.

STUDENT 6: I get really angry when I don't understand something, so I don't do it.

COORDINATOR: *You* get frustrated. Well *I'm* frustrated right now.

STUDENT 6: You don't get as frustrated as we do.

COORDINATOR: We have a problem. We're talking about something as simple as reading six pages and doing a few questions, sometimes only one question!

STUDENT 4: But it's a hard one.

COORDINATOR: Then see me! Come to my office! I worked on this [list of assignments] till 12:30 last night from 4:00 in the afternoon. It goes both ways. . . . You need to do the homework and do the reading before doing the time lines and questions so that you are able to ask questions about other stuff.

STUDENT 2: Why not do the questions and reading in school?

COORDINATOR: Because it's better to do that work at home. Any confusion can be dealt with in school where you have students and [your teachers] to help.

STUDENT 6: But it's better to read in school because you can ask questions in class.

COORDINATOR: It appears that the time lines and oral history projects are things you have questions on. So do the things you understand outside of class and do other things in class. We've set up a schedule so you will finish the work. And you're behind schedule.

PROFESSOR: Does anyone have anything to add?

STUDENT 5: Give us time to do work in class. Other teachers do.

COORDINATOR: We gave it to you last week. The idea behind the homework was simple. First, you'd read it. Second, you'd answer questions. And third, we'd discuss it in class. We're talking about simple homework assignments—fifteen to twenty minutes to do the reading and ten minutes to answer questions.

STUDENT 5: But we have other classes.

COORDINATOR: But other kids have classes too! This is a fact of life.

PROFESSOR (addressing Student 1, who had recently completed a project after having done few assignments for most of the first two quarters): Why did you decide to do the work?

STUDENT 1: I didn't want to get further behind.

STUDENT 8: We're still wasting time. Lots of kids have got jobs.

STUDENT 3: We've got cleaning and cooking to do.

COORDINATOR: It's a tension between having a job and responsibilities at home and doing the work you need to do to get a good, quality education. We need to move on.

By this class, most students were still doing little course work. Of the seventeen U.S. history students, only one had finished the oral history—ostensibly the year's first project. Collectively, students had submitted about 20 percent of the work that, according to the syllabus, should have been completed, including the now-required homework. Every student but one received a grade of incomplete for the first two quarters. Furthermore, students still expressed concerns about their ability to understand the work. As one student maintained, "It's so confusing in this class that you don't know what to do." Another claimed that the variety of work teachers expected further complicated matters. Moreover, students described their predicament as inequitable and blamed the teachers. One student threatened to leave the class and school.

This vignette also illustrates that students continued to support one another in their negotiations, taking turns challenging the teachers and reinforcing one another's arguments. Because negotiation took up a substantial portion of class time, the teachers covered less material than planned, and their frustration increased, in part because they had to defend the course rationale and discipline students so often. In addition, this episode revealed how the teachers had begun to modify their course. Mandatory homework assignments, for instance, now included "something as simple as reading six pages and doing a few questions."

This shift in pedagogical and curricular approaches continued for the remainder of the year. By early June, the consequences of this shift were apparent, and student negotiation was much less evident. From the teachers' perspective, students were less contentious and more productive because assignments were now structured in smaller, more manageable segments that would culminate in the completion of in-depth research projects. Other factors, however, contributed to this less contentious atmosphere. First, much more student work was deemed satisfactory by the teachers. In part, this occurred because those students who persevered now understood how to do the work and were doing higher-quality work. Indeed, by spring a few students reported that they enjoyed the class very much. But teachers also appeared more lenient in their grading. What may have been inadequate in the fall, was now more likely to be accepted. Furthermore, the teachers seemed to accept that students who had done little all year would receive incompletes and focused their attention on students who could pass the course. Finally, almost as an answer to the student request in December to "give us time to do work in class," the teachers provided substantial class time to work on projects: during May and June students concentrated almost entirely on project-related work in class.

During one June class, a student named Thomas presented his "special project," the final project required for the course. It was "special" in that students were allowed considerable latitude in defining their topic. Although he had been an outspoken critic of the performance-based structure, as the year progressed, Thomas was one of the first students to complete projects his teachers deemed satisfactory. (He was also one of eight students to pass the course that year.) Sitting at the front of the room, he began his special project by playing a tape of a symphonic overture. After a minute or two of music, students' attention drifted. Somewhat insulted by their inattention, Thomas chastised his peers: "If you're not going to listen to my report, I'm not going to give it." From the back of the room, the program coordinator waved his hand as if to say, "Let's get going." After the musical prelude, Thomas posed a question: "What is aviation?" Then he discussed the legend of Daedalus and Icarus and listed a series of significant dates from aviation history: the first flight of a helicopter, the breaking of the sound barrier, the first flight into outer space, and so on. When he reached the present he played another song, "Rock Steady" by Sting. While students again grew inattentive, Thomas sat in front of class appearing to enjoy the music.

After a minute or so of Sting, the coordinator approached the front of the class. Seeing this, Thomas reacted quickly, "Let's have a big round of applause for Sting." He then played a tape of a crowd roaring and announced, "Now, let's get back to the report." A student asked, "Why are you playing songs?" Thomas replied, "It's my special project, I'll do what I want." He went on to briefly mention the role played by aviation during war—from the use of balloons in the Civil War, to synchronized machine guns on propeller planes, to the aircraft carriers of modern warfare. After describing the use of air power in World Wars I and II, the Korean War, and the Vietnam War, Thomas dedicated a third song—a version of "War" sung by Bruce Springsteen—to the pilots who had fought in these conflicts. Again students' attention wandered: one girl read her recently received yearbook, a boy stole a girl's shoe and passed it to a friend, and three girls started a conversation.

When the song ended, Thomas announced, "That concludes my report." The student teacher asked why he chose this topic, and so he continued: "My whole family was in the service—the Air Force and Marines. They told me of the glory and the problems that they had and the great feelings that they had, and I got involved looking at their scrapbooks, which included a picture of my uncle standing next to a B-52 bomber. I started renting movies and getting into that, and I had some dreams about flying and was seeing it on television and hearing about it from my family and that affected me. It was a dream to my relatives too, but they didn't have the technology. But I have the dream and the technology so I can make it work." There were no further questions. For his ten-minute oral report and the paper that went along with it, Thomas received a grade of 95. It constituted one-seventh of his total course grade.

For the second half of this class the teachers divided students into two groups, those working on projects and those reviewing for the final exam. The review group worked with the student teacher. She first described the types of questions that would be on the final: multiple choice, definitions, and matching—adding that there would be no essay. She read examples of questions and students volunteered answers. (For instance, "Who was the 'father' of national labor unions?" "Name a former slave who led three hundred slaves to freedom?" "Which of the following was not a provision of the Missouri Compromise?") During the next class meeting, nine of the seventeen students took the exam, which included twenty-seven matching questions, twelve multiple choice questions, and ten identifications. The students had reviewed all of these two days earlier. Every student who took the exam finished in less than one period, no one scored below a 75, and the class average was 82.

ANALYSIS

LOWERED EXPECTATIONS IN STUDENT WORK AND CLASSROOM ACTIVITIES

One consequence of the student-teacher negotiation in this class was that the teachers lowered their expectations about the amount and type of work students would do. In one sense, these adjustments reflected the teachers' enhanced appreciation of their students' confusion and uncertainty regarding the performance-based assignments. Yet student negotiation and resistance played pivotal roles in this shift as well. Since students aggressively challenged the teachers' efforts to redefine their classroom experiences and did little work, the course gradually became more traditional and more typical of other Russell history classes. For instance, the teachers regularly postponed their class plans so students could work on projects or homework. In nearly three-quarters of the classes observed, students were given some class time to do their work. This was especially apparent in May and June, when the teachers covered no new material and students worked almost exclusively on their projects during class.

In an interview, a student whose work was regularly returned during the first semester but was later accepted, discussed why he felt this shift had occurred: "I got a time line done because of [one teacher's] help. If I made a mistake, [this teacher] told me so I wouldn't put it on the copy to be handed in. Plus, it's the end of the year, so I think [the teachers] are getting a little lenient. I've done all the homework. That's easy because I can use a book to look things up. Anyone can do that. All you had to do for homework was look up dates and people and write a sentence about them."

Thomas's special project also suggested that the teachers had become less demanding. The syllabus indicated that this project should fulfill three criteria: display in-depth understanding of a topic, draw some intelligent conclusions from the past about students' life choices as a U.S. citizen, and display a sense for their place in U.S. history. Thomas cited no sources, read directly from a prepared text, refused to answer a student's question, and had to be prompted to say why he had chosen his topic. Nearly half his presentation involved playing taped music. Nonetheless, he received a 95. The final exam, too, suggested that standards had been lowered. This exam, for which every question was reviewed during the class before its administration, took no student more than one period to complete, contained no essays, and consisted primarily of multiple-choice and short answer questions. As one of the seven course projects, it represented one-seventh of the total course requirements.

In addition to student negotiation and resistance, other factors made it difficult for the teachers to adhere to their original expectations. For instance, the curriculum and pedagogy were new to the teachers as well as to the students. The course was taught by a team of three teachers, and this structure required extensive coordination, which meant making time for meetings when the three teachers could reach consensus about multiple course-related concerns. Further, having three teachers provided students with three persons with whom they could negotiate and probe for inconsistencies. In an interview, the professor said: "As long as the three of us were taking turns teaching, no one teacher was able to establish and maintain the positive working relationship with the kids that they clearly needed in order to take the significant risks—and to put in the necessary effort. From our experience, I'd suggest starting slowly [in terms of the assignments given to students] and devoting considerable time and effort to establishing a positive classroom climate."

Although the teachers lowered their expectations, this was not caused by a lack of effort. Throughout the year, they devoted substantial time, effort, and thought to the class. The teachers acknowledged that they encountered difficulties implementing a performance-based curriculum, but a major problem may have been that they were overzealous, that they tried to do too much.

Differing Views on the Performance-Based Curriculum

As the vignettes make apparent, students and teachers held different views about many aspects of this course. At the heart of their differences was the performance-based curriculum. For the teachers, the course objectives—including the interconnections between homework, class work, projects, and exams—were readily apparent and desirable goals. As the student teacher told the class, "The assignments should help you discipline yourself and get the time line done by doing it with brief homework assignments—a little bit at a time so it won't seem like such a big thing that takes a long time." To clarify what they expected on the time lines, the teachers provided students with a sample and a handout on criteria for evaluating their time lines. The teachers also felt that the Essential School's policy on incompletes neatly meshed with their curriculum and goals and provided an appropriate context for learning, that is, one of "unanxious expectations" (see principle 7, chapter 1). As they told students: "We don't expect you to get the time lines 100 percent right the first time. Sometimes things that are new and different need to be done over and over before they are fully understood." In addition, they expected that allowing students to be their own historians—defining historical periods in their own terms and writing their own histories—would be intrinsically interesting. As the team wrote: "The topic studied was irrelevant. Student choice was meant as the bait to get students hooked."[3] The teachers assumed that by outlin-

3. These teachers published an article on their course experiences. To protect their confidentiality, we provide no citation.

ing their course expectations beforehand, by specifying interconnections within the curriculum, by providing models of acceptable projects, and by allowing students the freedom to investigate topics of personal interest, students would become interested and engaged. They were so confident that at first they did not require homework.

Students saw the course differently. When they first encountered the curriculum, they began to negotiate with the teachers. They questioned the clarity of the directions, whether work was inadequate or wrong, and whether being confused was part of learning. When the student teacher created a sample time line essay to inform their writing, students responded quickly: "It's a waste of time." "I ain't doin' it." "This is stupid."[4]

In interviews, students criticized multiple aspects of the performance-based curriculum. Many found the work of being their own historian disconcertingly unfamiliar. This led to various problems, the most pervasive being that students were uncertain how to approach the work. Recall the class in which students had little idea how to use the handouts and didn't realize that they needed to take notes to complete the time lines. As a student told the coordinator in December: "It's so confusing . . . that you don't know *what* to do." Another student said: "[The time lines] are very different from the things I used to do. Last year, I answered questions in a book and took tests. Now, I have to read books, find important events and dates, do an oral history, and write essays." A student who completed her work promptly but had assignments returned shared a similar perspective: "[The teachers] need to explain it better. . . . They said to do the time line one way. . . . Yet, when I did, they said it wasn't right so I had to do it over. That's why there are so many arguments and fights in that class and people are upset. . . . [The teachers] make it so complicated."

Not only did students find the work confusing and unfamiliar, but their uncertainty and frustrations were heightened when the teachers

---

4. In discussing assessment, the Coalition central staff maintain that grading criteria should be specified so that students understand how assignments will be evaluated. For instance, the sample time line was designed to show students what a satisfactory time line looked like. Yet the teacher who developed this model mentioned that problems arose because of the discrepancy between the teachers' expectations and the students' abilities, which made the model incomprehensible for many students.

outlined the entire course during the first class meetings and then expected students to work on multiple projects simultaneously. One student remarked in December: "But we have oral history projects, time lines, and tests. We don't even know where to start." Another student made a similar observation in an interview: "I don't like the class very much because they put all this work on you. They never give assignments to you one at a time and when you see it all you kinda get depressed and you just want to throw it away. If they gave it to you one at a time, it would be better. . . . It's not so much that it's confusing as it's tiring and depressing so when you mix it all up in your mind, you get confused. I've never had it presented in this format before [i.e., being told what an entire course would entail at the start of the year]. . . . I can never remember being given as much as two weeks' advance assignments before."

Even students who did well in the course were challenged. The student who received the highest grade in the class, a 98, described the course as "very challenging . . . the hardest Essential School course I've taken." And in an article the teachers readily acknowledged that "students [were] right in their assessment that the curriculum ask[ed] something of them, above and beyond hard work, that they should [have found] frightening. [It] ask[ed] that they look for their own place in U.S. history, using the skills and methods that historians say are appropriate for the task."

The students' feelings regarding the complexity and difficulty of the course structure were often exacerbated by a common reaction to confusion: doing nothing. Only a few students did nothing all year. Most attempted to complete the work. But, when course work proved different from "questions in the back of the book," when teachers returned work to be redone, and when students were asked to be their own historians, many gave up. As one girl told the teachers when asked why students were doing little work: "When you did the time line, you said we could do it like this, and then when we did it, we got confused. . . . It makes us mad and we're so confused that we just might not do it." In an interview, another student said: "I have an incomplete now and it's my fault. Because of all the frustrations, I just said, 'Forget it. I'm not doing work for awhile.' . . . When I was upset, I didn't work for two weeks and just made excuses not to do the work." The pervasiveness of such strategies was evident in the responses to a student survey the teachers administered in January. One question asked: "What do you think will happen to you if you don't hand in your homework and time lines?" All of the eleven respondents acknowledged that they would receive an incomplete, stay back, or fail the course:

I probably would get an incomplete, but I don't care because their rushing me to do everything, they never give you time to finish what you started.[5]

I would get incompletes until I finish. In other words, I'll stay in U.S. history until I complete this work.

Nothing. Just stay back. Never graduate until 1991.

I will fall behind and fail miserably.

I'll fail and have to complete U.S. history next year.

The Essential School's policy on incompletes may have contributed to this reaction. If students had trouble completing assignments, the incomplete offered an out, albeit temporarily. Students often selected this option, postponed their work, and fell behind. But the amount of work that accumulated after one postponed assignments, combined with the difficulty of the work, often proved daunting. As one student remarked: "Often, I let homework go to the last minute, but with this class the work is so substantial that once I get to the point of doing the work, it appears so insurmountable, that I don't do it."

Other students resisted doing this work because they considered the teachers' expectations to be unrealistic and unfair.

Everyone argues about this U.S. history class. They all want to go to Mr. Nolet's class because you just work from the book—read the book, answer questions, and have tests. We have tests on time lines and it's not fair. And the teachers know it. Everyone in U.S. history says there's too much work and it's too confusing.

There's so much work . . . and [the teachers] have never explained much of anything. . . . We don't understand all this stuff. Though [the teachers] tried to make it simpler for us by shortening their handouts and changing the words [to those we understand]

5. Grammar and spelling on these surveys reflect the exact student responses.

and giving us target dates [for our work], it's still garbage. It's not something you'd expect an average tenth-grade U.S. history class to do. I have cousins at Bryant High [another city high school] and they don't do anything like what we're doing—why should I?

To further complicate matters, some students held a different view of the policy on incompletes than the teachers. Many who received incompletes after attempting an assignment felt that they were being asked to do something above and beyond what was commonly expected in Russell classes. In their experience, teachers accepted whatever work students submitted. Being told that their work was inadequate and had to be redone heightened some students' feelings that the course was unfair. As one student commented: "Every time I did something, it got handed back. Usually, I did it twice. After that, I said, 'The heck with it. I'm not going to do it.' It just gets frustrating after a while."

The problems the teachers faced were exacerbated by one other development: their requests for students to complete work were often reacted to collectively. In effect, the students' reactions validated and stimulated the shared sense of confusion, frustration, and inequity created by this innovative schoolwork.[6] And this resistance took a toll on teachers.

Much of what occurred in this U.S. history class can be understood by framing the changes that the teachers attempted in the context of Russell High School. Active research was not common in Russell classrooms. Moreover, homework and academics were not high priorities for many Russell students, as suggested by a failure rate that exceeded 40 percent.[7] The teachers' goals differed from what students had come to expect as part of "real" school (Metz 1990),[8] and many students were ill-prepared to meet these expectations. Others felt that they were being treated unfairly. Student reactions generated by both these conditions made teaching difficult.

This case study shows that students are key to any school reform

6. That students can gain support and esteem from one another is well documented (e.g., Coleman 1961; Woods 1983: 11; Yates 1987: 214).

7. The failure rate was determined by dividing the number of courses Russell students failed by the total number of courses Russell students took.

8. On a related point, numerous researchers have argued that students can promote values among their peers that run counter to institutional goals (e.g., Coleman 1961; Fordham and Ogbu 1986; Willis 1977).

effort. Their actions, just like those of teachers, administrators, or parents, may influence multiple aspects of a school's efforts at change. In some of the same ways that resistant teachers have slowed, altered, or subverted the intentions of those promoting change, these students questioned the intent of the changes, denied the need for things to be different, and challenged efforts to implement Coalition practices.

10

> Behind these generalized problems lies the belief that
> high schools as they are conventionally organized create an-
> onymity and make it very difficult to achieve the kind of
> one-on-one engagement that good learning and teaching re-
> quire. Students differ, and, though this is inconvenient, such
> differences are an essential part of our humanity and must
> be addressed. . . . Members of the Coalition see no problem
> as more troubling than that of impersonality, for the chance
> of provoking excellent work from any youngster without
> understanding him or her as an individual is remote—a
> matter of pure chance or the result of home influences.
> —THEODORE R. SIZER, "Rebuilding: First Steps by the
> Coalition of Essential Schools"

In chapters 8 and 9, two perspectives of Coalition classrooms were
presented. In this chapter we present two additional examples of classroom settings and activities designed according to Coalition principles,
particularly those of student-as-worker and personalization. The
classes are humanities (English and history) classes. On the days described here, both teachers emphasized the more historical aspects of
these interdisciplinary courses. The descriptions are of a day-in-the-life
variety. Although admittedly limited, this approach offers another lens
by which to view Coalition efforts. When combined with Neil Allen's
four-year developmental history and Russell High's year-long history
class, it helps to create a multileveled analytic narrative about classroom

experimentation with Coalition ideas in our study schools.[1] These two humanities classes are the results of extended efforts by the teachers to reconceive classroom activities and curriculum using Coalition philosophy. In particular, we examine the work done by students and teachers, the classroom structure, and the atmosphere promoted by these teachers, including the relationships between students and teachers and among students. This chapter focuses on the work of individual teachers, but we shall also frame their work in a broader context of how their faculty colleagues and the school administration viewed their work and CES philosophy. In the final section we explore shared dimensions and key differences between the two classes.

A Ninth-Grade Class Looks at World War II

In 1990, Laura Gardner was in her fifth year of teaching, her third at Barrett Preparatory School, the only private school in our sample. She had received a master of arts in teaching degree from Brown University, and her interest in Coalition philosophy and practice dates to her time at Brown. She applied for and accepted the job at Barrett in part because it was a Coalition school. At Barrett, Gardner took advantage of professional development opportunities to continue learning about Coalition principles and practices.

The ninth-grade English/history course examined in this chapter was, like all classes at Barrett, heterogeneously grouped, with a range of skill levels present. Although the ninth-grade English/history curriculum was devoted to classical times—from the Greeks to the Fall of Rome—Gardner decided to insert a short unit on World War II toward the end of the school year (it was then May). She had three reasons for doing so. First, she wanted students to experience the more visceral aspects of war and felt that more contemporary examples of warfare might achieve this. Second, she wanted to use World War II to help

---

1. The value of these examples for generalizing across school experiences is limited given (1) the increasing awareness of student-teacher interaction and negotiation as ongoing features of school life (Hammersley 1980; Pauly 1991; Woods 1978, 1980) and (2) our observation of the different emphases and organizations of individual teacher's classrooms over the five years of our study. Nevertheless, the examples convey some sense of classroom activities designed with Coalition principles in mind.

students develop their ability to compare and contrast. And third, Gardner wanted to continue building student competence with formulating,
articulating, and defending their beliefs in both written and oral form.

An advocate of Coalition philosophy, Gardner was frustrated because her students often seemed minimally engaged in their learning.
She reported that she had tried throughout the year to get them to stay
on task while working in groups and to take greater responsibility for
their work, but she felt her success had been limited. The class had
struggled through a reading list of Greek and Roman classics with mixed
success. Hoping to pique students' interest and engage them more deeply
in discussions about the functions of war, Gardner decided to devi-
ate from the established curriculum and to devote some class time to
this comparative examination using materials written about World War
II. She had assigned excerpts from Studs Terkel's *The Good War* to some
of the students and the "Four Freedoms" speech by President Franklin
Roosevelt to the remainder for homework the night before.

As the ninety-minute class began, students handed out journals and
writing folders (individual folders containing all of a student's writing
for the academic year), while Gardner collected a homework essay assignment. The ten students in the seminar, five boys and five girls, were
seated at three long tables put together to form a U. Gardner explained
that the day's task was to look again at war, this time at modern images
of war and its heroes. She asked the students to respond in their journals
to the question: "Why is it important to you to learn about war?" She
added, "Write the answer you want to write, *not* what you think I
want."

A few minutes passed quietly as some students wrote. Others were
not writing, but they appeared to be thinking about what to write. A
female student asked, "Can we talk about the story we read [last night
for homework] in our answer?" A male student asked, "Can we write
why we think it [war] is interesting?" Ms. Gardner said yes to both
students, then wrote on the board: "If your society were to consider
'getting involved in a war' what would be your criteria for supporting or
opposing it?" She added, "Getting involved can mean: fighting . . . or
sending or lending money." She gave the students more time to write
then told them the questions were a warm-up, a chance for them to think
individually about why they would be examining war. She added, "It is
important to make our own decisions based on what we know and what

we learn, rather than on what someone else tells us, especially if we do not take the time to check what they say." After allowing students a total of fifteen minutes to answer the questions, Gardner said: "Today we are starting our comparison of World War II with the ancient wars we have already studied. I gave the class two readings with very different perspectives last night. Each of you read one of the assignments. What I would like is for you to share with each other the views from the readings." The teacher divided the class into two groups of five and wrote on the board: "Group task: What were the *purposes* of World War II (especially the U.S. efforts toward and in this war)? From whose point of view is the story being told? Share each article's points (stated reasons for war) with your group. When have we seen these reasons/purposes before?"

The two groups approached the task in distinct ways: in one group each person began by writing answers to the questions on the board; in the other, students explained the readings to one another. Ms. Gardner told the class she would stop them after ten minutes to see how they were progressing. After five minutes, the group that began by writing answers to specific questions started to discuss what they had written. Gardner worked with the other group, helping them generalize about why people go to war. She tried to help students consider why people go to war, and she also worked to help the students remain focused on the questions and avoid getting sidetracked.

After the first group exchanged written summaries, they seemed confused about the question "From whose point of view?" and called for Ms. Gardner to help clarify its meaning. After doing this, she assisted both groups, moving between them to answer questions that arose, occasionally making general announcements, for example, reminding the class that they had discussed several reasons for the ancient wars and that they should draw on those reasons where they were relevant and, later, asking each group to select a leader.

After the groups had been working for ten minutes, Gardner called for the class's attention again. Having worked with both groups, she seemed to sense that they were encountering a similar problem. She told the class: "I can see a problem. Struggle to stay on topic. Try to get the *purposes* down. Each group member should write them down." The classroom remained quiet as both groups appeared to have difficulty distinguishing between perspectives and goals. Students seemed to feel awkward sharing what they knew about the readings and to have difficulty determining what was important. They were particularly troubled by the concept of point of view. At times their discussions were wholly unrelated to the assigned topic. When this occurred, one or two students from the group would generally remind the group of its assignment.

One student asked Ms. Gardner if they could exchange readings that night because the one she had not read sounded interesting. It was the first she had heard of the notion of "conscientious objector," and she found it quite interesting. Before taking a break midway through the double period, Gardner told the class: "Everyone should write something in their journals that they said during the discussion that was important. Write down something from this discussion that was striking in your opinion."

During the break, Gardner drew the following diagram on the board:

Goals/Purposes for War

| FDR | John Abbott's View | View of Axis Powers (Germany, Japan, Italy, Spain) |

When the class returned she asked each student to add a point to the diagram about the goals of war from the article that they had *not* read. Based on their earlier group work, the students made the following observations, which Gardner wrote on the board. For Roosevelt's goals and purposes for war students noted:

1. Security for the nations of the Allies. Protect lives and culture.
2. End dictatorship and secure democracy.
3. Secure economics [i.e., protect the world's economies]; advance standard of living.
4. Civil liberties—freedom of speech, dissent, worship. Also, promote morality—a God.
5. War to end all wars. No more war.

The students disagreed about the fourth point on this list, civil liberties. After some discussion, "promote morality—a God" was added because some students felt the first phrase was so open as to be misleading. The problem the group had was whether Roosevelt meant complete freedom in each of these matters, particularly religion, or whether he wanted to promote the Christian notion of morality and God. Although brief, this discussion was interesting because students appeared to apply what they had learned from reading the Terkel excerpt about the conscientious objector to what their classmates had said about the Roosevelt speech. That is, Roosevelt expressed a need to protect citizens' rights to freedom of speech, dissent, and worship, but the Terkel reading offered a different perspective on World War II—one that revealed that all religious beliefs, particularly those that ran counter to the government's position, were not fully tolerated. Students also questioned whether people would willingly pay more taxes to attain these ends, especially because all taxpayers might not support these ideals. When it became apparent that this issue was related to the excerpt by Terkel, Gardner postponed discussion until after the class had listed the key points concerning John Abbott. She also reminded the class that only people who had not read the article were to respond. These students then came up with the following points regarding John Abbott's view of war:

1. To murder
2. To end dictatorship
3. To further the aims of a society that classifies, sorts, imposes order, in the name of "God," i.e., morality
4. Pulls society together
5. Causes change—in culture, individual spirit, and economic status

After the class enumerated these points, Gardner asked, "Is Abbott speaking for a lot of people or a few?" One student responded, "himself." A second replied, "He is speaking about global responsibility."

The class then turned its attention to the Axis powers and their reasons for going to war. All students were free to suggest reasons for war, and the following list emerged:

1. Cultural power [control]
2. Economic power
3. The political power that comes through dictatorship

After establishing these points, one student likened the sorting out of the weak from the strong in ancient times [probably a reference to the class's work on Sparta] to Nazi Germany's effort to purify the Aryan race. Gardner commended him and suggested that in both cases "individual dignity was not respected." The student added, "Maybe it is one of the stages that countries go through as they evolve." During this exchange, Gardner interrupted herself briefly and asked the class, "Is there a problem?" because, for the first time in the ninety-minute period, the noise level had risen as students discussed topics unrelated to the topic at hand.

Toward the end of the period, as part of a more general discussion about the effects of World War II on "common everyday people," the class turned its attention to why Veterans' Day and May Day celebrations occur in the United States and the Soviet Union and what the popular attitudes are toward these celebrations. "Fun" and "remembrance" predominated as explanations. The same student who earlier had questioned whether nations go through evolutionary stages asked a clarifying question, "Is it the 'effects' or the 'affects' that we are talking about now?" [That is, was the class discussing the "outcomes" of these celebrations or how they made people feel? Distinguishing when to use these terms had been part of earlier classes.] Following up on this issue, Gardner wrote a question on the board for students to address in their journals: "How does war *affect* our beliefs, i.e., who we are and what we stand for?"

While the class copied the question into their journals, one girl who had read the John Abbott excerpt raised her hand and said it reminded her of a book she once read. Gardner asked her the book's name, but she could not remember. From her brief description of the conflicts a student faced because of his nonviolent stance, though, it was clear that she was thinking of *A Separate Peace,* a book that had not been part of the reading for this academic year. Gardner praised her for the observation, saying that there really were a number of similarities, although she did not elaborate.

Fifteen minutes before the end of class, Gardner gave students more excerpts from the Terkel book to read. Ten minutes later, she asked them what they thought of the readings. Most had not gotten too far, but two girls remarked that it was "gross." Gardner acknowledged that many descriptions were graphic, but she asked students to keep in mind a question as they read: "Is there a way to discipline someone without hurting them?" (The readings had included descriptions of Nazi atrocities.) As they gathered their belongings to go to the next class, students made a few casual comments about the question. For homework, Gardner told the class, "Please write a letter to me on this subject of war. Tell me three things: the purposes of World War II for us (the United States), the effects of the war on people's beliefs and values, and whether or not you have changed your mind about when we should become involved in a war and why." Then she dismissed the class. The text of one of the letters she received follows.

Dear Ms Gardner,

Studs Terkel is a storyteller. His purpose is not to provide historical information. He wants to bring across the various feelings on one topic: war. Abbott's story shows his hatred of war. Galina's [*sic*] story shows the destruction caused by war. Roger states that putting yourself to the limit makes you feel "you're something."

I've personally changed my opinion of the importance of war. War is not productive and causes death and destruction. How can the United States condone war? If, however, a country is in a war, we should aid them in some way if we believe in what they are fighting for.

Abbott felt that the purpose of war was to separate the "men" from the conscientious objectors. Another reason is that "People needed a change, and a war promised to make things different." I think he's pointing out that a war changes the way we think, believe and judge. World War II is a good example. This war makes people think about what war is, how it offends moral laws and whose right it is to decide who lives and who dies. Galena feels the purpose of war is to murder. He describes the gory things that happen in a war. I think that murder is more of an effect than a purpose. It seems that Roger feels that war forces us to recognize ourselves and our potential. At least Studs Turkel [*sic*] gives both sides of the story.

The effects of war are not worth fighting for according to Galena and Abbott. Galena knows the bloody details of war and Abbott is against murder. He would resort to anything to avoid it. His belief is, "why fight for death?" A war pulls the country together. What about the peace-lovers? They withdraw even farther. Roger feels war is an incentive to make us aware. The question is, are we becoming aware of ourselves or of the destruction we can cause?

Perhaps the most prominent feature of this ninth-grade class was the teacher's emphasis on active student learning. Gardner and her students remained focused on two articles and the questions of goals and perspectives for most of the ninety-minute period. Throughout the lesson students were asked to formulate, interpret, assert, and defend their ideas. In doing so, the class demonstrated many features of the active, personalized learning that Coalition philosophy advocates: they cooperated in groups; they made connections between material they were studying and what they had already studied; they were respectful of one another and the teacher; and they sought help when they encountered problems.

Further, embedded in the class structure was an emphasis on writing that Gardner had maintained throughout the school year. In this particular class, writing was used to help students clarify their thoughts and prepare for discussion, to record key points raised in group discussions, to summarize and reflect on what had been learned in class, and to formulate judgments (particularly in the homework assignment). Each time students wrote, they were to assert and defend personal beliefs. Gardner's use of multiple activities allowed her to accommodate a variety of learning styles, an especially relevant strategy given the range of ability levels in the class. For instance, students had opportunities to express themselves in writing and through small and large group discussion. Moreover, by providing means to address varying learning needs, the class involved variety, another factor that appeared to foster student engagement. Students seldom seemed bored or distracted.

In terms of teaching style, Gardner tried to adopt classroom roles that were consistent with her goal of active student learning. She viewed herself as coaching her students, not directing them or thinking for them. She spent minimal time addressing the class. She was a moderator for class discussion, not the final authority. She set tasks for the class, asked questions, and prompted students concerning where they might look for relevant information. If their attention strayed, she reminded students of their responsibilities and, when necessary, helped clarify assignments. When she saw uninvolved students, she asked them to contribute to the discussion. If a group wandered from the task, she tried to help them refocus. She tried to be impartial and allow students to reach decisions on their own, but in interviews and informal discussions she frequently remarked about the difficulty of doing so, especially when students seemed headed in unproductive directions or when one or two members did most of a group's thinking.

In adopting this teaching orientation, Gardner became aware (as had Neil Allen) that success in such an interactive classroom was dependent on student preparation. As she often remarked, class was fulfilling only when students were adequately prepared and took responsibility for classroom learning. Otherwise class discussions and group work tended to founder. Gardner also realized that addressing topics that piqued student interest helped to engage them in class work. When she sensed that students felt distant from the Greek and Roman wars, she added readings with more contemporary perspectives.

In adopting a student-centered teaching orientation, Gardner realized that she would need to help students develop the appropriate academic skills. In this class, for example, Gardner regularly reminded students of the need to respect one another's opinions and ideas, and to do this not only by letting everyone speak, but also by listening thoughtfully. She helped students understand these expectations by highlighting behaviors that were consistent with these ideals and by coaxing and questioning students when their actions seemed inappropriate.

As the year progressed, classes like this—where students were involved and self-initiative dominated—became more common for Gardner. Nevertheless, this class represented the culmination of a long, struggle-filled process; it had not been typical to that point in the school year. Although Gardner felt that the class had gone well, she saw room for improvement and expressed hope that the class's performance was due to increased comfort with Coalition pedagogy, not simply to the readings she had inserted. Student behavior for the remainder of the year bore out her hopes; productive group interaction and active student engagement grew increasingly common. She later commented: "It occurs to me that this very diverse class . . . got very close and that that closeness among kids and teacher may ultimately be the single most influential factor on growth. How or why was it created? Smallness, much class time with peer sharing. We had done project work there more than I ever had. Also because of smallness, I was more willing to take risks."

In their English/history class the following year, these students often requested group work, possibly because they had developed the skills essential to effective cooperative learning and saw benefits to such an approach. Moreover, many of their tenth-grade teachers reported that these students both worked productively in groups and were more respectful toward each other and their teachers than many previous tenth-grade classes.

In spring 1990, Laura Gardner was selected as one of the first Coalition Citibank teaching fellows, an appointment that recognized her teaching expertise and one that has allowed her to work with other schools interested in Coalition philosophy. That spring she also resigned from Barrett and accepted a job at a newly formed alternative school in a nearby public school system.

TENTH-GRADE INTERDISCIPLINARY: CONSERVATIVES AND LIBERALS ON THE EVE OF THE FRENCH REVOLUTION

An excerpt from the history section of a tenth-grade Western civilization interdisciplinary course at Evans Hill High School gives a flavor of the activities undertaken as part of that school's SWAS program. The history teacher, Alice Mathis, used several simulation exercises—reenactments and mock trials, for instance, that explored history and literature through role playing—throughout the year to immerse students in the issues of the periods under study. Like the curriculum at Barrett, the Evans Hill interdisciplinary curriculum is a chronological study of modern Western European history that combines textbook readings with relevant materials from the period under study, including primary sources. For example, in their previous unit students read excerpts from Hobbes, Locke, and Rousseau to supplement their textbook.

In a forty-seven-minute class in October 1987, Mathis gave a final quiz about the philosophers and introduced the French Revolution. The desks of the eighteen students (eight males and ten females) were arranged in a U-shape around the teacher's desk. Mathis rarely sat at her desk; instead, she perched on a nearby student desk. The class began with the ten-minute quiz that asked students to: "Explain how the French philosophers felt about Hobbes, Locke, and Rousseau. Use specific examples." While students wrote, Mathis collected homework.

After the quiz, she gave the class a handout, "Can This Marriage Be Saved?" saying: "Today we are going to start something new. Please read the handout and then be ready to tell me how you feel about the situations described in it."

Can This Marriage Be Saved?

John tells his side:

When I married Mary we pledged to "love honor and obey, till death do us part." But Mary has taken a job as a stewardess; she's neglecting the house and the kids; she says she no longer loves me and wants a divorce. At the moment she's staying at the Tri-State Hotel. I want her to come back and resume life the way it was described in our marriage vows.

Mary tells her side:

John is unreasonable. I want my freedom. I used to believe in that nonsense about the marriage vows, but now they no longer apply. Why should I stay tied down to housework, snotty kids, and a husband I no longer love and whose financial support I can now do without?

The students discussed the handout as a class for twenty-five minutes, offering their opinions, restating the facts of the case, and suggesting solutions for the couple. Everyone offered an opinion about what John and Mary should do.

M1 (male student 1): The marriage could be saved. He's supposed to love, honor, and obey as well.

F1 (female student 1): But she's a stewardess: that means she's never home. . . .

F2: She chose that job. She cannot neglect her children. They must share responsibility. Maybe they could get a housekeeper.

F3: Mary has an attitude problem—she's selfish. But John doesn't recognize that she has a right to a job. Can they compromise? . . .

M2: Mary used him for financial support. Now she's independent. . . .

M3: John is also using Mary—he wants to have her keep taking care of him.

F4: An outsider can't save the marriage. You can try to force it, but they won't be happy. They are both being jerks. John is a little calmer, but really they're both being jerks. . . .

F1: Mary is running away from her problems—her kids, her home. If the kids are snotty, it's partly her fault. She just wants to get away. It almost sounds like Mary never liked them in the first place and that she can't handle responsibility.

M1: Divorce for the children's sake. Mary didn't plan ahead; she changed her mind. John loves his children but neglects the house. He says Mary is neglecting her job.

F3: Is that implying a woman's place is in the home?

M2: I never said that. She doesn't have to work.

M4: Mary's not doing her job.

F5: Mary wants a job; he wants her with him. John is inflexible. She's not being flexible either.

M4: He's at the office. It's natural that she would be at home. . . .

F6: They need to make some changes in their lives. . . .

M1: But she promised to love, honor, and *obey*.

F3: Women have to obey men?[2]

From time to time, Mathis interjected comments, but students carried the discussion. Finally, one male student named Philip said: "Marriage is more Rousseauian. But John is being more Hobbes-like. Maybe they should separate for a while." Everyone agreed with him, although no one asked for further clarification, which seemed surprising given the previous interaction. A female student added: "Both are thinking of themselves too much. Neither is thinking about kids much. At least they should think about them." The same male responded: "He's considered it. He wants it to be like it was. She's the one who changed everything. She's being unreasonable."

Soon after this exchange, Mathis stopped the discussion and said:

As Philip pointed out, John and Mary represent more or less conservative and liberal positions on this issue—although they are exaggerated. Some of you have articulated attitudes for or against change or toward freedom and responsibility that are more or less

2. The students in this exchange are identified by their gender because of the content of the conversation. In previous chapters, student responses have been numbered but not usually more completely identified.

compatible with these positions as well. These issues—change, freedom, and responsibility—were all values at the heart of what led to the French Revolution. Tomorrow we are going to begin a simulation of the French Revolution. This simulation builds on the discussions we have had about Hobbes and Locke and about conservative and liberal stances. This handout ["The French Revolution: A Simulation"] explains what we will be doing. Think about John and Mary and the stance you took in the previous discussion as you read it.

The French Revolution: A Simulation

Beginning Thursday . . . you will be divided into three groups. *But each day, your group will play a different role*—either liberals, conservatives, or judges. Each day we will consider a different crisis in the French Revolution. When your group is *conservative* for the day . . . you will support the general views of Hobbes and you support monarchy over any republican form of government. When your group is *liberal* you support the general views of Locke (or Rousseau) and prefer "the people" to rule, not the king. When you are a *judge*, you listen to the arguments, question the debaters, and then vote on who is right in that crisis. For *homework*, you will write a paper explaining why you voted the way you did.

Readings: Our Western Heritage, pp. 193–212; *Sources*, pp. 58–78; Pamphlets; Handouts[3]

Crisis #1: Explain from your group's point of view the situation in France in 1789, the reasons for calling the Three Estates and the voting method you prefer: by head or by order. . . .

Crisis #2: Explain the Tennis Court Oath and the Fall of Bastille. Are these events beneficial to France? . . .

Crisis #3: National Assembly: Declaration of the Rights of Man, Civil Constitution of the Clergy, Assignats—Are these examples of Liberté or License? . . .

---

3. Students had a textbook for the course (*Our Western Heritage*) and a supplemental book of primary source reading material (labeled *Sources* on the handout). They also received other handouts and reading assignments for the unit, as Ms. Mathis deemed appropriate.

>*Crisis #4:* Flight to Varennes and foreign wars; what should we do with the King and Queen? . . .
>
>*Crisis #5:* The Convention and Reign of Terror
>—Levve en Masse
>—Law of the Maximum
>— "Terror is virtue"—Robespierre . . .
>
>*Crisis #6:* The Directory: Is this better than what we started with? . . .

For the remainder of the period, Mathis assigned students to groups, reviewed the handout, and explained her expectations for the exercises students would soon begin. The class was attentive, most took notes, and students who had questions asked for clarification.

DISCUSSION

Simulation exercises comprised much of the tenth-grade interdisciplinary. The John and Mary discussion introduced the French Revolution and set the tone by establishing a sense of conservative and liberal based on discussing such issues as openness to change, responsibility to self and state (in this case to the state of marriage), and freedom and its relation to personal responsibility. This tone was mirrored in class give-and-take. In the days ahead, Mathis would remind the class of the John and Mary discussion, encouraging them to ground their interpretations of the complexities of and motives for people's actions during the French Revolution in their understanding of the John and Mary case.

Mathis expected students to talk in class—to offer their impressions and opinions, then defend them—and to engage in several role-playing projects. Unlike Gardner's students, Mathis's classes rarely complained to her about the work assigned, the standards by which they were graded, or the class's distinctive formats. Compliance with classroom expectations was virtually universal; overt resistance (such as was seen in the Russell history class) was absent. Even the gradual acceptance of a new classroom structure, the day-to-day unevenness in participation, and the other impediments that Gardner described were rarely noted by students, teachers, or observers at Evans Hill. As a consequence, problems experienced by Laura Gardner and Neil Allen—indeed by many of our study teachers—such as getting students to take individual or group responsibility for completing assignments, were not critical issues at

Evans Hill. This was true of both Coalition and non-Coalition class-rooms, and so classroom management issues were minimal for most Evans Hill teachers.[4] But, even though Evans Hill students may have done the required work diligently, teachers at Evans Hill recognized their students in Sizer's descriptions of passive, nonengaged students in *Horace's Compromise*. One of the goals of Coalition supporters at Evans Hill was to design classroom activities that would draw students into the curriculum materials, in part by helping students understand difficult issues through drawing parallels to issues that resonated with students and to global themes with adolescent appeal. The tenth-grade interdisciplinary course, for instance, began the year reading *Lord of the Flies* in their English class, and they studied *Summerhill* and explored issues of liberty and responsibility—civic and individual—in social studies and in Seminar. (Chapter 5 discusses the Seminar program, Evans Hill's advisory program.)

Like Gardner, Mathis tried to be provocative and to serve as a guide and resource for students. Also like Gardner, Mathis was fairly new to teaching; she had returned to school mid-career to finish her teacher education. She had taught at the alternative school where Mary Ellen Smith had been principal before coming to Evans Hill. When a vacancy arose at Evans Hill, Smith recruited Mathis, hoping to "stir things up." Smith had high regard for Mathis's professional work and subsequently hired her to be a consultant and teacher mentor at the next site where she served as principal.

Mathis and the English teacher with whom she teamed for this tenth-grade interdisciplinary class struggled to develop projects that bridged the two disciplines. Even with summer planning time and some common planning time during the school year, this proved difficult as the two women had different teaching styles and classroom management techniques. The English and history components of this class ran chronologically parallel, but the teachers rarely combined classes or utilized the services of art and music teachers who worked with the interdisciplinary program. Each of the teachers pointed out parallels and other connections between the material under study in English and

4. However, this was not true for substitute teachers. When respect was discussed at the Student-Faculty Legislature and in Seminar (see chap. 5), the treatment of substitute teachers by students was often used as an example of the students' disrespect.

history for the students in her own classroom. Occasionally students articulated links between the materials from the two classes as well.

FINAL THOUGHTS

We have presented two different interpretations of humanities classrooms where active learning was expected of students. Laura Gardner stressed group work, followed by sharing, summarizing, and discussing with the whole class, all structured by writing tasks that asked students to consider, then reconsider, their views and to provide supporting evidence. Alice Mathis relied more on whole-group discussion, debate, and simulations. Gardner, whose class lasted ninety minutes, taught both components of the English-history curriculum and strove to make the skills, themes, and expectations for her course consistent across the two disciplines. She was able to hold common expectations across the courses (for instance, with regard to how students should behave while doing group work), to integrate similar themes (such as the goals of war), and to develop and reinforce academic habits (such as writing and comparative analysis). Mathis taught the single-period history component of an English-history course, and she worked to make connections between two curricula that reflected goals, topics, and texts of two different teachers from two different departments. Further, Mathis's colleague in this course had an approach to teaching and classroom management that tended toward maintaining the role of teacher as authority. Consequently, the integration of course themes, the standards for student work, and the skills students developed varied between the two classrooms.

One key to promoting active student learning that was apparent in both classrooms was the belief that students' skill development was an ongoing process, something which the teachers (especially Gardner) had to attend to regularly. Both teachers adopted pedagogical styles that they felt promoted active student learning. They provided students with questions or issues to address, and they worked to support student inquiry, rather than to direct student thinking. And both teachers identified this as being critical to active learning and difficult to maintain, especially when they felt it important to cover course content.

The emphasis on active student learning meant that student commitment and involvement was critical in both classes. As Gardner noted throughout the year, when students were prepared (which usually meant that they had done the assigned reading or writing), classes were far more productive. This was not such a concern for Mathis: students at Evans Hill generally did their assignments. Nonetheless, both teachers relied on similar strategies to promote student engagement. In these two classes, for example, they drew parallels—one historical and one philosophical—with the work students were doing. In both instances, the intent was to offer students another perspective by which to understand course materials. To make Greek and Roman wars more real, Gardner injected readings from World War II; to help students appreciate the differences between conservative and liberal positions on the French Revolution, a parallel was drawn to a strained marital relationship.

To promote student engagement, both teachers relied on multiple research sources. The textbook was but one source. Outside readings offered alternative perspectives on the topics being studied. Furthermore, the teachers employed a variety of teaching strategies, which allowed them to accommodate multiple learning styles. Gardner's students wrote in their journals, they addressed questions related to their readings in small groups, and the groups both reported their findings and engaged in classwide discussion. Although Mathis's class was half as long as Gardner's, her students took a quiz, held a class discussion, and collaboratively clarified the work they would do in the next unit.

These vignettes from two Coalition classrooms describe how two teachers sought to create classrooms where students were actively involved in learning. Although they are fairly representative of the activity we often observed in these two teachers' classrooms, we do not present these as typical of activities in Coalition classrooms more generally. Our point in this chapter was to provide some sense for how two teachers had tried to apply Coalition philosophy and ideas to their classrooms. More specifically, we sought to illustrate the expectations two teachers had of their students in two different settings and to provide descriptions of students at work.

Both courses were somewhat unique at their respective schools, yet students made accommodations to their teachers' different styles and approaches. The term *heterogeneous grouping* was used to describe the two classes' compositions, but the meaning of that term differed considerably in the two sites. The Evans Hill tenth-grade Interdisciplinary self-selected to participate in the class. Although a range of abilities was present, it did not match the complete range that comprised Gardner's class. There were several sections of history available—though only one Interdisciplinary—into which the approximately seventy-five Evans Hill sophomores might be scheduled. The time block for this class coincided with a free block that allowed students in advanced math and science classes to enroll. In addition, there were remedial and English-as-a-second-language classes at Evans Hill; so students in need of these forms of extra assistance were not in Interdisciplinary. According to the tenth-grade faculty and the administration, most students in Inter-disciplinary would be taking AP courses next year, suggesting that these students were among the more academically inclined of Evans Hill's tenth-graders. In contrast, all ninth-graders at Barrett were registered in Ms. Gardner's class; there were no remedial classes at Barrett. Regard-less of the differences in student composition, however, the two exam-ples show that once students became involved in class assignments, they could accomplish the tasks given to them and engage in thoughtful discussion about difficult topics.

The two classrooms presented in this chapter are in Coalition schools in which schoolwide consensus about the need for change and the form it would take was not achieved during our fieldwork. Further, neither Barrett nor Evans Hill has been designated as a second-step, or more fully articulated, Coalition school by the central staff. Nevertheless, these examples of change at the classroom level were observed at both schools (and at all the schools we studied). Thus, although there was minimal schoolwide support for CES membership and philosophy and although Coalition affiliation may have had a limited influence school-wide, individual teachers redesigned their classrooms and teaching styles in ways that reflected many aspects of Coalition philosophy, even if they were constrained by aspects of the larger school (for example, the schedule) that had not changed.

11

"You Can't Always 'Do Change' on Top of Everything Else"

A Comparative Look at the Role of the Principal in Coalition Schools

So "vision" alone isn't enough. It must be tempered by the habit of thinking clearly and critically and systematically about how change comes about. We might begin by ridding ourselves of the fatal belief that because we're "good people" who seek to improve our school, barriers will crumble and everyone will flock to our cause. Better to assume that we're quite ignorant about "the system" we work in, that we're politically naive and need to get smarter fast. We must learn to do business with people—all kinds of people. —STUART TUCKER, principal of Green Valley

So you stir everybody up and create these great expectations and that makes your job more difficult because then everyone's out to get you because they say you aren't doing it [change] right. —KATHERINE SHAW, principal of Silas Ridge

In this chapter we examine the role played by the principal in implementing Coalition-based reforms at Silas Ridge High School and at Green Valley Junior-Senior High. Both principals—Katherine Shaw and Stuart Tucker—were newly appointed to their positions. Both were committed to educational reform, were attracted to Coalition philosophy, and contacted Ted Sizer about joining the fledgling Coalition. Both embraced the opportunity to promote change at their schools and encouraged their faculties to help plan for this change. The similarities end here; the schools' experience with Coalition reform diverged markedly. Silas Ridge adopted a school-within-a-school approach that first expanded but eventually became so bogged down in controversy that the program was suspended and the school's Coalition membership was placed in question. Green Valley's approach to change was more inclusive; the entire faculty was involved in discussions about the school's mission as well as in experiments with change. Although things proceeded smoothly initially, challenges to reform were raised by community members who were displeased with aspects of change and with Tucker's leadership. Once these issues were resolved, the faculty renewed its commitment to the school's vision and to change.

To some extent the diverging paths at the two schools reflect the differing contexts within which the principals operated. Silas Ridge is a large urban school that offers its diverse student population a wide range of curricular offerings. In the local community, the school enjoys a solid reputation for academic achievement. Green Valley is a small rural school that serves a white working-class student population. Before Tucker's arrival, the school had a high dropout rate, many discipline problems, and few graduates attending college.

In addition, each principal's role in the change process and personal style influenced what occurred at the schools. Although both saw themselves as collaborating with teachers to promote reform, each interpreted the role and responsibilities differently. Relying on volunteer committees to drive change, Shaw at first worked closely with Coalition supporters to develop a new vision and structure for Silas Ridge. A vocal proponent for reform, she became a focal point for much frustration and resentment disaffected faculty felt toward the change process. When it proved difficult to sustain her initial level of involvement and when allegations of top-down manipulation of the change process arose, she stepped back from the school's reform efforts, asserting that teachers needed to own and defend the changes being undertaken. Using an active, assertive style, Tucker defined a vision for Green Valley and "encouraged and cajoled" faculty to embrace and develop this vision or to leave the school. His aggressive style and unorthodox manner made him the target of community fear and confusion about changes occurring at the school.

SILAS RIDGE HIGH

Located in the heart of an eastern city of 65,000 inhabitants, Silas Ridge High enrolls slightly more than one thousand students and has a staff of teachers, guidance counselors, and administrators that numbers around eighty. Although most students are white and middle class, the school has a sizable percentage of students from Southeast Asia and Eastern Europe, and nearly half the student body qualifies for the school lunch program. Thus, the school serves a population that includes students headed for Ivy League universities, students from the city's poorest neighborhoods, and students with little understanding of either English or the United States. To meet its students' needs, Silas Ridge has implemented a five-tier tracking system—advanced placement through basic—as well as programs in English-as-a-second-language, special education, and vocational training. The school also offers an array of extracurricular activities. Approximately 90 percent of Silas Ridge students graduate, and most pursue some form of higher education.

In the opinion of many faculty, students, and community members, Silas Ridge is a fine school whose staff—75 percent of whom have advanced degrees—has consistently sought to improve itself. Before Katherine Shaw became principal, for instance, the school had instituted a professional development program for faculty and had created an honors program for students with advanced skills and a remedial program for those with academic deficiencies. Moreover, Silas Ridge has been publicly recognized for its accomplishments; its students were named National Merit scholars and it was designated a James Madison High School by then-Secretary of Education William Bennett.

COALITION MEMBERSHIP

Silas Ridge High's association with the Coalition began in March 1984 when the school department invited Ted Sizer to speak to faculty from all city schools. Following this visit, a group of Silas Ridge teachers decided to explore the pedagogical and curricular implications of Sizer's ideas, as well as the possibility of Coalition membership. This group included Katherine Shaw, a respected teacher who had left Silas Ridge for Texas five years earlier but who had recently rejoined the faculty. As a sign of the regard accorded Shaw, she was named an assistant principal in fall 1984. In January, she was appointed acting principal, the first woman principal in Silas Ridge's one-hundred-sixty-five-year history.

As principal, Shaw immersed herself in the literature on school reform and became an advocate for change. The changing nature of public school populations, coupled with the shifting needs of society, convinced her that schools needed to change significantly. As she explained to a central staff member, "We are involved with school restructuring, not just school improvement. School improvement is just a Band Aid for the problems that exist in education today." Outlining her rationale, Shaw wrote to a local journalist: "Educators agree that our student populations have changed. . . . Our students come to us needing many things—personal attention, nurturing, discipline, basic social skills, and a deeper sense of responsibility. [Moreover,] our nation and world need a more highly educated population. The educational programs . . . that were successful in the factory age are not adequate for the high-technology, information-processing age. We now need to . . . teach ALL students how to problem solve, how to make reasonable and defensible decisions, how to communicate articulately, how to learn independently, and how to be responsible citizens."

Acting on her concerns and in conjunction with a volunteer committee composed of teachers supportive of Coalition philosophy, Silas Ridge applied for membership in the Coalition of Essential Schools and became one of the original twelve members in January 1985. Once a member of the Coalition but before implementing any specific reforms, Silas Ridge undertook various planning activities intended to lay a foundation for schoolwide change. Faculty met with a professor experienced with school reform to discuss teaching styles and school structures and the possibility of changing them. National Humanities Faculty— university professors funded by the National Endowment for the Humanities to work with educators interested in reconceptualizing English and history curricula—conducted seminars at the school on interdisciplinary instruction and Socratic dialogue. Teachers and administrators attended workshops sponsored by the Coalition as well as by the local Teachers' Academy. Silas Ridge teachers visited other schools to observe school reform in practice. The school also kept in touch with the Coalition central staff; Shaw and faculty members attended Principals' and Coordinators' Council meetings at Brown, and central staff members visited Silas Ridge. To help fund their work, Coalition proponents applied for several grants.

During the planning phase, Shaw appointed a Coalition coordinator and gave her minimal release time from teaching responsibilities. The school also established the Coalition steering committee, a volunteer committee open to any interested faculty and charged with overseeing Coalition-related work. In virtually all of these activities, Shaw took a central role: she initiated contact with National Humanities Faculty and the college professor; she helped author grant proposals; and she was active on the steering committee. To create an informal setting for discussing Coalition membership, Shaw hosted faculty dinner meetings at her home. In his field notes, Sizer described one he attended: "The spirit at the supper was extraordinary. . . . There was a camaraderie among colleagues, and it was hard to tell which staff were new and which were old. . . . Forty individuals gathered . . . to discuss [their reform plans] and throw questions at me. As has always been the case when I visited Silas Ridge, the questions were often tough, the kind that in other schools are not delivered in the presence of the principal. Clearly Katherine is perceived as a colleague, and able to take direct questions. . . . The tone was striking: one got a sense of a friendly group of colleagues who were engaging in important work together."

Many at Silas Ridge, especially Katherine Shaw and members of the steering committee, shared Sizer's optimism. In their view, faculty participation throughout the planning phase suggested there was substantial support for the program. As the reform effort unfolded, however, noninvolved faculty grew increasingly dissatisfied with the effects of change and actively resisted it.

THE SWAS PROGRAM

In September 1986, after planning for a year-and-a-half, Silas Ridge implemented a SWAS program that consisted of four teachers (English, history, math, and science) and an assistant principal who replaced the original coordinator and who added this responsibility to her existing work. The SWAS teachers taught four sections of ninth-grade students—two general-level classes, one honors, and one college preparatory. Initially, the SWAS seemed uncontroversial. Although Coalition teachers taught one fewer class and had no supervisory periods, the consensus was that this was a reasonable trade-off for teaching all freshmen, half of whom were general-level students.[1] Katherine Shaw remained involved with the steering committee; she attended their meetings and served on various subcommittees. She also met twice a year with the Coalition's Principals' and Coordinators' Council. At the same time, the city of Silas Ridge was promoting a $20 million bond proposal to underwrite renovations in city schools, and Shaw served regularly as a spokesperson for this effort.

As plans to expand the SWAS program became apparent to the entire faculty in spring 1987, problems arose. One aspect of this expansion proved particularly contentious: the steering committee decided that the SWAS would continue enrolling general-level, college preparatory, and honors students. Consequently, all SWAS teachers would have one honors class—with the rest of the faculty sharing any remaining honors sections. A few teachers who considered this practice unfair, claiming that SWAS teachers now had a near monopoly on honors classes, expressed concern to Shaw, but they were told that the decision would stand. So they would have input into future SWAS decisions, these persons and others joined the steering committee. Whereas previous committee meetings were attended only by Coalition supporters, by fall 1987 faculty who disagreed with various aspects of the SWAS program had joined the committee. Among those who opposed the SWAS were influential, experienced, and respected faculty members, including two department chairs and the teachers' union representative.

FACULTY DIVISIVENESS

During the 1987–88 school year, the divisiveness experienced by the steering committee spread to much of the faculty. Because of her close association with the school's reform efforts, Shaw became the focal point for much resistance and resentment. Faculty maintained that she accorded SWAS teachers favored treatment; they were assigned fewer students, no supervisory duties, and fewer classes. Others felt that Shaw hired only those willing to participate in Silas Ridge's restructuring efforts, including several young women with Ivy League backgrounds. An experienced teacher remarked: "[The SWAS] took new teachers and

1. At Silas Ridge, teaching freshmen and general-level classes was commonly viewed as less desirable than teaching upper-class students or honors classes.

put them in a position of privilege at the expense of older teachers who'd earned it. The only recognition teachers receive is through minor privileges and that was all revoked and given to new teachers in the Essential School.[2] This caused lots of resentment because these untrained, untried, and opinionated teachers—there was a certain arrogance on the part of Coalition teachers—thought they were experts because they had master's degrees from Brown University."[3]

Another contentious issue concerned whether the reform process at Silas Ridge represented a democratic change embraced by the entire faculty or an administrative mandate. In the words of one teacher: "The perception within the school was that it's not coming from the faculty, it's coming from Katherine. And that's how [the opposition] coalesced." Another teacher elaborated: "Katherine had this grant money that she held over our heads. . . . 'If you want to have eighty students and no nonteaching duties, you want the Coalition. . . . And we don't want to prevent anybody from having new ideas and having an opportunity to spend all this money and do things differently.' So if you were against this initial idea, you were against people trying new ideas. And who was? . . . What started out as tacit agreement—because why would you be against improvement?—all of a sudden turned into a school-within-a-school."

Further, although an open faculty committee created the SWAS program, not everyone felt that they had access to this forum. Some maintained that participation was restricted because those who could not attend the voluntary before- and after-school meetings were excluded. As one teacher said, "What created the problem was that the school began to make a major turn toward [the Coalition] . . . through a small number of teachers."

A third source of tension emerged from what many considered implicit criticism of their teaching practices embedded in Coalition rhetoric. In a newspaper article describing the school's reform efforts, a Silas Ridge teacher commented: "There was a feeling that what [experienced] teachers were doing and had been doing was not good and should be

2. Although all SWAS teachers taught one honors section, no faculty lost any other privileges nor were any forced to assume additional responsibilities. Still, this was a common perception among non-SWAS faculty.

3. Most SWAS teachers were experienced Silas Ridge teachers. Nonetheless, this too was a common perception.

changed, and the new people were doing things right." This perception was exacerbated by Shaw who was an outspoken critic of the status quo. She questioned whether the school's tracking system served the interests of all students, even countermanding an English department policy and allowing ninth-grade general students to enter tenth-grade college preparatory classes without passing ninth-grade college English, which had been a requirement. She promoted teaming and interdisciplinary teaching and, in her teacher evaluations, encouraged faculty to rely less on lecturing and to pay greater attention to gender issues in the classroom. Moreover, some faculty felt that those who were most active in the restructuring were publicly portrayed by Shaw as doing the most progressive work at the school.

After a series of emotional and complicated negotiations during the 1987–88 school year, the steering committee disbanded the SWAS program. Further, as a precondition to submitting a grant proposal to support school restructuring, the faculty conducted a needs assessment survey. The ensuing report noted that faculty expressed "broadly differing perceptions of the administration's role." The subcommittee in charge of the needs assessment recommended creating one faculty governance body to oversee all of the school's various change efforts, which by this time included the steering committee, a number of subcommittees, and a school-improvement team mandated by a state restructuring effort. The Faculty Forum, an elected, seven-member committee that subsumed the school's restructuring activities into a single effort, was created.

Reactions to this decision at Silas Ridge differed. In the opinion of one non-SWAS teacher, "The 'Forum' was a way for teachers to take back control. . . . We were told that we had control, but we didn't. . . . People were [also] feeling left out . . . that they were no longer an important member of the faculty." A Coalition proponent saw the same development differently: "What happened was that all of the forces who had been criticizing the Coalition really jelled . . . and an 'anti-Coalition' coalition was formed and proceeded to write this grant, and they related it to the needs assessment. . . . It was a debacle. . . . The grant . . . became a document to defeat the Coalition."

Silas Ridge's Coalition program spent the next two years in a state of uncertainty. During the 1988–89 school year Shaw attempted to team teachers who were willing to do so, but logistical constraints and faculty indifference hampered these efforts. During the 1989–90 school year, the school held a referendum on whether to remain in the Coalition. Although more than a third of the faculty did not participate, a majority of those who voted favored continuing Coalition affiliation. Since then, there has been little Coalition-related work at Silas Ridge.

In looking at Katherine Shaw's role in the change process three factors seem prominent: her shifting level of involvement in the restructuring effort; her ambivalence toward teacher empowerment; and the decision to use a SWAS structure as the basis to reform. In terms of Shaw's participation, perceptions were that it tended toward two extremes. At first she was intensely involved with all Coalition-related work, so much so that some teachers felt she was unwilling to delegate responsibility. Consequently, some faculty saw reform in terms of top-down, principal-directed change, and those who opposed the SWAS focused much of their disaffection on Shaw. But in the second year of the program, Shaw adopted a more hands-off approach. As the coordinator explained: "Katherine always came to [steering committee] meetings and she tended to be a dominant presence. And one of the aims we had that [second] year—because so much of the Coalition had become identified with Katherine, as Katherine's project—was to emphasize that this was a teacher-driven project. So in the beginning of the year, she said, 'Would you like me to come to meetings or not?' And I said, 'No, I think you should stay away for awhile.'"

Other factors contributed to Shaw's decision. After three years of overseeing reform at Silas Ridge, she felt unable to deal with a reform agenda on top of her normal responsibilities. As she noted in a letter to Ted Sizer: "You can't always 'do change' on top of everything else. The principal can't be the change agent because the community expects me to be at basketball games, to attend school committee meetings, to do evaluations at other schools, and to attend parent meetings. . . . The principal can't be the change agent, but can be a facilitator."

But letting SWAS faculty direct their own efforts generated problems as well. Many people had been attracted to Shaw's reform ideals, and her distancing herself from this effort left some SWAS faculty and Coalition supporters uncertain of their role and of her support. A local newspaper article raised this concern: "Katherine Shaw . . . believes that as principal she must allow ideas to percolate among the faculty rather than introduce change through the power of her office. [The program's third coordinator] applauds Shaw for being 'absolutely dedicated to sharing responsibility for making decisions about the school,' but acknowledges that Shaw's leadership style had made some of the faculty uncomfortable. 'Some people are anxious because Katherine won't say, "This is what I want." . . . She keeps asking, "Is this what we need?"'" In a later interview, the coordinator alluded to problems the SWAS faced during its tumultuous second year: "When things really started to go bad . . . Katherine didn't act. . . . I did say, 'Katherine, you really have to say clearly what is going to happen. . . . What procedures are we going to follow?' But she didn't. And she explained it by saying, 'No, I want to stay out of this. It has to be from the teachers.'"

Some teachers also questioned whether the school was ready for such a leadership style. A steering committee member explained: "Katherine is relatively new as principal here and the first woman principal, and she has a very different management style. . . . She's trying very hard to empower teachers . . . to have a nonhierarchical management structure. But that means that the lines [of authority] aren't clearly drawn. And it's very tough . . . because it's new for her and it's very tough for the faculty to accept."

This shift in her level of involvement brought Shaw the worst of both worlds. By supporting SWAS faculty and questioning traditional practices, she alienated many experienced teachers. When she later distanced herself from reform, some SWAS teachers felt abandoned and directionless, at the same time Coalition opponents organized and joined the steering committee. Further, those skeptical of Shaw's motives viewed her disengagement as more manipulation—while talking of empowerment, she still sought to impose her agenda. Ultimately, Shaw's relations with both parties suffered.

A second critical aspect of Shaw's leadership concerned her ambivalence toward teacher empowerment. On the one hand, she maintained that teachers had to own the change process and collaboratively address issues of reform. On the other hand, she acknowledged ambivalence, "There's a real tension. . . . How much freedom do you give [teachers]? And what will they do with it?" Shaw also felt that many teachers were preoccupied with their own well-being. When it was proposed in a

Faculty Forum meeting that all teachers receive an additional duty-free period, Shaw's ambivalence was apparent: "I'd like to do that, but I need accountability that things will happen. I don't want to give people a free period so that they can just go out for an extra cup of coffee." In discussing how she perceived the Forum's approach to change, Shaw outlined her differences with them: "The Faculty Forum wants to discuss Maslow's 'hierarchy of needs.' They say that the staff's security needs aren't being met. They say that kids are using bad language. . . . They can't see that as long as our school is like this—with a fragmented curriculum, where the day is divided into disconnected periods, where students are anonymous—that these problems will not go away."

As a consequence of her ambivalence, Coalition supporters as well as opponents felt that Shaw tried to orchestrate too much of the school's reform efforts. Moreover, faculty, including those involved with the SWAS program as well as the Faculty Forum, sensed that Shaw did not trust them to implement change. Thus, teachers were uncertain whether Shaw would support their reform efforts, while Shaw questioned the sincerity of their commitment to reform, and the school did little Coalition-related work.

The third critical aspect of Shaw's involvement with reform at Silas Ridge concerned her decision, made in conjunction with an assistant superintendent, to use a SWAS structure as the entry point to reform. This approach was appealing to a public school principal as it allowed the school to attempt change without appearing to conduct a wholesale experiment, an action that may have raised community concern. The SWAS structure would not require all faculty to participate, and for a school system on a tight budget, it was affordable. Yet this approach resulted in Silas Ridge's restructuring efforts becoming identified with Shaw and a core of faculty. Efforts were made to involve all teachers in discussions about Coalition membership and school reform, but when the program began, SWAS faculty directed most change-related work. In addition, these faculty were perceived as being accorded additional privileges and their work was publicly touted—two developments that alienated many who were not directly involved with the program. Furthermore, those who supported Shaw and the reform effort often had limited influence at the school; many were relative newcomers and women.

SUMMARY

Katherine Shaw sought to implement reforms that many in the educational arena consider appropriate and necessary. Yet many teachers did not share her views and perceived her as critical of the status quo. This generated resentment toward her as well as toward the change process, and it created divisions between supporters and opponents of Coalition reform. Moreover, when she lessened her involvement, Coalition proponents, many who were relatively new to Silas Ridge, felt directionless, and faculty who were skeptical of her motives suspected manipulation. When an opportunity to conduct a needs assessment arose, many who opposed Shaw's efforts used this as a means to increase faculty power by creating the Forum. In the following two years Shaw and the Forum, working together, initiated few Coalition-related activities.

Four additional points are important for understanding what occurred at Silas Ridge. First, establishing the success of the SWAS program proved problematic. Although Shaw touted SWAS efforts in various forums (for example, newspaper articles and education seminars), and many SWAS faculty were proud of their ability to motivate their students—particularly general-level students—these were not clear signs of success at a school that prided itself on the number of National Merit scholars and Ivy League students it produced. Second, the school relied on previous experience with change—such as creating a ninth-grade at-risk house, an honors curriculum, and a school-based professional development program—to inform their Coalition efforts. As with the SWAS, these changes involved voluntary participation, and most work was an add-on to teacher and administrator responsibilities. In all these cases, this approach proved adequate and nondivisive. Thus, the school's limited but relatively successful experiences with change obscured how time-consuming and potentially divisive it could be.

Third, during Shaw's six-year tenure, there was substantial administrative turnover. In the central office, there were five superintendents, three assistant superintendents, and three business managers. Silas Ridge had six different assistant principals. Clearly such turnover disrupted the continuity of understandings about and support for Coalition reform. Finally, in the spring of the second year of the SWAS program, when critical decisions were being made about the needs assessment survey, Shaw was ill and spent limited time at the school.

GREEN VALLEY JUNIOR-SENIOR HIGH

Green Valley Junior-Senior High School is a relatively small school, with three hundred fifty students enrolled in grades seven through twelve and a staff of slightly more than thirty. Located in the rural Northeast, the town of Green Valley has the second lowest per capita income in a state that provides little support for local education. Despite these economic circumstances, there is a sense of community and excitement about the school. When a student broke his neck in an accident, for instance, the school rallied to raise funds to buy him a wheelchair. To help students and faculty to get to know one another informally, some teachers hold cookouts with their students at the start of the school year. One student commented, "The cookouts are great. You get to see your teachers as real people. . . . We still respect our teachers . . . but we can laugh with them too." Describing an end-of-the-year gathering her team initiated, one teacher remarked: "We got all the kids together and it was the most heart-wrenching, incredible hour-and-a-half of my life. Each kid said something for one minute [about the school year] and it was quite a year. . . . By the end of the year, they were no longer just kids that came to school that I had to teach. Things had changed. . . . Now you begin to worry about this one and you keep in touch with that one, and they seem to feel the same way because we've heard from them."

This sense of community was apparent within the faculty. Reflecting on her first year of teaching, a Green Valley teacher explained: "I was taught [in college] that the first year of teaching is hell because you're so alone. But that's not true here. In doing my student teaching, I only had one mentor. Here, I have thirty-three [the number of faculty at Green Valley]. . . . The atmosphere is honest and open. There's lots of help available. I can go to anyone and count on them."

Much of what occurs at Green Valley Junior-Senior High emanates from its principal, Stuart Tucker. He came to the school in 1981 after ten years as a middle school principal. Green Valley had a troubled recent history. In the seventies and early eighties, the school faced many problems. School funding—on both the state and local level—was tight. Teacher salaries were low, with most teachers, even veterans, earning less than $20,000 a year. Furthermore, the school had one of the higher dropout rates in the state—20 percent—and sent only 8 percent of its graduates to college. The absentee rate was nearly 20 percent. Students roamed the hallways and lavatories and harassed younger students and sometimes newer faculty. The school building was plagued by vandalism and neglect.

In summer 1981, after he was appointed principal but before school began, Tucker tried to learn as much as he could about the school, modeling an inclusive approach to school change that has endured throughout his tenure at Green Valley. He met with all students (including recent dropouts) to hear how they felt about the school, to discuss their goals for the coming year, and to ask them how the school might be improved. He asked faculty for their impressions and held meetings with parent and community groups to discuss the school's role in the community.

At this time the school had a traditional structure—a seven-period day, a faculty divided into departments, and students who were scheduled individually. Over the next decade, with Tucker spearheading the effort, the school came to look quite different. At first, most work was directed toward changing the school's structure—decreasing the number of periods in the day, extending the length of each period, and doing away with study halls. The school also eliminated the D from its grading options after faculty agreed that it gave no indication that significant learning had occurred. The faculty streamlined the school's discipline policy by implementing a series of straightforward rules: students are suspended for fighting, using drugs or alcohol, swearing at teachers, stealing, and destroying property. Tucker explained: "We wanted to teach students to respect other students, to respect the faculty, to respect property, and to respect . . . their own well-being."

To promote active, in-depth learning and interdisciplinary teaching, Green Valley instituted the "two-week thing." Once a year, for two weeks the school breaks from business-as-usual and organizes itself into teams of teachers and students to address a common theme. One year the home economics teacher secured an $8,000 grant to underwrite the school's effort to examine the issue of "sustainability": how can the world be organized so that it doesn't exhaust nonrenewable resources and slowly self-destruct? To help faculty design curricula for this particular two-week session, a professor from a nearby college ran a curriculum development workshop. During this annual two-week break from routine, everyday teaching became a potential source of professional growth as teachers experimented with team teaching, interdisciplinary courses, group learning, and flexible schedules. In addition, the initial two-week things served as the basis for soliciting volunteers for Green Valley's first efforts at teaming teachers. That is, after experimenting during the two-week thing for several years, teachers willing to team for an entire school year were recruited, assigned a group of students, and given a block of time to structure however they considered appropriate. Because of the school's size, these changes could be made without disrupting normal routines. The faculty continued to learn from the two-week seminars and the initial efforts at year-long teaming. By the fall of 1991, virtually the entire school was teamed (except for some elective teachers).

In its reform efforts, Green Valley has made personalizing students' educational experience a priority. To provide each student with a faculty advocate, the school instituted an advisory system in which all staff— including Tucker—are assigned fifteen advisees with whom they meet daily during what most schools consider "homeroom." The school also implemented a course entitled "Life after Green Valley," a senior requirement that covers health and social issues (such as AIDS prevention and sexual discrimination), as well as exposes students to such practical life choices as finding a job, managing a budget, and interviewing for a job. The apprenticeship program was another innovation intended to make school relevant for students. Through having students work as newspaper reporters, teacher aides, auto mechanics, and secretaries, the program seeks to engage them in actively learning about relevant professional skills while offering them a chance to develop socially and intellectually outside the school setting. Explaining the rationale behind the program, Tucker said: "The more I talked to students, the clearer it became that all their needs could not be met within the existing school. We lacked the staff, the materials, and money to provide the broad range of courses and experiences students needed. The traditional curriculum just didn't inspire every student . . . nor did it meet the expectations of some highly motivated . . . students. So we began looking outside the school and into the community for help." Although many changes implemented at Green Valley reflect Coalition philosophy, the school did not join the Coalition until 1984, three years after Tucker arrived and after some of these reforms were already underway. In many respects, Coalition membership offered Tucker a means to further his existing ideas as to how schools should be organized and run.

Although Tucker and the faculty have changed much about Green Valley Junior-Senior High, this has not occurred without incident. Green Valley is a conservative town, and difficulties arose, in part, because some residents disliked Tucker's appearance, demeanor, and approach to education. Sporting bushy hair and a beard, Tucker never wears a coat and tie at school, instead preferring flannel shirts worn over brightly colored T-shirts. He has two doctorates and is highly educated in a town where some are skeptical of intellectuals. Moreover, some programs implemented during Tucker's tenure were considered inappropriate. A faculty member who lived in the town commented: "Some people . . . feel that doing something different in school means that we are treating the kids like guinea pigs. Some feel that the high cost of education is tied to our reform-minded teachers. Some school board members have commented that they think the journals that we use in some classes are intrusive into the private life of students."

Lingering tensions eventually coalesced. In his third year as principal, the school board did not renew Tucker's contract. When he challenged their right to do so in court, the reservations of some residents (including school board members) surfaced. There were accusations that Tucker's unconventional dress and relaxed manner promoted a lack of discipline at the school. Board members observed that many students referred to teachers by their first names and often addressed Tucker as "Doc." Others claimed that students were allowed to play boom boxes and listen to obscene rock songs in class. His detractors maintained that Tucker was too liberal and too lenient. To highlight all that was wrong with his leadership, these persons regularly cited the case of a pregnant girl who was allowed to design her own independent study course and examine community attitudes toward teen pregnancy. Green Valley's membership in the Coalition was also viewed with disfavor by those who saw it as a progressive, university-based experiment. After a bitter court battle and a highly contested school board election, Tucker was reinstated as principal.

Why Has Change Endured at Green Valley?

A variety of factors have worked in concert to promote and sustain Green Valley's restructuring efforts. Leadership has played an integral role. Unlike most Coalition programs we studied, Green Valley has no Coalition coordinator. Since his arrival, Stuart Tucker has been the impetus behind most change. The apprenticeship program, the two-week thing, the Life after Green Valley course, and the advisory system were all ideas that originated with Tucker. He also directs much of the school's professional development work, often both designing and leading sessions aimed at helping teachers reassess aspects of their work.

Although Tucker was often the driving force in introducing change, faculty commitment enabled it to take root. This aspect of Tucker's leadership—his ability to coalesce support for reform initiatives among teachers—has been a critical factor in sustaining change. For instance, the teaching teams at Green Valley have had nearly total freedom to develop curricula, design schedules, and organize their students. The home economics teacher took the initiative to organize and obtain funding for the two-week thing on sustainability. Moreover, Tucker was attentive to teachers' concerns and created multiple forums in which to discuss them—summer workshops, faculty meetings, teacher journals, and during classroom visits and team meetings. At one point, for example, Tucker was considering an idea that few would associate with public education—securing an endowment to underwrite such projects as summer professional development work or buying (or having students build or renovate) a house to serve as a dormitory for college interns working at Green Valley. As Tucker noted: "There are a lot of things that I'm doing too much thinking about by myself. For the good of the idea, it needs more minds. So I'm thinking of taking a day every two weeks and just ordering pizza and picking a topic [to discuss]. And I'll tell teachers, 'I really don't care if you come. Don't come to make me happy.' We're just going to sit around and eat pizza and talk about school. . . . If we do it that way, the idea can go further."

Green Valley teachers offered various reasons to explain Tucker's ability to enlist faculty support. One veteran, who was at first skeptical of Tucker's leadership style but later came to support him, noted: "Stuart is a great persuader. . . . He can convince you to do anything. He told me that the program *needed* me. . . . He's the reason behind much of my professional change because he's been encouraging me to do more." Along the same lines, another teacher remarked: "Stuart is concerned about all the faculty, both professionally and personally. I always thought of the principal as a figurehead. I never even met the principal at the school where I student taught. But I see Stuart every day. He's very much a part of my day. He's involved with everything at the school, and that's important to the teachers and the kids." A third faculty member reflected on Tucker's ability to work with his faculty: "I see Stuart more as an educator than an administrator. At other schools where I have worked, the principal was generally very impersonal. . . . [Stuart] knows where he wants to go and how to find people who want the same thing. . . . He spends his life thinking. . . . I have three kids and they're my top priority. Stuart has 350 and they're his top priority. . . . Stuart gets the most of the people who are working for him. His life is consumed with it. . . . He is the energy behind the school. . . . Stuart is always pushing for teachers and the superintendent to get better. He won't allow his family of 350 to be ignored."

One way Tucker has kept faculty enthusiastic and energized is through continually promoting professional development. Indeed, much of what transpires at Green Valley might constitute professional development. Every Wednesday, for instance, the faculty meet and address administrative as well as pedagogical and curricular issues. Tucker encourages faculty to reflect on their work through journals. Teachers often submit these to Tucker, who responds to their thoughts. He also tries to visit teachers' classes regularly. One new teacher said: "He plays a big role on our team because the three teachers on my team are new to Green Valley. . . . Stuart helps to direct my thinking, and I have no hesitation to say, 'I'm stuck.' He never lets me rest and I like that. He meets with us as a team at least once a month. Sometimes, he'll just stop in when we're working together. He's helped us adjust to teaching seventh grade and establishing an exciting and worthwhile curriculum."

In addition, Tucker regularly seeks summer funding to enable teachers to meet for a week or two to discuss such matters as goals and curricula for the coming year. One grant, for example, funded an effort by five teachers to develop a flexible schedule that allowed the school to integrate critical thinking skills across the curriculum and develop individual education plans for all students. Another summer the school received funding for ten teachers to "define in measurable, performance terms, both entry- and exit-level academic requirements." One year, Green Valley faculty ran a three-week professional development session on the West Coast to help teachers develop curricula collaboratively—

using "essential questions" as the overarching framework.[4] Moreover, Green Valley teachers frequently offer workshops at Coalition conferences. These professional opportunities have complemented the school's restructuring efforts because, through articulating their educational goals, developing materials, organizing workshops, and instructing other teachers, faculty have fine-tuned their skills and developed further insight into their own work.

Creating multiple forums for experimentation and reflection has had an additional benefit: Green Valley faculty have evolved a sense of shared philosophy that, in Tucker's view, has made their work more effective: "If every person doesn't believe in the philosophy, then we are being inconsistent and working against each other. This doesn't mean we are all the same, but it does mean that we are all driven by similar philosophy and goals." Excerpts from informal professional development sessions indicate how Tucker has helped faculty generate a sense of common purpose and shared philosophy. In one, Tucker and an English teacher discuss the teacher's goals for his students in the coming year:

TUCKER: Talk to me for two minutes about a kid who is your brightest kid and is proficient in what you want him to do. Tell me about your dream kid.

TEACHER: This kid will have been thoroughly introduced to at least the four genres of literature.

TUCKER: Put it in terms of what the *kid* is saying—not what you're introducing to them. . . .

TEACHER: OK, I know about four different types of literature. . . . I know the structure of each. I know the process of theme and character development in each of these genres.

TUCKER: How do you know this? . . . For example, one student sat with me for an hour and was able to not only write her own poetry and not only show me five poems she wrote, two short stories she wrote, and an outline for a novel, but she talked about the different styles she used in all of those and referred to how she picked up things from O. Henry and Haiku poetry.

TEACHER: Not only was I introduced to these different types of literature but I learned what makes them up. Also, I wrote in at

4. See note 3 to chapter 6.

least three of these forms. I presented outlines for ideas. I presented finished products in paragraph form and in longer forms. . . . I did some research and I learned how to follow through on an idea and develop and crystallize it in a final form, in a form that others could read.

Meeting with a different team of teachers, Tucker made a case for developing students' study skills:

We get frustrated when a kid does a half-assed job. A lot of our disappointments are because a kid's not finishing something or not knowing how to do something. What we tend to do, too often, is just get angry rather than seeing that the kid does not have the skills to do it. It's interesting that most of us have not planned study skills as part of what we're doing, but actually . . . it's probably the key to everything we do. . . . Rather than saying these kids fell on their face . . . let's give them another shot, maybe let's try to figure out whether they didn't know how to find books in the library, or they didn't know how to listen. And although it's not doing science or not doing English, that time spent [developing study skills] might be more worthwhile.

In addition to promoting support for reform among faculty, Tucker has made students a part of the change process, and this appears to have aided the school's reform efforts. One of the first things Tucker did as principal was to meet with students to discuss their educational plans and hear their suggestions for improving the school. Interested students were hired to do much of the cosmetic repair work on the school building, mostly painting. When Green Valley first teamed students and teachers, Tucker and teachers from the teams met with students to see how they felt about the change. As he explained: "I did a thing with groups of five kids and one teacher and myself. We put five kids around a table and asked questions like, 'What were your expectations of the program? What did come through? What did not? What were the highlights?'. . . . And kids were very open. We just ran about a twenty-minute session every day for that week. And for the last five minutes I asked the teacher to leave, to see if there was anything else students would say. And there was really nothing else they said. It was pretty open."

The school also implemented various incentives for students, including a student of the month award and an annual academic awards banquet for students and their parents. Through Tucker's connections with local businesses, Green Valley honor students receive discounts at some stores. Students have increased responsibilities as well. When one team took a trip to Walden Pond, for example, students determined what the cost would be, set up the schedule, arranged the car pool, and collected all moneys. At various symposia and workshops attended by Green Valley representatives, students usually go along and participate in most activities.

The school's signs of success have helped sustain change at Green Valley. For instance, by 1986, after five years of school reform, the dropout rate sank to 3 percent and daily attendance improved to over 95 percent. In addition, the number of students who attended college tripled. Three years later, half of Green Valley's graduating class went on to college, the most ever for the school. These developments have been touted in magazines and newspapers, and Tucker was featured in a PBS special and a made-for-television movie.

Another reason Green Valley has sustained change appears connected to a lack of resistance to reform. In an historically nonunion state, the local teachers' union has had little influence at the school. At other schools, unions sought a clear delineation of teachers' work responsibilities, but at Green Valley Tucker has been able to, as he puts it, "encourage and cajole" his teachers into going beyond the normal eight-to-three routine. The school also had no special programs—such as magnets or advanced placement offerings—and departmental ties were generally weak and have been further diminished as many teachers have developed strong interdisciplinary ties with team members. In changing institutional structures, therefore, there was less likelihood of violating existing interests. Also, Tucker has been able to hire many staff members according to his philosophical interests and has let go teachers who were not committed to his reform ideals. Because few faculty had tenure (in part, due to Green Valley's recent history and low pay scale), as of the 1991–92 school year, approximately two-thirds of the faculty had been hired by Tucker.

SUMMARY

A few factors appear to have played integral roles in implementing the reform agenda at Green Valley. First, Stuart Tucker is an educator with a vision who has constantly promoted his educational ideals—among students, faculty, and community members. As he wrote in a letter to the superintendent and school board in 1986: "My life commitment at this time is Green Valley Junior-Senior High School." Second, Tucker gained grassroots support for his educational plans. Although he was the catalyst for much change, faculty commitment combined with multiple opportunities for professional growth allowed these changes to develop and expand. In addition, grassroots support included Green Valley students, many of whom cite aspects of their more personalized learning environment as reasons for their support and engagement. By consistently promoting his educational ideals and enlisting broad-based support for reform, Tucker and the faculty transformed a school with a typical, multiperiod day organized according to discrete departments into a more integrated and personalized, teamed approach to learning. In doing so, the school community has evolved something of a common philosophy, which has informed and been shaped by its ongoing experiments with change.

SILAS RIDGE AND GREEN VALLEY:
A COMPARATIVE PERSPECTIVE

Perhaps the most significant difference between these two efforts to undertake substantive change was that reform at Silas Ridge was viewed as an exclusive process whereas at Green Valley all faculty participated in at least some aspects of reform. Although reform began as a schoolwide effort at Silas Ridge, it came to be identified with a core of teachers and the principal. When the school discussed program success or secured funds to promote further change, those who were excluded grew alienated. Moreover, after Silas Ridge instituted its SWAS program, there was little schoolwide discussion about reform. Many teachers who were not directly involved with the SWAS were initially indifferent, but as the consequences of change began to affect their lives and as hostilities developed, many came to oppose the effort. In contrast, at Green Valley there were multiple opportunities—faculty meetings, professional development activities, and team meetings—for faculty and other members of the school community to develop a common philosophy. Although certain reforms began with volunteers, restructuring gradually included the entire school. Moreover, Tucker secured funds so all faculty could participate in professional development work. As faculty evolved a sense of common purpose and philosophy, success became something they all shared, and this further reinforced their sense of common purpose.

The principals' level of involvement with reform also invites comparison. Both principals actively supported reform at first, but because of her workload, faculty skepticism, and a desire to make the effort more teacher-driven, Katherine Shaw stepped back from the change process. When this occurred, SWAS faculty felt uncertain and directionless. In contrast, Tucker remained the driving force for change throughout his tenure at Green Valley. In a related vein, trust appears to have played a crucial role at these schools. At Silas Ridge, faculty felt that Shaw did not trust them to enact change. Instead, she tried to oversee much of the school's reform efforts. When she limited her role during the second year of the SWAS, many SWAS teachers were uncertain of her support and skeptics saw it as more manipulation. When the Faculty Forum was created, trust was such an issue that the school undertook few efforts at change because faculty and administration reached consensus on very little. At Green Valley, Tucker delegated substantial responsibilities to teachers—devising schedules, setting course goals, and so on. It may have been easier for him to allow teachers such autonomy because he could monitor much of what happened at this small school.

The matter of scale also played a role in the relative success of reform efforts at these schools. Silas Ridge is roughly three times larger than Green Valley. Tucker worked with teams of teachers to develop course goals and design schedules, but this was more difficult for Shaw, who was overseeing a large high school with a five-tier curriculum, an ESL program, vocational education, special education, and an array of extracurricular activities. Given Tucker's ability to maintain contact with all aspects of reform, it may have been easier for him to trust his faculty. Further, Tucker could hire persons with similar educational philosophies. Shaw also hired new faculty, but these teachers represented a much smaller portion of the faculty. Attempting to change the faculty ethos at Silas Ridge through hiring was more difficult, and it actually exacerbated divisions within the school because many veterans felt that new teachers were given privileges traditionally accorded experienced faculty.

Reputation was another contextual feature that influenced these two reform efforts. Silas Ridge has a solid community reputation and a faculty that prides itself on curricular offerings, disciplinary expertise, and the achievements of exemplary students. In contrast, Green Valley had no special programs in place, a teachers' union with limited influence, and weak departmental ties. The school also had a poor reputation before Tucker's arrival. For Green Valley, then, success was more easily attained as the school lowered its dropout rate, improved daily attendance, and sent increasing numbers of students to college—signs of success that helped build support among skeptical faculty and community members. At Silas Ridge, the dropout rate, daily attendance, and college acceptances were less of a concern, making the issue of what constituted success for Coalition efforts problematic.

12

INDIVIDUALS, CLASSROOMS, AND LEADERSHIP IN EDUCATIONAL REFORM

In Chapter 7 we summarized findings derived from five case studies that looked at change from a schoolwide perspective. The smaller, more focused units of analysis presented in later chapters not only reinforced some of these findings about the school change process, but also suggested further insights that were not as apparent from the broader schoolwide perspective. For instance, the schoolwide studies revealed that politics played a significant role at every school, and they described the nature and structure of these political dimensions. The more focused studies provided a sense for how the political elements influenced day-to-day life at these schools, including their effects on students, teachers, and administrators. Taken together, these two analytic perspectives enrich our understandings of school reform by offering complementary views of the school change process. Given the nature of CES reform, this approach is particularly appropriate; that is, while schools that join this reform coalition are expected to initiate some degree of institutional restructuring, individual teachers and students are also expected to change. Examining both units of change—individual and schoolwide—therefore allows us to more fully assess the effects of CES reform efforts.

TEACHERS AND CHANGE

We presented certain specific teacher case studies—Neil Allen, a U.S. history classroom, and two humanities classes—because they illustrate many of the dimensions of classroom practice that can be influenced by Coalition-based reform. For instance, these teachers all adopted different approaches to curriculum, pedagogy, and assessment. They changed *what* they taught, often focusing on fewer topics and exploring them in greater depth. Laura Gardner hoped to enrich students' appreciation of war as a pan-human phenomenon by injecting contemporary perspectives on warfare into the study of classical Greece and Rome. Others allowed students a greater say in what they studied, as the teachers in the U.S. history course did by helping students define their own research topics. These teachers also changed *how* they taught: group work and cooperative learning became more common. New forms of assessment were introduced. Traditional exams were still common, but so were such alternatives as research projects, group presentations, and exhibitions. Furthermore, it is important to note the nature of these changes because the classroom relationship among student, teacher, and subject matter was the original focus of Coalition reform efforts. In fact, the common principles were designed to focus attention on this relationship.

NEW EXPECTATIONS AND SKILLS

As was evident in the classroom vignettes, when teachers made shifts in pedagogy, curriculum, and assessment to emphasize active student learning, they created new expectations and roles for themselves as well, which in turn changed the nature of their classroom experiences. Rather than directing class and relying extensively on lecturing, teachers tended to adopt roles that allowed them to support students in their learning—what in Coalition terminology is referred to as teacher-as-coach. They posed higher-order questions and let the questions direct student learning. They designed more long-term projects and guided students through the research process, from identifying and selecting topics to preparing oral reports. These teachers helped students develop their intellectual abilities—supporting a point of view with evidence, asking questions to clarify one's understanding of a topic, and planning and writing research papers. As some of the schoolwide case studies made apparent, many teachers took on the new role of adviser—helping students with future plans, addressing concerns that arose at their schools (such as Russell's policy on incompletes or the issue of racism at Wade), and generally supporting students in their educational development.

While our more focused case studies did not examine this topic in depth, many Coalition teachers also adopted different roles outside the classroom vis-à-vis their colleagues. This may have been most pronounced for Coalition teachers who were teamed, as they had to collaborate and devise group decision-making processes for issues ranging from grading practices to substitute teacher policies to student discipline.

Furthermore, experimenting at the classroom level and being part of a collaborative reform effort commonly increased teachers' commitment to Coalition philosophy as well as to school change in general, at least initially. Like Neil Allen, teachers often reported that their Coalition involvement, which generally included time to collaborate with one's colleagues and the chance to know students better, increased their sense of professional commitment. Many teachers said they had become more reflective about their work, took greater responsibility for student progress, and became more involved in the life of the school.

Although our more focused case studies did not emphasize this point, we should mention that all of these teachers were encouraged to implement changes through Coalition membership. In particular, they felt they benefited from belonging to a network of schools that were exploring the same ideas, particularly when faced with questions arising from their reform work and attempts to change classroom practices. For them, Coalition membership could be both a spur and a support mechanism for change and experimentation. For instance, Coalition central staff (or consultants to them) sometimes visited schools—often to provide feedback on classroom or schoolwide experiments. (The Neil Allen case illustrated, however, that as the Coalition grew, visits to most of our study schools decreased.) The CES network also offered teachers a means to share ideas and strategies with others at conferences and workshops. Teachers at all the study sites repeatedly alluded to the important function of Coalition gatherings—as providing support and encouragement, as offering a forum to exchange ideas, and as an opportunity to learn about the Coalition's expanding work and influence throughout the country. (In fact, Laura Gardner and the three teachers from the U.S. history course made presentations describing their classroom-based reform efforts at CES symposia.) After attending such gatherings, teachers often expressed a sense of revitalization, from encountering new approaches to teaching as well as realizing that others were struggling with similar issues and tensions.

Across our eight study sites, the majority of teachers who became involved in SWAS programs or participated on committees implementing Coalition ideas schoolwide were experienced teachers. But they had also begun to question whether what they had been doing for years was really working for their students, often because they sensed a lack of engagement on the students' part. In some schools they had evidence that they were not reaching many of their students: dropout and absenteeism rates were high, and disorder and violence on school property had reached a point, as one teacher decried, "where security not curriculum revision was a top priority." The traditionally successful schools we studied, with virtually universal graduation and college attendance rates, were not problem-free, but faculty at these schools were attracted to Coalition philosophy as a means of making their students' learning more active, not to find ways of getting them to attend to their work in the first place. Incorporating student-as-worker and personalization principles into their classrooms often revitalized teachers at all of our schools and demonstrated a potential for personal efficacy in the classroom that many said had seemed lost.

Many teachers we interviewed, however, had reservations about giving up their role of authority in the classroom, citing professional responsibility, enjoyment of their craft as practiced, and the desire to share their knowledge and understanding of subject matter as reasons why they resisted adopting student-centered instruction. Other teachers' opposition to the student-as-worker philosophy was rooted more in a concern about giving up control of their classrooms, no matter how temporarily, to students.

Many teachers also had concerns with the Coalition's notion of less-is-more. The concept of less-is-more proved particularly difficult for teachers to rethink at the classroom level and for them to use as a possible entry point into schoolwide change. At the classroom level, teachers were uncertain whether they should teach a few concepts in detail or survey a range of concepts; schoolwide concern centered on whether schools should adopt a core curriculum or strive to be comprehensive and offer a broad array of electives. Less-is-more proved especially contentious among disciplines, such as math and science, whose curricula were viewed as sequential and developmental. Faculties often divided on these issues, and the contexts within which teachers were rethinking classroom content grew increasingly tense. The distance between emerging factions often grew as the reform-minded cut back on the breadth of their curricula at the same time that their colleagues continued to question whether focusing on a few subjects or topics represented an improvement over survey and elective courses. Further complicating the issues, as we saw in the school-based case studies, in some instances accommodations made to the schedule to promote in-depth learning meant that other teachers' schedules changed, whether or not they requested it.

The issue of academic standards also proved contentious and raised questions about new expectations and skills for teachers. While the teachers described in chapters 8, 9, and 10 did not confront these issues directly, teachers in individual classrooms frequently faced questions of how to assess student performance when course work could vary widely. For instance, when there were several options for final projects, how did one compare writing and performing historical vignettes with a traditional research paper? Teachers also worried about how new standards would be integrated with existing district- and state-level requirements and with parents' expectations for their children's education. And as reform proponents wrestled with these concerns, those skeptical of proposed changes continued to question whether such changes were even appropriate.

Tensions, uncertainty, and divisiveness commonly accompanied these efforts at change, yet the changes teachers made and attributed to CES philosophy and practices could be impressive. One principal commented: "The change in the approaches to teaching that occurred in a few staff members . . . was the most significant professional development activity that I've [ever] seen. They really transformed their approach[es] to teaching."

In sum, teachers' reasons for supporting Coalition membership were focused for the most part on the positive consequences they perceived for students and themselves, particularly in terms of their changed classroom experiences. The successes teachers noted often inspired confidence in reform ideas. Further, teachers' sense of their increased reflectiveness about their work could become intertwined with a desire to be more involved in the school's decision-making processes as well as to increase personalization and active student learning. Indeed, perceived success at classroom-based change could be a powerful positive outcome of a school's participation in the Coalition, regardless of the outcome of schoolwide efforts at change.

Increased Commitment, Increased Workloads, and Lack of Time

Coalition-based changes—such as promoting greater closeness with students and other faculty—reinvigorated many teachers and increased their sense of commitment to their work, but they also meant teachers were confronted with issues and problems that they had previously not addressed. This increased experimentation and the new classroom roles required time on the part of teachers—time to design changes, time to assess their effectiveness, and time to adjust methods. Teachers who became affiliated with Coalition-based efforts expected to change how they taught, but many felt strained to find time and assistance to translate their inclinations into daily practice. For example, although Coalition teachers generally appreciated the opportunity to work collaboratively, most acknowledged that this entailed problems. Neil Allen noted that he found it difficult teaching to "other people's rhythms." In the Evans Hill humanities class, the teamed teachers were provided summer time for designing their course, but they had little integration in the classroom once the school year began. And the three teachers who taught the U.S. history class felt that one problem they faced was the limited collective time they had to reflect on the effectiveness of their course.

For teachers attempting change, success could bring increased workloads and a heightened sense of being pressed for time. For instance, because teachers at the more troubled schools sought to improve student attendance *and* to challenge students academically, when they succeeded in getting more students to attend school regularly, faculty had more students to teach. And once students did more school work, teachers had more work to review and assess. A similar development occurred with teachers who incorporated active learning into their classroom routine. Many were satisfied with the changes in student performance, but it took time to find appropriate materials and develop new lessons. Encouraging parent involvement and developing new forms of assessment also strained teachers' schedules.

Further, success with new practices was often rewarded with an increased work load and concomitant time commitment. As one teacher remarked during her second year of Coalition involvement: "It's still very demanding. If I'm doing things right it means that I'm spending even more time on my work. I go home now expecting to work and fall asleep. The kids are now doing work, and I've got to be ready for them."

Moreover, the challenges and the sense of being pressured that derived from rethinking what to teach as well as how to teach it could be intensified by an uncertainty as to how to assess one's performance and how to evaluate student learning. As Neil Allen noted, when he taught more didactically, he knew the signposts that indicated whether students were learning what he wanted them to know. His goals and expectations changed after he adopted a more active approach to student learning, and these signposts were no longer adequate. The same difficulty was apparent in the U.S. history class with the seven performance-based projects that were new not only to the students, but to the teachers as well.

The increase in workload and uncertainty with change—both in the classroom and in their collegial relations—coupled with disillusionment when political controversies arose, led some teachers to return to previous teaching practices or otherwise disengage from reform work. The combination of experimentation, professional self-reflection, and more active involvement in school decision making caused Neil Allen to feel overloaded. As was also apparent in his case, teachers involved with school restructuring often felt unsatisfied with their classroom efforts because more of their time was now directed elsewhere. And, as the U.S. history class revealed, teachers could become disillusioned when students resisted their efforts at change.

A sense of frustration and disillusionment led some teachers to revert to previous practices or otherwise disengage from reform efforts. Their reactions were usually not based on a disagreement with Coalition ideas but rather on a perceived inability to achieve their desired ends or because doing so offered a means to cope with increased workloads and the associated stress. As Neil Allen said, "When I get tired or pushed, I go back to old habits." In the U.S. history class, a similar trend was evident—as students resisted innovations, the teachers increasingly relied on more traditional approaches, to the point that the final exam emphasized students' ability to recall facts and assessed few other academic skills.

Somewhat ironically, frustration and disillusionment with reform could emerge from an initial period of program success. That is, as

Coalition programs began to take hold, opposed teachers often intensified their resistance to these efforts while the workloads of involved
teachers continued to increase. When manifestations of success were
dismissed as the result of preferential treatment or special conditions,
exasperated teachers felt even more attacked and vulnerable. Further, as
programs were implemented, opponents began to use specific examples
from the school to challenge the Coalition's ideas rather than the more
hypothetical ones that had accompanied preimplementation debate.
These criticisms were taken personally by pro-Coalition teachers, and
communication between pro- and anti-Coalition factions worsened. In
an attempt to reduce the pressure they felt or to regain some semblance
of control, some teachers returned to aspects of their previous classroom and schoolwide practices. Others maintained their new activities
but assumed no additional responsibilities. Thus, although teachers
often took pride in what they and their students had accomplished,
some questioned whether they could maintain the pace and their
peace of mind at the same time. When there was limited institutionalized
time to support school reform, personal costs for those involved were
high.

In sum, teachers cited three factors as reasons for backing away from
CES reform work in their classrooms and schoolwide: the cumulative
effects of the increased workload associated with implementing reform;
the disillusionment they experienced when students did not respond or
when teaming with other teachers proved problematic; and the emotional drain they experienced as they dealt with their colleagues' opposition.

Finally, regardless of how one views the curricula, pedagogical styles,
or assessment strategies employed in the classroom-based case studies,
in these instances, the scope of change generally did not spread beyond
individual classrooms. Coalition proponents at these schools adopted
aspects of the common principles that individual teachers (or small
teams of teachers) could implement on their own with little disruption
to the school as a whole. In particular, the emphasis on personalization
and active student learning may have kept the change process focused on
the teacher–student–subject matter relationship and away from issues
of schoolwide change, such as changing the schedule, lowering the
student-teacher ratio, or restructuring schoolwide into houses.

STUDENTS AND CHANGE:
NEW EXPECTATIONS BY AND FOR STUDENTS

As the case studies make apparent, students' experiences in Coalition schools changed, and student reactions to these changes varied. Students were often some of the more supportive proponents of change—a reaction that seemed connected to the increased sense of personalization that many experienced. At virtually every school (except where student-teacher ratios were already low) students were uniformly positive in their response to increased personalization. Moreover, the increasingly personalized relations students experienced with their teachers enhanced their willingness to accept the new forms of school work.

In addition, teachers found that their efforts to promote active learning were reinforced by personalizing students' educational experiences and that students were more diligent when they were provided with opportunities to connect course work with their lives outside school. At our study sites teachers used cooperative learning techniques, peer editing, and other forms of group work to foster an environment of trust and decency—both between students and teachers and among students—so that students would feel comfortable taking the risks teachers felt were necessary for serious and consequential learning. Moreover, a more personalized educational experience often led students to raise their expectations for the work they would do in high school as well as for their post–high school plans, which often came to include a college education.

Teachers, however, sometimes found that their expectations for students were overly ambitious. Instead of embracing changes, students—who were usually accustomed to schools with very different practices—could seem ill prepared for what Coalition teachers envisioned. As in the U.S. history class, when students considered changes to be radical departures from their previous experience, they resisted teachers' efforts. And as Neil Allen commented on his efforts to promote active learning: "The students hated it. . . . They saw it correctly as more work for them." One math teacher described a common problem that pro-Coalition teachers encountered: "Without a book, students were very insecure. They were always trying to get me to tell them how to do this rather than discovering the processes for themselves. They just wanted to find out the answer rather than to understand the essence of things.

For instance, when we worked on statistics, students wanted a book. . . . They kept saying, 'I'm supposed to be in algebra class, where's my algebra book?' They wanted to cover traditional topics."

The classroom-based case studies also reveal that students could be critical collaborators in enacting school reform, regardless of whether schools or teachers accorded them official roles or responsibilities in the change process. This was most apparent in the U.S. history class: when students resisted, they had a serious influence on the teachers' efforts to change classroom practices. Further, both humanities teachers acknowledged that student engagement (for instance, their willingness to do assigned homework) had a clear effect on the quality of classroom learning. When teachers opted for more active forms of student learning, the student's role became more critical because what occurred in the classroom depended more on what students did and less so on the teacher. Whereas structural and cultural constraints often restricted student participation in the change process, when student involvement was encouraged and nurtured, classroom and schoolwide changes were more likely to be sustained and deepened.

THE PRINCIPAL'S ROLE

For the most part, the principals in our study schools were central to the school change process; they were often *the* central person. Individual teachers made changes in pedagogy, curriculum, and assessment, but by themselves these efforts never provoked change beyond one or two classrooms. Only in schools where the principal was an active and ongoing participant were the experiments of individual teachers incorporated into schoolwide change.

Yet, the principal's role was often less directive than traditional conceptions of this position would suggest. As teachers' and students' roles changed when faculty attempted to implement the common principles, so too did the role of the principal. At schools that sustained their Coalition reform efforts, the principal's role involved a balancing act, one that required knowing when to be directive and assertive and when to back off and allow faculty to direct change efforts. In many respects, the Coalition's emphasis on the triangle of learning, personalization, and the quality of schools as experienced by students reinforced these principals' belief that they and their faculties needed to collaborate and that they had to keep student interests clearly in mind as they designed and implemented change. Further, beyond collaboration, principals ultimately had to enlist faculty support, for without that support, change did not occur.

Principals at the second-step schools—where reform efforts were sustained—worked to strike a balance between top-down decision making and grassroots change. For the most part, they were able to support reform but avoid the charges of favoritism and inequity that divided faculties and effectively ended the change process at some schools. This was evident in our schoolwide case studies, and it was reinforced in our more focused look at leadership. When Katherine Shaw, the principal at Silas Ridge, shifted her involvement with school reform, she lost the support of Coalition proponents as well as those skeptical of change. In the end, the school effectively ended its affiliation with CES, and all structural changes that had been introduced were dismantled. In contrast, Stuart Tucker gradually gained widespread faculty support for change at Green Valley (in part by not rehiring those who were reticent to change), and reform was more widespread.

It also appears that striking a balance between top-down decision making and leadership with grassroots support was dependent on trust. As noted in our comparison of Silas Ridge and Green Valley, Tucker adhered to his stance on reform throughout his tenure whereas Shaw was perceived as wavering when she found it difficult to maintain her initial level of involvement. Of course, the size of the school may have played a critical role in these developments: it may have been easier to promote trust at Green Valley, which has a faculty of about thirty and one hundred sixty-five students, than at Silas Ridge, a comprehensive high school with nearly three times more teachers and a thousand students.

Change is an ongoing process, not something that is attended to once and forgotten. This was apparent in our school-based studies (chapters 2–7) and in our chapter on the role of the principal (chapter 11). Because schools are such complex organizations, it seems inevitable that change will be perceived negatively by some persons. In addition, resistance is likely to emerge merely from longstanding differences and distrust held by some faculty toward their administrators. Principals who remained in their position for an extended tenure were more likely to encourage and nurture change to the point at which commitment to reform among the faculty expanded. Indeed, at schools with no turnover in principal or Coalition coordinator, Coalition programs tended to sustain their efforts, as these persons were able to design, implement, and shape programs that reflected their goals and vision, as well as their faculties' conceptions of necessary change.[1] Specifically, these persons promoted change by encouraging involvement in the change process. In our case studies of schools that sustained their reform efforts (except Lewis), principals offered faculty multiple forums for discussing the many dimensions of change. Also a principal's extended tenure at a school allowed him or her to generate trust, to adjust school-based initiatives, and to garner the level of grassroots support necessary for change to endure and be refined.

Just as teachers can do little in the classroom without student support, so too principals are dependent on teachers' support and trust if reform efforts are to endure. These principals helped their faculty to become the ones who directed change on a regular, day-in and day-out basis, much as students who accepted innovations in their classrooms assumed greater responsibility for their learning.

More inclusive reform efforts deepened schools' commitment to change at our study sites, but we want to stress that the individual teacher and his or her classroom was a key unit of this change. The teachers we have described attributed personal and professional transformations to their work with CES ideas. They also mentioned benefits for their students and themselves that they felt derived from changed patterns of interactions that accompanied their efforts at personalizing students' educational experiences. Further, many teachers felt—at least initially—empowered by their participation in schoolwide decision making. We offered these glimpses of changed classrooms and emphasized the teacher's perspective because at some of our schools, and for most of the CES staff, this was the point of change—the intended focus of

1. In fact, of our three study schools designated as second-step exemplars of Coalition practice, two had the same principal and Coalition coordinator throughout our research. At the third—Lewis High—the principal was promoted to the central office for one year but was later reassigned to the school. Further, during his tenure at the central office, he maintained close contact with Lewis's Coalition program.

reform. The reality of political controversy, the difficulties of building consensus for change, and the inability of most study schools to alter their structural realities often impeded CES-based reforms. Nevertheless, even in those schools where few, if any, changes endured schoolwide, there were teachers and classrooms that implemented CES ideas.

Likewise, we included case studies of principals to shed more detailed light on phenomena mentioned in the earlier schoolwide case studies. Most significant, these cases reinforce our understanding of the central role principals played at all our schools effecting change. The two case studies in chapter 11 illuminated the difficulties that accompany inconsistency in reform advocacy. Further, they hint at a possible connection between leadership style and issues of school size, as well as the importance of honoring the starting points of all faculty who will be involved with or affected by change.

Personalization was often a source of inspiration for teachers and students in our study schools. The case studies in the first part of the book illustrated the role personalization could play in promoting and reinforcing change; the chapters in this section further demonstrated the effects this approach had on individuals and on school and classroom climates—effects most immediately and apparently noted in the schools with troubled backgrounds and histories. Students and teachers in these schools appreciated lower class sizes and felt able to innovate in the classroom and make closer connections as a result of smaller student-teacher ratios (although implementing such smaller class sizes across an entire school could be impeded by financial constraints).[2]

It is common to use the "school" as the unit by which to assess change—to determine whether change has been institutionalized—yet we found that the schoolwide perspective provided an important but limited view of what happened at our study schools. Although school structures and decision-making processes might change little, individual classrooms often changed markedly. (The opposite was also true.) Indeed, success at classroom-based change could be a powerful positive

---

2. Although we did not discuss this issue in detail, it is evident from the case studies that in each school fiscal issues, tied to these smaller class sizes, waxed and waned in visibility, if not in importance. Nevertheless, during our research period, class size and relations between students and teachers at the more troubled schools generally came to resemble those in traditional "good" schools.

outcome of a school's participation in the Coalition, regardless of the schoolwide outcome. A schoolwide perspective yielded one set of insights into educational reform, just as these case studies yielded another. To neglect either perspective limits one's understanding of the school change process.

IV

13

SOME FINAL THOUGHTS ON SCHOOL REFORM

In this book we have examined multiple dimensions of the school change process as a means to identify and understand influences that occur across different levels of the educational system and which thereby may be presumed to represent significant factors in the change process. Throughout our research we found that looking at reform from the individual classroom level produced a different interpretation of Coalition-related change and its effects than when we employed a more schoolwide perspective. At all our study schools, discussions about reform and efforts to implement change became part of the political life of the school, raised questions of belief and philosophy, and often produced controversy; but within individual classrooms, teachers and teams of teachers made changes that led to a more personalized and student-directed approach to education.

FINDINGS COMMON TO BOTH THE INDIVIDUAL AND THE SCHOOLWIDE CASE ANALYSES

Although Coalition reform efforts looked quite different when examined at the classroom and schoolwide levels, some of our findings were shared across both levels of analysis. We discuss these findings further because they are likely to be quite significant to most school change efforts.

1. The popular and academic views of American education are dominated by a rhetoric of change. Yet we found that whether change was necessary or desirable and whether individuals who questioned both the need for change and the specific nature of reforms could be compelled or persuaded to participate were almost always points of contention.

2. Reform rhetoric may stress pedagogical, curricular, and structural

priorities, but because all reform efforts involve shifts in power, prestige, and responsibility, they can have political consequences for all involved.[1] All change efforts we studied became embedded in the political life of schools and contributed to increased political contentiousness, within faculties and between teachers and administrators. Many of the political issues that emerged reflected concerns that arose from participants' cultural values and challenges to accepted practices, as discussed later in this chapter.

Political tensions emerged not only among the professional staff; comparable tensions were apparent in student-teacher classroom interactions. In general, teachers found that personalizing students' education complemented their efforts to promote active learning and that students were generally receptive to such innovations. In some instances, however, students for whom certain changes represented radical departures from previous experiences were often ill prepared for—and at times resistant to—what Coalition teachers envisioned. The political life of these classrooms could then become hostile; expectations of student work became a matter of continual negotiation. Furthermore, in the same way that political conflict at the school level could drain the enthusiasm and energy of pro-change teachers and administrators, political disputes in the classroom could diminish a teacher's willingness to experiment with change and thereby undermine efforts at school reform.

3. Our study schools with troubled histories differed in what they attempted as part of their Coalition reforms from those with reputations as successful or good schools. Most schools with poorer reputations lowered their student-teacher ratios; required more writing, research, and active learning; and increased graduation requirements—in effect, the schools became more like traditional college preparatory programs. At the schools with reputations for excellence, Coalition membership served as an impetus for faculties to reassess the existing philosophy and practice, but not necessarily to change them.

4. Success proved to be a relative phenomenon across our research sites. Schools with higher dropout rates, poor attendance, and few graduates pursuing higher education could achieve some measure of success

1. In particular, and as we saw in several cases, attempts at reform may also revive latent hostilities within schools, further intensifying the political nature of school change at the site by tying it to earlier controversies.

by improving performance in these areas, but at schools where these factors were not a concern, what constituted "success" was often a contentious issue.

5. The more inclusive the Coalition reform effort—that is, the more levels in the educational system, participants in that system, and school programs that were brought together—the more likely it has been to endure. Although individual teachers made substantive changes in pedagogy, curriculum, and assessment, these efforts by themselves rarely provoked change beyond one or two classrooms. Only when the principal was an active and ongoing participant in directing and negotiating school reform were the experiments of individual teachers incorporated into schoolwide change. Of course, the question of cause and effect is at issue here because those more inclusive efforts incorporated more of the school and the local educational system as means by which to deepen and secure their work. This finding suggests that if reform efforts are to endure, the traditional divisions and the associated mistrust between administrators and teachers will need to be addressed, since it is clear that these persons will need to work together to effect lasting and institutionwide change, particularly given the increasing emphasis on teacher empowerment (at least rhetorically) as one means to advance school reform.

6. In a related development, all of our study site schools experienced some similar problems during their change efforts, but creating school-within-a-school programs generated additional tensions. In particular, "us versus them" divisions—often resulting from philosophical differences about schooling—were embodied in the institutional structure and heightened as the alternative program bumped up against the larger school structure within which it was embedded.

7. Time for planning and reflecting on change was in short supply and great demand in virtually all our study sites. In school after school, a lack of time consistently created impediments to developing and sustaining individual and schoolwide change. Moreover, this lack of time combined with the continual controversy that surrounded many reform programs and the increased workloads and new expectations teachers faced gradually led to the disillusionment of many reform proponents and to a return to some aspects of previous (pre-reform) practice. In most of our study sites, some who supported school change came to view their reform work as unrealistic and its goals as admirable but, for

various reasons, unattainable. Although experimenting at the classroom level generally increased teachers' commitment to Coalition philosophy and school change in general, it also increased teacher workloads. This increase, coupled with the disillusionment many experienced when political controversies erupted, led some participating teachers to return to previous teaching practices or otherwise to disengage from Coalition reform work. In many cases, this was a marked change in the stance of reform proponents who had earlier viewed themselves as revitalized or transformed by participating in reform-related activities.

8. Regardless of a school's previous reputation, the form chosen for implementing CES ideas, and the tensions that emerged, faculty and administrators often felt that, as a consequence of their school's involvement with Coalition-related reform, there was a greater acknowledgment of the value of professional self-reflection, both for individual classroom teachers and for the school as a whole. Many said that their personal as well as their schools' values, beliefs, and mission(s) were clarified through deliberations associated with the school reform process, regardless of the eventual outcome of their schools' reform efforts.

9. Whether to deepen existing efforts or broaden participation in reform work was a tension that existed throughout the various levels of the reform effort—in the Coalition central staff's planning, in individual schools' decisions whether to expand SWAS programs or deepen the work of the already participating teachers, and so forth. When depth and breadth were perceived as alternatives, breadth was consistently the chosen strategy: more member schools, another grade added to a SWAS program, another level of support staff for CES reforms, another interdisciplinary unit added to the curriculum. On the one hand, this emphasis on breadth over depth resulted in steady growth of program size and membership at both the school sites and for the Coalition as a whole. On the other hand, constantly expanding program size and continually striving to do more in the classroom contributed to the sense of overload and the desire for more preparation that teachers consistently noted.

The findings discussed above were common to both individual and schoolwide analyses, but we want to emphasize that overall quite different understandings about the nature of school reform emerged from looking at change from either one or the other perspective. Structural changes implemented at some of our study schools, for instance, could obscure the fact that there were few coincident changes in classroom practices. At some schools, teachers were teamed and shared the same students, there was time for collective planning, and the class periods were longer. Yet, classrooms in these schools might look little different from those described by Sizer in *Horace's Compromise*. The school structure may have changed, but the substance of classroom life could remain much as it had been.

In contrast, our focus on the efforts of a few teachers in other schools who had reorganized their curricula, pedagogy, and assessment techniques might suggest that Coalition philosophy had taken root throughout the school. Within the larger institution, however, there might be few concomitant developments—course offerings and schedules could remain the same, there may have been no professional development to support change, and there may even have been no facultywide consensus on the need or desirability of change.[2] In sum, an incomplete picture emerged at our sites if only one view of reform was examined. Therefore, to understand the nature and degree of change experienced in restructuring schools more thoroughly, the effects of structural, institutionwide changes as well as changes in individual classroom practices should be examined.

POLITICS AND SCHOOL REFORM

Americans assert that their schools are fundamentally educational institutions; yet political factors play prominent roles in what occurs within them on a day-to-day basis. This somewhat unpleasant and often overlooked reality takes on additional significance for schools involved with reform because differences of opinion, philosophy, and pedagogy typically left undisturbed or taken for granted are often stirred up through the change process. This also suggests to us that if change is to take root, those involved must confront the political dimensions of change. As we found, the initial apolitical stance of reform advocates (for example, focusing on classroom-centered change) left many unprepared for political disruptions that arose, tensions which in some instances over-

2. Further, as Cohen (1991b) maintained, self-assessments of reform implementation can overstate the degree of change.

whelmed the pedagogical, curricular, and structural aspects of change. Moreover, as the philosophical and political became entwined, these issues became divisive and dismaying for many Coalition proponents, and they were ultimately draining on the school's restructuring effort. Participants in schools considering change may want to consider such issues as how their resources (including time) are (or are likely to be) redistributed as a consequence of reform initiatives, how participants and nonparticipants are being publicly portrayed, how decisions are being made, and so on. Although the particulars will vary according to local contexts, ignoring the political context of a school and denying its potential role as an impediment to change may lead reform advocates to approach a formidable challenge with unwarranted optimism and naivete.

Given the pervasiveness of political concerns in school reform efforts, we offer an additional finding: at our study sites, it was difficult for school personnel to distance themselves from the effects of the changes and from the ensuing political tensions. In school after school we noted an embeddedness in one's own perceptions and a concomitant difficulty in taking the perspective of the other (Schutz 1967). This was most apparent during disagreements or misunderstandings regarding school change or Coalition membership. Because change and the desire for change are not value-neutral, the effects of this tendency could be seen the moment schools began discussing Coalition-based reform. Efforts to effect change simultaneously created a sense that there were winners and losers among the faculty, that some would benefit from change while others were disadvantaged. Further, being an advocate for school reform seemed to preclude neutrality: advocates were vested in viewing change as improvement and were generally perceived as judgmental by those not directly involved with reform. Local adherents of Coalition ideas may have considered themselves open-minded about teaching or specific plans for change, but they were rarely viewed that way by those less interested in change. The tensions generated by these perceptions within faculties were often intensified by a closely related development: advocating change was perceived as implicitly critical of the status quo and created perceptions of judgmental dissatisfaction, regardless of intention. As one teacher remarked, "To a degree, 'we can do better' was the statement. But I think the message that people seemed to get was,

'What you're doing is all wrong'. It was a negative message rather than a positive message, and it really put people on the defensive."

The tendency of faculties to view change and its effects judgmentally seems connected to three developments that arose at most of our research sites. First, most schools did not establish a working consensus about the need for change before implementing a Coalition program. Whether change was necessary or desirable was therefore continually contested. Second, although Coalition proponents experienced some positive aspects of change, faculty who were not directly involved often experienced negative (from their perspective) consequences. Finally, the tensions raised by political divisiveness tended to restrict communication between Coalition advocates and opponents. Consequently, there were few common understandings regarding program goals and developments since such topics were seldom the object of joint reflection or problem solving.

Yet it would seem that awareness and careful monitoring of people's perceptions about change represent important elements of the process. Unless faculty members and administrators establish a working consensus about the need for change, the goals of their reform efforts, the specific forms that change will take, and how they will work to realize this shared vision, individuals tend to become vested in their own views of their school's reform effort and change in general. When the taken-for-granted was under examination and some portion of the faculty was not embracing, encouraging, or participating in the discussion, these people often felt threatened professionally and acted somewhat in concert to resist aspects of the reform agenda.

Looking at the experiences of our study schools, then, it would seem critical that schools seek informed and supportive outside perspectives while developing, implementing, and assessing any efforts at change. Outsiders may perform an important role by helping school personnel gain some distance on their reform efforts. Because they are not formally associated with any particular domain of school life, outsiders may be able to see, and to clarify for others, the multiple perspectives that are informing (and perhaps impeding) discussions about and efforts at reform. To the extent an outsider understands existing political divisions and the perspectives common to various factions within schools and is respectful of all parties, he or she can help promote understanding and possibly engender greater trust, two vital elements for any school attempting change. It is worth noting that the three second-step schools in our study made extensive use of CES central staff throughout our research.

EDUCATIONAL REFORM, THEN AND NOW

A flurry of reports criticizing the American public school system and students' academic performance were published in the early 1980s, the most well known of which was *A Nation at Risk*.[3] These reports, many produced by blue-ribbon panels, stressed that American high school graduates were ill prepared for either higher education or the world of work, that America was becoming increasingly unable to compete internationally as a result of flawed schools, and that worse social ills would follow if the "rising tide of mediocrity" (National Commission on Excellence in Education 1983: 1) were not addressed. Later in the decade these attacks on American public education expanded to include the impersonal atmosphere of the schools, the lack of standards and low standardized test scores by American students, and the deplorable working conditions as well as the teachers' lack of professional preparation.

The initial response by state legislatures and school boards was to include more top-down, bureaucratic mandates—assuming, as Edward Fiske wrote, that what was needed was "more of the same: more core academic courses, more standardized tests, a longer school year, more money for teachers" (1991: 25). By the late 1980s, reformers began to assert that local autonomy, greater responsibility, and more authority might make reform efforts more palatable to educators and more effective overall (Steffens 1990: 1).

By the early 1990s the rhetoric had again shifted. Headlines in newspapers and magazines summed up ten years of responses to this call for reform and proclaimed a general sense of disappointment: "Results Below Expectations," "Report Raps American Education," "10 Years Later, Many Educators See Little Progress."[4] To explain the apparent

3. Other reports were issued by such groups as the Twentieth Century Fund Task Force on Federal Elementary and Secondary Education Policy (1983), and the Task Force on Education for Economic Growth (1983).

4. Henry (1993); Business Wire Features (1993); Zook (1993).

lack of effective reform, reporters and educators proposed myriad cul-
prits: a lack of funding,[5] inadequate and ineffective schools of education,[6] the entrenched bureaucracy, and, of course, teachers[7]—as well as
a critical lack of support for teachers.[8] The reform rhetoric on the tenth
anniversary of the publication of *A Nation at Risk* did not celebrate ten
years of accomplishment. Rather, as one article concluded, "Ten years
later, the nation is still at risk, still looking for answers."[9]

While it is convenient to use the most recent waves of school reform
efforts as the context for understanding CES reform efforts, they provide
a limited perspective for one important reason: reform and "tinkering"
(Tyack 1990) have been an almost constant feature of the American
educational system for over one hundred years. Throughout these ongoing efforts to change various aspects of the educational system, numerous studies have been done to try to understand what transpired and
why.[10] It is well beyond the scope of this book to compare our findings
to this massive literature on school change.[11] However, we offer a qualified comparison of our findings with those of an evaluation conducted
over twenty years ago on another reform initiative: the Ford Foundation's study of its effectiveness in educational giving conducted by an
independent evaluation team, the results of which are summarized in a
report entitled "A Foundation Goes to School" (Ford Foundation
1972).

5. Kantorwitz, for example, wrote: "Sadly, despite all the talk of reform, real
change has been remarkably slow. Money—the lack of it—has been the biggest
obstacle" (1993: 46).

6. Zook, a professor of education, wrote, "The most serious source of the whole
mess is in the schools of education" (1993: A24).

7. As reported by Business Wire Features, "Many dedicated teachers work long
and hard ... but most lack the training needed to help their students learn to
analytically read, write, and think critically" (1993: B20).

8. Kantorwitz reported, "There's been a critical lack of support for teachers"
(1993: 47).

9. Ibid.

10. See, e.g., Cuban (1990), Fullan and Miles (1992), Kirst and Meister (1985),
James and Tyack (1983), Newmann (1993), Orlich (1989), and Tyack (1990).

11. Gibboney (1994) is an interesting example of this type of comprehensive
assessment of reform efforts. It is, though, only the most recent of these efforts, which
include the volumes that emerged from the Eight-Year Study and several impressive
histories of American education. (See, e.g., Aikin [1942], Chamberlin et al. [1942],
Cremin [1964, 1965], Giles et al. [1942], Perkinson [1968], Ravitch [1983], Smith et
al. [1942], and Tyack [1974].)

In certain respects these two reform initiatives are quite different. The Ford Foundation limited its involvement to twenty-five projects and made specific requirements of them. The Coalition made few requirements of individual schools and adopted a membership policy that led to rapid growth. Also, Ford Foundation funds were given directly to school districts, state education agencies, or cooperating universities; funds raised by the Coalition have usually been administered by the central office. These differences noted, the reforms shared similar goals. The following excerpt from the Ford Foundation report, which outlined the goals of the Comprehensive School Improvement Program, reflects many of the reform ideals promoted by the Coalition's central staff and Ted Sizer:

> to break down the isolation of the self-contained classroom, to facilitate professional interaction . . . [to] change . . . the nature and structure of the curriculum . . . [to incorporate] the use of technology, [to reconsider] the habitual one teacher/one classroom-for-55-minutes format, to rearrange learning spaces within traditional school buildings and to alter uses of conventional school facilities. . . . Despite the multiplicity of program objectives, the Comprehensive School Improvement Program was first and foremost a teacher-development effort. In all the projects, the teacher was seen as the key to school improvement. The teacher's skill and attitude were identified as the central factors in moving a school beyond the status quo (18–25).[12]

In addition, the findings of the Ford Foundation's independent evaluation team parallel many findings from our ethnographic research. First and foremost, the evaluation team discovered that four years after the implementations were in place, "In many instances, innovations that had been implemented were no longer in use" (5). This team also found that the foundation's projects often created a "significant context for professional growth" (20); that significant conflicts often resulted from

---

12. The two efforts shared another key feature: tens of millions of dollars were invested in each. The Ford Foundation invested more than $30 million in its reform effort during the 1960s, and a number of funding organizations and businesses have invested well over $30 million in the Coalition since its inception. Further, in December 1994 the Annenberg Foundation awarded the Coalition of Essential Schools $50 million to support its efforts at school reform.

"innovations in scheduling [which] tended to affect all or nearly all staff members" (23); and that "innovations in staff utilization clearly emerge[d] as the most successful and most permanent [changes], since changes in teacher behavior and attitude could be effected within a school or inside a few classrooms with a minimum of disruption, and often without the community's full awareness" (25). Expectations that newly developed curriculum materials would become a permanent part of individual teachers' classroom activities were met only when they were accompanied by "systematic teacher training" (25).

The study also described reactions to reform that were remarkably similar to what we found among our traditionally successful schools: "Innovations relating to the use of time (such as flexible scheduling) and to student groupings have also disappeared from several of the projects. These, too, demand different teaching behavior, and they impinge more directly than other changes on intra- and extra-school relations. Modular schedules and independent study, for example, create an atmosphere that challenges the notions of order, discipline, and learning traditionally associated with schools. As students of any age are given more freedom to talk, to move, and to decide where, when, how, and what to study, parents, community, and even teachers become apprehensive that the culture is being eroded" (25).

Two other findings paralleled conclusions that we drew from our research. One is the importance of continuity in leadership. As the report concluded: "Projects that were most effective in the short run and after outside assistance ended were those whose directors were present at the planning and remained through the implementation, evaluation, and adaptation phases. The leadership of capable directors and the continuity they provided appear in retrospect to be at least as important as organizational or policy structures, experimental models, the organization's original commitment, or the depth and length of funding" (42). The second finding concerned the complexity of school structure and was summarized as follows: "Not surprisingly, the less complex the school system's structure, the more easily innovations were introduced and accepted initially. Small schools changed faster than large ones . . . [a development] often attributable to the efforts and convictions of a single dynamic leader" (43).

The significance of the similarity in findings between these two reform efforts would seem to be that the opportunities, impediments, and processes we saw in our case studies have both specific and generic relevance.[13] Our findings also reveal that research on educational reform often rediscovers the wheel, finding out what has already been learned in previous studies. This may reinforce one's faith in the validity and reliability of those research findings, but it raises a critical question: Don't new reforms build on findings from those previously undertaken?[14] The Coalition central staff, including Ted Sizer, maintain that they have examined and used the literature on educational change to help guide their work. We suggest that many of the problems and issues that arose during the study schools' reform efforts may be inherent to school change processes. But we also maintain that a tendency to emphasize the current conditions facing schools and new approaches to educational change can be understood more fully by locating school reform in the larger context of American culture, a culture that emphasizes success and avoids failure (including discussions of failure).

AMERICAN VALUES AND EDUCATIONAL REFORM: A CULTURAL PERSPECTIVE

American culture had a multidimensional influence on the school change process: it contributed to constraining what schools undertook; it created expectations for what change would entail and how difficult or easily it would be realized; it colored how people perceived these efforts; and it provided a language for debating the merits and drawbacks of educational reform. For example, much of what the Coalition of Essential Schools proposes—in terms of philosophy and practice—as well as the factors that appear to enhance the likelihood of change taking root, run counter to many institutional values and accepted prac-

13. Some Ford Foundation findings differed from our findings, most particularly those suggesting that medium-sized suburban districts could implement changes more quickly and with longer lasting effects than other districts. More research would be needed to understand these differences, but we suspect they might be tied to how funding was allocated in the two projects and to the differences in emphasis at the start of the project. The early Ford Foundation project schools were considered "lighthouse" schools, exemplars in their districts. The thrust of CES reform was viewed (by many) as saying, "No matter how good you are, we think you are deficient in several important regards."

14. Seymour Sarason (1982, 1990, 1993) has discussed this question in his substantial body of work on educational change.

tices in American education and society. Consider the oft-repeated Coalition goal: to help students learn to use their minds well. This is
ostensibly a reasonable and valued goal for American high schools, but
in practice, making an "intellectual focus" (common principle no. 1) a
school's top priority has proven difficult. Although some faculty welcomed it, others (such as elective teachers and coaches) felt marginalized
by this philosophical tenet and so resisted aspects of reform efforts. At
some schools there was also a cultural disjuncture between this goal and
community expectations. When the central staff suggested that member
schools cut athletic budgets as a means to free up funds for reform
efforts, one principal remarked, "If my school board read this, we'd be
out of the Coalition in a minute. Haven't they [the central staff] read
Anti-Intellectualism in America? That's what the community wants."
An anti-intellectual (read "pragmatic") attitude also constrained reform implementation when faculty suggested that academics were all
well and good, but that students needed jobs. As an elective teacher at
one study school stated: "My fear is that if we go completely [to the]
Essential School program, our students are not going to be prepared for
the world of work. And if you look at our community, you look at our
students, you can see where the need is. . . . Every student is not college
material." Marketable skills versus academics was most often a debate
in the historically troubled schools, but it also occurred in schools where
multiple program offerings existed to meet the needs of less academically inclined students.

Community values and associated expectations could also restrict
the nature and degree of change. Although a relative lack of organizational complexity made it easier for some schools to enact reform, this
conception of the American high school is antithetical to society's expectations: schools are far more likely to promote individual choice
through creating programs tailored to the unique needs of different
students than they are to adopt a simpler structure and a more limited
institutional focus. In fact, many of our study schools had reputations
for excellence precisely because of the array of courses and programs
they offered. Their reputations created expectations among students,
faculty, and parents that made it difficult for them to embrace schoolwide reforms because the reforms were seen as limiting student choice
and as promoting equality of experience but not opportunity.

Further, even factors that were critical to spreading reform could be undermined because they challenged existing practices and ran counter to current manifestations of American values in those settings. For example, including multiple actors in the change process broadened participation and helped create a sense of common purpose and vision about the nature of (and need for) change, but accomplishing this concerted action was difficult. Collaborative decision making between faculty and administrators is not common to American schools. The professional responsibilities of teachers and administrators are quite different. Typically, administrators mandate and teachers are expected to carry out those decisions. Communication between the two groups tends to be infrequent. Such relationships seldom engender trust. Somewhat predictably then, at our study schools teachers often questioned their principals' motives for embracing reforms. Some felt that their principals had pre-set agendas they wanted to foist on the school. Others saw administrators as résumé builders, joining the Coalition only to enhance their professional marketability. Principals commonly viewed some faculty members with a similar skepticism, seeing them as endorsing only those reforms that they expected would make their lives easier. It was difficult for teachers and administrators to work together effectively when trust was so often an issue.

Cultural values also influenced how people perceived reform. At the outset of their reform efforts, Coalition proponents were often idealistic and somewhat naive. Many reform advocates, both teachers and administrators, assumed that successful change could be realized by working harder, by adding additional responsibilities to their existing work loads. This attitude toward school reform fit neatly with school systems' traditional commitment to reform and professional development: they had little money to support such efforts but welcomed teachers who were willing to accept additional responsibilities. Over time, however, the enthusiasm of Coalition proponents often waned; and those who were initially skeptical about the need for reform were unlikely to change their minds when the benefits of doing so seemed uncertain and the drawbacks readily apparent.

People's interpretations of American values, too, could serve as touchstones for debate about both the goals and effects of school reform, thereby contributing to political and social contentiousness at the study schools. Issues of freedom, individual choice, and autonomy—

values integral to debates about American identity—framed faculty debates at our study sites. For example, teachers asked if adopting Coalition reforms would free teachers to work in more engaging and effective ways or constrain them to using only pieces of their existing repertoire of pedagogical techniques. The same tension surfaced regularly when faculties discussed the relative merits of adopting a core curriculum as opposed to offering students an array of electives. Those who supported having a rich selection of electives claimed that such course offerings would free students to explore and create their individual paths through the school's curriculum, rather than constraining them to the limited options of a core curriculum. Drawing on the same beliefs, proponents of a core curriculum maintained that their curriculum would free students to explore topics of personal interest in more detail through student-as-worker approaches to learning where they had been limited by traditional curricula. Cultural values then did not simply impose limits or create impediments to reform; they were used to construct and communicate expressions of pro- and anti-reform sentiment.

The prominent role played by the concept of success and the desire to appear successful in so many domains of the reform movement is a particularly revealing illustration of just how embedded educational reform processes are in American culture. Then-Secretary of Education Lamar Alexander exemplified this concern when, in outlining the need for educational reform, he remarked, "This is the nation that likes to be first. This is the country that grew up reading *The Little Engine That Could*" (Klein 1991: 5). For various reasons, not the least of which is their continued existence, Coalition programs and the reform movement as a whole have sought to be visibly successful. Although successes have been important for establishing the Coalition's credibility with teachers, administrators, funders, parents, and students, determining what constituted success and highlighting alleged successes of Coalition programs often led to increased difficulties in many areas of school life.

One fundamental difficulty revolved around the question of whether Coalition schools and programs had been successful. This issue proved contentious, in part, because as a society, Americans are not clear about what they want from secondary schools. Some maintain that high schools should create responsible citizens, socializing students for a democratic society; others see school as a place to prepare students for occupations later in life; still others, such as CES, maintain that schools should be first and foremost sites of academic learning. These philosophical divisions are reflected in the different types of high schools (for example, vocational, comprehensive, and college preparatory) and in the many divisions and tracks within them. Within schools, then, various persons see the goals of schooling in different terms, each of which may produce its own measures of success. Introducing change is likely to accentuate these differences. Determining what constituted success at changing schools, then, highlighted the political contentiousness at most of our study sites and—except for such traditional indicators as improved dropout and attendance rates—success remained an unresolved piece of individual schools' change issues.

The criteria of success were not the only contested issues; problems could arise when programs succeeded in certain domains. For instance, when Coalition programs expanded and came to influence more and more of school life, resistance could intensify. Coalition proponents welcomed program expansion, but those skeptical of or opposed to reform sometimes reacted by strengthening their resistance. Moreover, when the alleged successes of Coalition teachers were publicly touted (often in local newspaper articles that discussed a "new and innovative" educational program), other faculty who felt that they had taught well for years without formal recognition often became alienated, in part because they sensed an implicit criticism of their teaching, a reaction that often distanced them from the reform effort.

This concern with success presents those who would attempt to reform American schools with a difficult dilemma. To attract financial support and members (either schools or individuals), a reform movement must assert an understanding of existing problems as well as an ability to address them. An apparent optimism can create unrealistic expectations about what change will entail and how quickly it will occur—in a society that is often optimistic, idealistic, and rather impatient. Mistakes are not easily tolerated. Yet to serve students better, any change effort must determine what works and what doesn't. And discovering what does not work is seldom satisfying. In American culture, failure is something to be avoided, not studied. The history of educational reform reflects this tendency: when reform ideals have not been fully realized, the efforts have lost both momentum and credibility.[15] Rather than evaluate the obstacles these efforts faced, the tendency has been to move on to a new, more pressing interest.

Similar tendencies have been present in the media coverage that marked the tenth anniversary of the publication of *A Nation at Risk.* The following excerpt from a newspaper article illustrates the importance of success in portraying America's school reform efforts:

Educational Reforms Do Too Little Too Slowly

> Ten years after a landmark federal report rallied the nation around attempts to reform schools, the United States remains "at risk" of losing its competitive edge to countries with superior educational systems, leading educators say.
>
> Authors of the widely publicized 1983 report, *A Nation at Risk,* said . . . that although some progress has been made in strengthening graduation requirements, improving curriculum and increasing the pay and quality of teachers, the United States continues to lag far behind the goals identified in the report. . . . "Our results have been disappointing," said Terrel Bell, former secretary of education. "I can't say we've had a dismal failure, but we're a long, long way from what many of us thought we'd have" (Kleffman 1993).[16]

This quote embodies many aspects of American culture and parallels how school reform has been approached historically. It draws on a sense

15. In contrast, Seymour Sarason (1990) has observed that the field of medicine has made a "virtue of its ignorance." The medical community is expected to learn from the dead ends and temporary setbacks, not to ignore them. Another contrast is the Federal Aviation Administration's extensive study of airplane crashes (Stringfield and Teddlie 1991: esp. 375). Those authors argue that American educational reform efforts should be subjected to the same intense study. We agree. Historically, however, reaction to perceived disappointments in educational reform has been to abandon and ignore them (see Cuban 1990 in particular).

16. Here we are drawing on the presentation of this issue by the popular press, which has tended to portray the present situation as a disappointment. Within the education community, there are a wide range of opinions as to the success of America's response to *A Nation at Risk.* Nonetheless, we feel that it is revealing that so many newspaper stories (and often headlines) stress this rather pessimistic opinion.

of competition—the United States competing with other countries to establish their educational prominence. The article also threatens failure, the counterpoint to success. It proclaims the effort a disappointment, in great part because ten years have passed since the movement was initiated. According to American time frames, reform should have taken root by now. And, as in the past, educators in the the United States seem poised to declare the most recent reform initiatives a disappointment and to move on to other interests.

Just as American values are present in the schools, so too are they found in efforts to remake schools and in media reports about these reforms.[17] Our view of how these values structure and are structured in discussions of educational change is suggestive but not exhaustive. But when we try to understand why school reform efforts adopted particular forms and had the outcomes that they did, we should consider how the participants' taken-for-granted cultural values and beliefs served as lenses through which the change effort was envisioned, implemented, and assessed.

In this book we have used ethnographic descriptions at several levels of analysis to identify and understand influences that occur throughout school change efforts, across different levels of the educational system, and in very different contexts. As one would expect, academic concerns were central to school reform. Change and even attempted change can have multiple effects throughout schools, but political concerns also had a significant influence on the school reform efforts we observed. Moreover, the political dimensions were often intertwined with the cultural. Common American values figured prominently in these change efforts, particularly when various participants held different interpretations of these values.

Educational change of the scope and nature presently being undertaken nationwide and by such organizations as the Coalition of Essen-

17. This should not be a surprise, since arguably reform itself—in a variety of guises—is considered a pervasive theme or value in American life. The drive to better oneself (manifested at the individual level in the Horatio Alger story or in the children's book *The Little Engine That Could* and at the societal level in our belief in progress, improvement, and the concept of the "betterment" of society) is a pervasive theme in American life. See, e.g., Lasch's recent work, *The True and Only Heaven: Progress and Its Critics.*

tial Schools has little historical precedent. Many lessons—some of them painful—about how to effect meaningful change still need to be learned.[18] In addition, much of what has been learned about school reform efforts has been disappointing and occasionally painful. Yet as a society that esteems success we find it difficult to tolerate mediocrity or, even worse, failure. Historically, reaction to disappointing efforts at educational reform has been to abandon and ignore them, thereby neglecting the insights they offer as well as generating cycles of reform that are consistently stalled by many of the same problems. We hope that our efforts to document and interpret the processes and outcomes at our eight study sites will clarify and deepen the education community's understanding of the change process and help reformers and educators create a more satisfying and effective educational system. There are no quick fixes or miracle panaceas for American education. We urge ongoing and future reform efforts to study closely and learn from the experiences of these Coalition schools—including those some might consider disappointments—rather than simply dismissing them on the way to catching the next wave of educational change.

18. See, e.g., work by Wehlage, Smith, and Lipman (1992) and Firestone, Fuhrman, and Kirst (1989).

METHODOLOGICAL REFLECTIONS

Rather than citing the specific techniques we employed to collect and analyze data, we have chosen to discuss our perspectives about what ethnography is and how we approached the conceptualization and conduct of our work in this methodological chapter. In one sense, then, this chapter is another level of contextualization for the ethnography that precedes it. But it also emphasizes pieces of the work we did—data collection, analysis, and writing—and how we got funding for the research that will be of interest to other researchers and, we hope, to those people who asked us (often and with vague expressions of confusion) what ethnography is and why anthropologists were studying schools.

A HOLISTIC VIEW OF ETHNOGRAPHY

Ethnography, literally the writing (graphy) about groups of people (ethnos), is a form of qualitative research commonly undertaken by anthropologists. In our view, this type of qualitative research is more than simply a set of techniques for collecting data, it is an approach to research design, data collection, analysis, and interpretation. Doing ethnography generally entails: using ethnographic methods to collect data (not just relying on interviews but drawing on observational data and cultural artifacts, for instance); a *long-term commitment* to your research focus; adopting the stances of *cultural relativism, taking the native's perspective,* and *holism* in the collection and analysis of data. (See chapter 1 for a more in-depth discussion of these features of ethnographic research.) It also involves incorporating a "model of cultural process in both the gathering and interpretation of data" (Spindler and Spindler 1987a: 151). We follow the Spindlers in conceiving of culture (cultural process) as: "a continuing dialogue that revolves around pivotal areas of concern in a given community. The dialogue is produced as social actors apply their acquired cultural knowledge so that it works in social situations—they make sense. . . . Neither the knowledge nor the situations replicate themselves through time, but both exhibit continuity. The dialogue occurs at several levels simultaneously—from the most explicit and obvious to the tacit and sometimes very hidden" (153).

Within qualitative research, including to some extent within ethnography, there are two distinct perspectives about how to do and make sense of research. These perspectives—the *quantitative tradition* and the *interpretive tradition*—reflect a larger philosophical tension about how we "know" something. As John Smith and Lous Heshusius describe the differences between the traditions:

> The quantitative tradition, with its realist orientation, was based on the idea of an independently existing social reality that could be described as it really was. Truth was defined as a correspondence between our words and that independently existing reality. Common to this perspective, which allowed that facts were separate from values, was what Hilary Putnam (1981) calls a "God's Eye" point of view. The interpretive tradition, based on an idealist temperament, took the position that social reality was mind-dependent in the sense of mind-constructed. Truth was ultimately a matter of socially and historically conditioned agreement. Social inquiry could not be value-free, and there could not be a "God's Eye" point of view—there could only be various people's points of view based on their particular interests, values, and purposes. (1986: 5)

The manifestation of the first of these perspectives comes through rigorous and systematic data collection, with an emphasis on constructs like validity and reliability—concepts that have embedded within them a belief in a realist view of truth. An example of the latter perspective is the hermeneutic process, based on an understanding that there is no definite beginning or end points to the interpretative process and that, according to Smith and Heshusius, the methodological procedures one uses "are related to the context of a particular inquiry and what it makes sense to do in that particular context" (9) not to a concern for rigor per se.

Our approach to ethnographic research was a particularly open-ended one, allowing themes and emphases to emerge from the observations and the data, rather than specifying from the start the relationships under study and the expected outcomes. We began our work with several framing questions. Throughout our research, we reexamined the appropriateness of these questions and considered incorporating others into the design. In sum, our research, as with most ethnography grounded in anthropology, was more interpretive than quantitative in nature. This may be most evident in the presentation of our case studies, which are written to emphasize the key points as they emerged in the sites, not as they might have been if strict comparative analysis had been our goal.[1]

Paul Rabinow's reflections on the nature of data are particularly relevant to our research:

> We can pretend that we are neutral scientists collecting unambiguous data and that the people we are studying are living amid various unconscious systems of determining forces of which they have no clue and to which only they have the key. But it is only pretense. . . .
>
> The "facts" of anthropology, the material which the anthropologist has gone to the field to find, are already themselves interpretations. The baseline data is already culturally mediated by the people whose culture we, as anthropologists, have come to explore. Facts are made—the word comes from the Latin *factum,* "made"—and the facts we interpret are made and remade. (1977: 152, 150)

Ethnographic research seeks to understand its object of study through immersion in the life of the object—be it a culture, a family, or an educational reform project. A long-term time commitment is a hallmark of ethnographic research, yet at the same time there is an explicit awareness that one's data are but *samplings* of the universe of activities, impressions, and material culture of the object of study, not the universe itself. Given this, it is important to collect data that represent various

---

1. We acknowledge, though, that we moved cautiously between the two perspectives (interpretive and quantitative), recognizing that this approach also has its limits. For one view on the dangers of combining approaches, see Smith and Heshusius, 1986.

perspectives concerning an issue, various categories that have meaning for participants, and various occurrences that take place during the research period. A further goal is not to privilege one group or perspective in the data collection process, through one's analytic approach, or in the written descriptions. Because the object of study is rarely as neatly bounded as one would like, what constitutes "representativeness" and "privileging" is always an issue in this type of research, one that is never totally resolved but is worked out partially—largely through the negotiation of the content of the final products of the study.

Through the construction of narratives and the process of sharing them with the people involved in the study, ethnographic researchers can attain some degree of comfort that the world they create on paper is at least partially recognizable to the people who participate in it. Rarely, however, do one's informants suggest that "you've got it just right." More likely, people will see themselves in the product but still question many analyses.[2] In this work, the process of sharing and reflecting on drafts of our chapters has clarified and sharpened our cases (and in some instances, our school-based collaborators' understandings about the change processes at their schools).

FUNDING THE RESEARCH

As the Coalition began to create its network of schools, the central staff became interested in creating a detailed record of its work, both to learn from what happened and to help schools plan for and effect change.

---

2. They may see things they are uncertain about or have strong reactions to (positive or negative) in the written products. This stance is consistent with a worldview in which the emphasis on all members of a society or culture having to share cultural understandings, meanings, and knowledge is incomplete. Certainly "nonsharing" is a component of our lives: no one has complete knowledge about the worlds he or she lives in. We follow A. F. C. Wallace (1961) on this point. Respectful attention to places or interpretations that participants in the system view as too far out is another goal of most serious ethnographic inquiry (and incidentally a reason why people with a strong theoretical predilection rarely produce "good" ethnography—though their work may in fact be admirable and valid from different contextual standpoints). This attention to one's informants' reactions to ethnographic narratives is more prominent in some fields, such as educational anthropology, than others, such as, for instance, symbolic anthropology.

Conversations between the Coalition and us began in 1986, and by the end of summer, we had submitted a proposal for a longitudinal research project to the central staff. During the preparation of the proposal and for much of the first year of research (1986–87), the Coalition provided seed money for our work. At the same time, conversations were initiated with the Exxon Education Foundation, which also saw value in this endeavor. In 1987, Exxon awarded the Coalition a grant to support one year of our ethnographic research. The following year, as part of a sizable multiyear grant to the Coalition, the Exxon Education Foundation agreed to fund three more years of our research. The foundation continued its generous support with two grants during the data analysis and writing phases of this work.

Because we intended to study the reform effort from the perspective of both school personnel and the university-based central staff, it was essential for our work to be independent of the central staff. With the agreement of both the Coalition and Exxon, we established ourselves as a separate entity formed to study the Coalition. A statement of our rights and responsibilities as researchers studying the Coalition central staff and its member schools was prepared and shared with the central staff; the Principals' and Coordinators' Council; an advisory board to the Coalition composed of researchers, policy makers, and practitioners; and relevant persons in the participating school sites (the principal, faculty, and, if necessary, the board of education or the board of trustees [in the case of the private school]). This statement was revised a number of times before the conditions of our research were totally agreed upon.

We recognize that the Coalition's endorsement of our proposed research and help in finding financial support were key factors in our obtaining the resources and access necessary to do the ethnographic study. Throughout the project we had an independent budget and complete autonomy to decide what to study and how to allocate our research, analysis, and writing time. We recognize that this is an unusual situation; the grants we received were in effect brokered by the Coalition, but the use of funds and all research- and writing-related decision making were left to us. The level of trust and concern that our work not be compromised shown by Coalition members was impressive, especially given the high risk of failure in educational innovation projects.

As with most ethnographic research, the researchers were the primary instruments of data collection. Through observation (alone and occasionally with the assistance of audio or video recording), collection of artifacts, interviews, and one student survey, we amassed the data set—ten filing cabinets in size—that is the source for this book. It was not, however, simply the product of the two ethnographers.

Throughout the data collection process, we were assisted by "ethnographic reporters," students and teachers whom we worked with in workshops each summer and who collected data about their schools during the year. These students and some teachers kept journals, designed and carried out research projects, interviewed their peers, made observations at their schools (and in some cases, at other schools), and collected materials that were used or handed out in their classes. These data augmented our understanding of what was going on at our study sites. The ethnographic reporters' work was particularly informative for us in the third and fourth years of the project when students and teachers became more comfortable with their work and began to collect data of interest to them (rather than simply the data requested by us).

We learned throughout our research, and particularly through our work with the ethnographic reporters, that undertaking ethnographic research results in the researchers' exerting influence on the persons and the setting being studied. Also, teaching others to use ethnographic models can (and did) result in these methods becoming a part of the change process itself. Further, whether or not the people studied are directly involved in the writing that follows, the research and writing are a collaborative effort.[3] In general, research on school reform can be viewed as a continuum from those efforts explicitly directed toward research for change to those focused on research about change. Our work, even our efforts to promote and enhance schools' efforts toward self-documentation, was conceived as and is most accurately viewed as research about change. At the same time, even the most objective, non-interventionist, documentary work inevitably creates change in the setting studied (Dobbert 1982). Research about change therefore can, in and of itself, become research for change.

3. For more about this perspective, see Van Maanen (1988); Marcus and Fischer (1986); Clifford and Marcus (1986); and Clifford (1988).

Some measure of collaboration was envisioned in our initial research design, particularly the ethnographic reporters, yet we were also concerned about preserving some distance (objectivity). From the outset, we conducted our research with a clear sense of what our role as ethnographic researchers should and could be—that is, to conduct research about change, not to act as direct change agents. In no way during our research did we dictate, direct, or make recommendations concerning what people should or might do in our research settings. Furthermore, we selected our sample schools with a sense that comparison on key dimensions would be helpful: we wanted both whole-school efforts and school-within-a-school projects; we included public and private schools; and we selected urban, suburban, and rural schools. In our school-based research, we were systematic in our interview schedules and protocols, and we were sensitive about contaminating our research through inappropriate feedback. At first, we were even fearful that the most innocuous remarks might influence, and therefore undermine, the "validity" of our research.

As our research progressed, however, we began to view many of our subjects as collaborators in the research process. In seeking the most encompassing ways to address our research questions, we incorporated some highly interactive research practices. We worked with students, teachers, administrators, parents, and other school personnel in a variety of ways to broaden our notions of what constituted data and to model effective strategies for eliciting and understanding alternative viewpoints.

Simultaneously, they began to consider us collaborators in the change process. We resisted this label for fear of being identified as proponents of Coalition philosophy. At the same time, we recognized that by doing our work and sharing our methods with others, we were contributing to the change process. We began, therefore, to document our own activities at each research site, believing that if our influence would be felt, it must also be systematically recorded.

We found that being interactive with people in our study schools, discussing our research methods and overall goals, generated a shared understanding of what we were looking at and why. Rather than undermining our research, we found that recognizing the inevitably collaborative nature of qualitative research allowed us to expand our methodological diversity, as well as facilitating the process by which those at the schools sites could assist us in our research. (This was an especially significant concern, given that we each worked at various research sites: receiving regular updates helped us understand developments that had occurred in our absence.) For example, initially few teachers, students, or administrators understood much about ethnographic research. As we conducted our research and had opportunities to explain ethnographic methods, at least some people at each of our study schools began to understand and appreciate our research methods. People came to understand our goals and to share with us what they felt might be useful or valuable, often volunteering their view on the situations as well.

To try to keep the influence of this interaction in perspective, we relied on a high degree of reflexivity in our research. As Martyn Hammersley and Paul Atkinson argue: "Rather than engaging in futile attempts to eliminate the effects of the researchers, we . . . set about understanding them" (1983: 17). This self-scrutiny forced us to continually question our methods, to ask ourselves: What is my social role in this study? How does my presence influence the data I collect? How are my choices of collaborators influenced? How am I determining what events are significant enough to document? When we took a reflexive stance, all these questions became integral parts of the research process rather than a priori abstractions.

We benefited as well from the advice of others, particularly members of an advisory board of educational researchers who offered us their perspectives on our research, analysis, and written products. These board members were an important component of our work, for they brought their combined expertise in educational anthropology, sociology, administration, and history to the table when debating with us how to make sense of our data. Accordingly, they helped to stretch us in a different direction: in addition to trying to get multiple perspectives on the Coalition's reform effort (through studying eight schools and the central staff), they pushed us to look at its effects from various analytic perspectives.

BOUNDING THE OBJECT OF STUDY AND DECIDING ON AN ANALYTIC FRAME

During early conversations with the Coalition staff and the principals of the charter schools we decided that the most appropriate foci of attention for our work would be the schools, the central staff at Brown University, and places or occasions where people from the two met. The Coalition was a school-centered reform. Other people with a stake in schools (parents, for instance) were invited to participate in the restructuring and communitywide involvement was applauded. But neither were actively sought by the Coalition's Brown University–based staff or by the charter schools. Therefore, we more or less bounded the school-based portion of our research at the front door of the school, incorporating parents and others when they moved into the school or joined discussions with people at the schools.

It is important to remember that our study was bounded in another way: the study schools were selected from the charter member schools, the original twelve schools that joined the Coalition in its early years. Over time, the Coalition became more aware of the importance of including participants in all levels of the education system in the reform process, and several initiatives were begun to achieve this. That we do not, indeed cannot, address these later approaches to school reform here is, in our opinions, as much tied to Coalition emphases when we began our work as it is to how we bounded our study. During CES's rapid expansion, we discussed the advisability of modifying our research design and opted, in the end, to maintain our original study, rather than risk compromising its integrity by incorporating more schools or network perspectives into an already ambitious research agenda.

Another crucial decision we made (and revisited time and again) was to use educational reform and American cultural values as our analytic frames for the book, rather than one or more of several equally important perspectives—race, class, or gender, for instance. Such analytic foci would offer additional insights, but we decided the reform context was the most appropriate framework because it offered the possibility of seeing continuities and discontinuities across very different sites in terms of the micropolitical issues that emerged and affected the course of reform work in each school. It was, more often than not, the frame that participants used to make sense of what was happening. And we do, albeit softly, allude to issues of socioeconomic status, race, and gender.

The decision to incorporate some discussion of how the reform mirrored American cultural values observed in other institutions or through the enactment of rituals stemmed in large part from trying to make sense of the strong emphasis on success that emerged throughout our fieldwork. As we read and reflected on other works about American cultural values and emphases and talked with our advisory board, we realized other of these so-called core values were at play as well. Although we do not delve into this discussion with anywhere near the attention it deserves, we felt strongly that it needed to be a part of the final "sense-making" we offered, as it helped us to understand why people framed their arguments (for and against reform) as they did.

A NOTE ON SOURCES

When writing this book we relied extensively on documents we collected at our study site schools and from the Coalition central staff. These included school newspapers, handouts created by teachers for their classes, and program assessments by external evaluators. Copies of all these sources are included in an archive we created from this research project. Nonetheless, the documents themselves are effectively unavailable. Because of our commitment to protect the confidentiality of those who collaborated in our research, few—if any—people reading this manuscript would have access to these materials. Consequently, we have not formally referenced these materials in our writing. Rather, we have provided a description of the material and, where relevant, a time reference.

REFERENCES

Adler, Mortimer J. 1982. *The Paideia Proposal.* New York: Macmillan.

Aikin, Wilford M. 1942. *The Story of the Eight-Year Study.* Vol. 1 of *Adventure in American Education.* New York: Harper and Brothers.

Bacharach, Samuel B., ed. 1988. "Education Reform: Change and Rhetoric." Special issue of *Educational Administration Quarterly* 24 (3).

Ball, Stephen. 1988. *The Micropolitics of the School: Towards a Theory of School Organization.* New York: Routledge, Chapman, and Hall.

———. 1980. "Initial Encounters in the Classroom and the Process of Establishment." Pp. 143–65 in *Pupil Strategies,* ed. Peter Woods. London: Croom Helm.

Ball, Stephen, and Richard Bowe. 1991. "Micropolitics of Radical Change." Pp. 19–45 in *The Politics of Life in Schools,* ed. Joseph Blase. Newbury Park, Calif.: Sage.

Barth, Roland S. 1990. *Improving Schools from Within.* San Francisco: Jossey-Bass.

Blase, Joseph, ed. 1991. *The Politics of Life in Schools.* Newbury Park, Calif.: Sage.

Boyer, Ernest. 1983. *High School.* New York: Harper and Row.

Brandt, Ron. 1988. "On Changing Secondary Schools: A Conversation with Ted Sizer." *Educational Leadership* 45 (5): 30–36.

Business Wire Features. 1993. "Report Raps American Education: Educator Says Students Can't Analyze." *Boston Sunday Globe,* Aug. 8, sec. B.

Chamberlin, Dean, Enid Chamberlin, Neal E. Drought, and William E. Scott. 1942. *Did They Succeed in College? The Followup Study of the Graduates of the Thirty Schools.* Vol. 4 of *Adventure in American Education.* New York: Harper and Brothers.

Clifford, James. 1988. *The Predicament of Culture: Twentieth-Century Ethnography, Literature, and Art.* Cambridge: Harvard University Press.

Clifford, James, and George Marcus, eds. 1986. *Writing Culture: The Poetics and Politics of Ethnography.* Berkeley: University of California Press.

Coalition of Essential Schools. 1989. *Prospectus.* Providence: Brown University, Coalition of Essential Schools.

———. 1985. *Prospectus.* Providence: Brown University, Coalition of Essential Schools.

Coalition of Essential Schools, Committee on Evaluation. 1988. "Report of the Committee on Evaluation of the Coalition of Essential Schools." Providence: Brown University, Coalition of Essential Schools, Sept. 1.

Cohen, David K. 1991a. "Educational Technology and School Organization." Pp. 231–64 in *Technology and Education: Looking Toward 2020,* ed. Raymond Nickerson and Philip Zodhiates. Hillsdale, N.J.: L. Erlbaum.

————. 1991b. "Revolution in One Classroom (Or, Then Again, Was It?)" *American Educator* 15 (2): 16–23.

Cohen, Marshall A. 1991. "An American Teacher's View of British Assessment Practice." Studies on Exhibitions no. 2. Providence: Brown University, Coalition of Essential Schools.

Coleman, James S. 1961. *The Adolescent Society.* New York: Free Press.

Coles, Robert. 1980. *Children of Crisis.* Vol. 5, *Privileged Ones: The Well-off and Rich in America.* Boston: Little, Brown.

Cremin, Lawrence A. 1965. *The Genius of American Education.* New York: Vintage.

————. 1964. *The Transformation of the School: Progressivism in American Education, 1876–1957.* New York: Vintage.

Cuban, Larry. 1990. "Reforming Again, Again, and Again." *Educational Researcher* 19:3–13.

Cusick, Philip. 1991. *The Educational System, Its Nature and Logic.* New York: McGraw-Hill.

Diffily, Ann. 1986. "Must Horace Compromise?" *Brown Alumni Monthly* (March), 22–27.

Dobbert, Marion Lundy. 1982. *Ethnographic Research.* New York: Praeger.

Doyle, Paul. 1979. "Student Management of Task Structures in the Classroom." Paper presented at the Conference on Teacher and Pupil Strategies, St. Hilda's College, Oxford.

Dreiser, Theodore. 1981. *Sister Carrie.* New York: Viking Penguin.

————. 1964. *An American Tragedy.* New York: New American Library/Dutton.

Elmore, Richard F., and Associates. 1991. *Restructuring Schools: The Next Generation of Educational Reform.* San Francisco: Jossey-Bass.

Firestone, William, Susan Fuhrman, and Michael Kirst. 1989. *The Progress of Reform: An Appraisal of State Initiatives.* East Lansing, Mich.: Center for Policy Research Information.

Fiske, Edward B. 1991. *Smart Schools, Smart Kids.* New York: Simon and Schuster.

Ford Foundation. 1972. *A Foundation Goes to School: The Ford Foundation Comprehensive School Improvement Program, 1960–1970.* New York: Ford Foundation.

Fordham, Signithia, and John Ogbu. 1986. "Black Students' School Success: Coping with the Burden of 'Acting White.'" *Urban Review* 18 (3): 176–206.

Fried, Robby, and Theodore R. Sizer. 1987. "Common Principles for an Uncommon Education." Unpub. paper. Providence: Brown University, Coalition of Essential Schools. Apr.

Fullan, Michael G., and Matthew B. Miles. 1992. "Getting Reform Right: What Works and What Doesn't." *Phi Delta Kappan* 73 (10): 745–52.

Futrell, Mary Hatwood. 1989. "Mission Not Accomplished: Education Reform in Retrospect." *Phi Delta Kappan* 71 (1): 9–14.

Geertz, Clifford. 1973. *The Interpretation of Cultures.* New York: Basic Books.

Gibboney, Richard A. 1994. *The Stone Trumpet: A Story of Practical School Reform 1960–1990.* Albany: SUNY Press.

Giles, H. H., S. P. McCutchen, and A. N. Zechiel. 1942. *Exploring the Curriculum: The Work of the Thirty Schools from the Viewpoint of Curriculum Consultants.* Vol. 2 of *Adventure in American Education.* New York: Harper and Brothers.

Goodlad, John I. 1984. *A Place Called School: Prospects for the Future.* New York: McGraw-Hill.

Greenfield, William. 1991. "The Micropolitics of Leadership in an Urban Elementary School." Pp. 161–84 in *The Politics of Life in Schools,* ed. Joseph Blase. Newbury Park, Calif.: Sage.

Guskey, Thomas. 1986. "Staff Development and the Process of Teacher Change." *Educational Researcher* 15 (5): 5–12.

Hammersley, Martyn. 1980. "On Interactionist Empiricism." Pp. 198–213 in *Pupil Strategies,* ed. Peter Woods. London: Croom Helm.

Hammersley, Martyn, and Paul Atkinson. 1983. *Ethnography: Principles in Practice.* London: Tavistock.

Hampel, Robert. 1986. *The Last Little Citadel.* Boston: Houghton Mifflin.

Hargreaves, Andy. 1991. "Contrived Collegiality: The Micropolitics of Teacher Collaboration." Pp. 46–72 in *The Politics of Life in Schools,* ed. Joseph Blase. Newbury Park, Calif.: Sage.

Hargreaves, David. 1980. "The Occupational Culture of Teachers." Pp. 125–48 in *Teacher Strategies,* ed. Peter Woods. London: Croom Helm.

Harrington, Diane, and Peter W. Cookson, Jr. 1992. "School Reform in East Harlem: Alternative Schools vs. 'Schools of Choice.'" Pp. 177–86 in A. G. Hess, *Empowering Teachers and Parents: School Restructuring through the Eyes of Anthropologists.* Westport, Conn.: Bergin and Garvey.

Hart, Ann Weaver. 1990. "Impacts of the School Social Unit on Teacher Authority during Work Redesign." *American Educational Research Journal* 27 (3): 503–32.

Healey, Ann Macari. 1988. "A Plan to Unshackle Schools: 'Re:Learning' Program Invites Rhode Island and Others to Experiment with Change." *Providence Journal Bulletin,* Aug. 18.

Heller, Joseph. 1989. *Something Happened.* New York: Dell.

Henry, Jules. 1965. *Culture against Man.* New York: Vintage.

Henry, Tamara. 1993. "Results below Expectations: Analyzing the Lack of True Gains." *USA Today,* Mar. 17.

Hofstadter, Richard. 1974. *Anti-Intellectualism in American Life.* New York: Knopf.

Houston, Holly M. 1988. "Restructuring Secondary Schools." Pp. 109–29 in *Building a Professional Culture in Schools,* ed. A. Lieberman. New York: Teachers College Press.

Irving, John. 1990. *The World According to Garp.* New York: Ballentine Books.

James, Thomas, and D. Tyack. 1983. "Learning from Past Efforts to Reform the High School." *Phi Delta Kappan* 64: 400–406.

Kantorwitz, Barbara. 1993. "A Nation Still at Risk." *Newsweek,* April 19, 46–49.

Kelly, Dennis. 1993. "Saving Schools from 'Mediocrity': Improvements Hard to Measure after Ten Years of Reform." *USA Today,* Mar. 17.

Kirst, Michael, and Gail Meister. 1985. "Turbulence in American Secondary Schools: What Reforms Last?" *Curriculum Inquiry* 15:169–86.

Kleffman, Sandy. 1993. "Educational Reforms Do Too Little Too Slowly." *Providence Journal Bulletin,* Apr. 9.

Kohlberg, Lawrence. 1985. "A Just Community Approach to Moral Education in

Theory and Practice." Pp. 27–87 in *Moral Education: Theory and Practice*, ed. M. Berkowitz and F. Ozer. Hillsdale, N.J.: L. Erlbaum.

———. 1984. *Essays on Moral Development.* Vol. 2, *The Psychology of Moral Development.* San Francisco: Harper and Row.

———. 1981. *Essays on Moral Development.* Vol. 1, *The Philosophy of Moral Development.* New York: Harper and Row.

———. 1980. "High School Democracy and Educating for a Just Society." Pp. 20–57 in *Moral Education: A First Generation of Research and Development*, ed. R. Mosher. New York: Praeger.

Lasch, Christopher. 1991. *The True and Only Heaven: Progress and Its Critics.* New York: Norton.

———. 1979. *The Culture of Narcissism: American Life in an Age of Diminishing Expectations.* New York: Warner Books.

Lewis, Sinclair. 1989. *Babbit.* San Diego: Harcourt Brace.

———. 1982. *Cass Timberlane.* Laguna Beach, Calif.: Buccaneer Books.

Lieberman, Ann, Linda Darling-Hammond, and David Zuckerman. 1991. *Early Lessons in Restructuring Schools.* New York: Teachers College, Columbia University, National Center for Restructuring Education, Schools, and Teaching.

Lightfoot, Sara L. 1983. *The Good High School: Portraits of Character and Culture.* New York: Basic Books.

Little, Judith, W. Gerritz, David Stern, J. Guthrie, Michael Kirst, and David Marsh. 1987. *Staff Development in California.* San Francisco: Far West Laboratory.

Lortie, Dan. 1975. *Schoolteacher: A Sociological Study.* Chicago: University of Chicago Press.

Marcus, George, and Michael Fischer. 1986. *Anthropology as Cultural Critique: An Experimental Moment in the Human Sciences.* Chicago: University of Chicago Press.

McDonald, Joseph A. 1991a. "Three Pictures of an Exhibition: Warm, Cool, and Hard." Studies on Exhibitions no. 1. Providence: Brown University, Coalition of Essential Schools.

———. 1991b. "Dilemmas of Planning Backwards: Rescuing a Good Idea." Studies on Exhibitions no. 3. Providence: Brown University, Coalition of Essential Schools.

McLaughlin, Milbrey. 1990. "The Rand Change Agent Study Revisited: Macro Perspectives and Micro Realities." *Educational Researcher* 19 (9): 11–16.

McQuillan, Patrick J. 1989. "The Tensions of University Intervention in Secondary Education." Paper presented at the meetings of the Northeastern Anthropology Association, Montreal, Canada, Mar.

McQuillan, Patrick J., and Donna E. Muncey. 1994. "Change Takes Time." *Journal of Curriculum Studies* 26 (3): 265–79.

———. 1991. "School-within-a-School Restructuring and Faculty Divisiveness: Examples from a Study of the Coalition of Essential Schools." Paper presented at the annual meeting of the American Educational Research Association. Chicago, Ill., Apr. Working Paper no. 6. Providence: Brown University, Coalition of Essential Schools, School Ethnography Project.

Meier, Deborah. 1992. "Reinventing Teaching." *Teachers College Record* 93 (4): 594–609.

Metz, Mary. 1990. "Real School: A Universal Drama Amid Disparate Experience."

Pp. 75–91 in *Educational Politics for the New Century: The Twentieth Anniversary Yearbook of the Politics of Education Association,* ed. Douglas Mitchell and Margaret E. Goetz. Philadelphia: Falmer Press.

Mooney, James. 1896. "The Ghost-Dance Religion and the Sioux Outbreak of 1890." In *14th Annual Report of the Bureau of American Ethnology, 1892–93,* pt. 2. Washington, D.C.: Smithsonian Institution.

Muncey, Donna E., and Patrick J. McQuillan. 1993a. "Preliminary Findings from a Five-Year Study of the Coalition of Essential Schools." *Phi Delta Kappan* 74 (6): 486–89.

———. 1993b. "Education Reform as Revitalization Movement." *American Journal of Education* 101 (4): 393–431.

———. 1992a. "The Dangers of Assuming Consensus: Some Examples from the Coalition of Essential Schools." Pp. 47–69 in *Empowering Teachers and Parents: School Restructuring through the Eyes of Anthropologists,* ed. G. Alfred Hess, Jr. Westport, Conn.: Greenwood.

———. 1992b. "Findings from the Field: What Happens When Schools Restructure? A Five-Year Study of Eight Essential Schools." Working Paper no. 3. Providence: Brown University, Coalition of Essential Schools, School Ethnography Project.

———. 1991. "Empowering Nonentities." Paper presented at the Ethnography in Education Research Forum, Philadelphia. Feb. Working Paper no. 5. Providence: Brown University, Coalition of Essential Schools, School Ethnography Project.

———. 1990. "Some Observations on the Possibility of Major Restructuring in American Schools: An Ethnographic Perspective." Paper presented at the American Anthropological Association Meetings, New Orleans. Nov.

National Commission on Excellence in Education. 1983. *A Nation at Risk: The Imperative of Educational Reform.* Washington, D.C.: National Commission on Excellence in Education.

Neill, A. S. 1960. *Summerhill.* New York: Hart.

Newman, Frank. 1988. Remarks delivered at the coordinators' meeting for original Re:Learning states, sponsored by the Coalition of Essential Schools and the Education Commission of the States, Milton, Mass., August.

Newmann, Fred. 1993. "Beyond Common Sense in Educational Restructuring: The Issues of Content and Linkage." *Educational Researcher* 22 (2): 4–13.

Orlich, Donald C. 1989. "Education Reforms: Mistakes, Misconceptions, Miscues." *Phi Delta Kappan* 70 (7): 512–17.

Pauly, Edward. 1991. *The Classroom Crucible: What Really Works, What Doesn't and Why.* New York: Basic Books.

Perkinson, Henry J. 1968. *The Imperfect Panacea: American Faith in Education, 1865–1965.* New York: Random House.

Piper, Watty. 1981. *The Little Engine That Could.* Greenport, N.Y.: Harmony Raine.

Potter, David. 1954. *People of Plenty.* Chicago: University of Chicago Press.

Powell, Arthur G., Eleanor Farrar, and David K. Cohen. 1985. *The Shopping Mall High School: Winners and Losers in the Educational Marketplace.* Boston: Houghton Mifflin.

Purkey, Stewart, and Martha Smith. 1983. "Effective Schools: A Review." *Elementary School Journal* 83 (4): 427–52.

Putnam, Hilary. 1981. *Reason, Truth, and History*. Cambridge: Cambridge University Press.

Rabinow, Paul. 1977. *Reflections on Fieldwork in Morocco*. Berkeley: University of California Press.

Ravitch, Diane. 1983. *The Troubled Crusade: American Education, 1945–1980*. New York: Basic Books.

Re:Learning. 1989. *The Conversation: From Schoolhouse to Statehouse*. Denver: Education Commission of the States.

Richter, Conrad, ills. 1966. *The Light in the Forest*. New York: Knopf.

Sarason, Seymour. 1993. *Letters to a SERIOUS Education President*. Newbury Park, Calif.: Corwin Press.

———. 1990. *The Predictable Failure of School Reform*. San Francisco: Jossey-Bass.

———. 1982. *The Culture of the School and the Problem of Change*. 2d ed. Boston: Allyn and Bacon.

Schlechty, Philip C. 1991. *Schools for the 21st Century: Leadership Imperatives for Educational Reform*. San Francisco: Jossey-Bass.

Schutz, Alfred. 1967. *Collected Papers*. The Hague: Martinus Nijhoff.

Sennett, Richard, and Jonathan Cobb. 1972. *The Hidden Injuries of Class*. New York: Vintage.

Shanker, Albert. 1993. Letter to the Editor, "He Likes Head Start." *Providence Journal Bulletin*, May 11.

Sinclair, Karen. 1976. "Maramatanga: Ideology and Social Process among the Maori of New Zealand." Unpub. Ph.D. diss., Brown University.

Sizer, Theodore R. 1992. *Horace's School*. Boston: Houghton Mifflin.

———. 1991a. Letter sent to all CES schools. Nov.

———. 1991b. "No Pain, No Gain." *Educational Leadership* 48 (8): 32–34.

———. 1989a. Letter sent to all CES schools, Jan. 17.

———. 1989b. "The Nine Common Principles." Remarks at the Fall Forum, a conference sponsored by the Coalition of Essential Schools, Re:Learning, and the Education Commission of the States. Newport, R.I. Nov.

———. 1988a. Remarks made at the annual meeting of the Education Commission of the States, Baltimore, Aug.

———. 1988b. "When a Teacher Says 'I Quit.'" Speech given at a conference on teaching at-risk youth, Johns Hopkins University, May 5.

———. 1987. Remarks made at a meeting of CES schools in Baltimore, Oct. 19.

———. 1986a. Précis of statement on the improvement of American secondary schools to the National Governors' Association. Feb. 23.

———. 1986b. "Rebuilding: First Steps of the Coalition of Essential School." *Phi Delta Kappan* 68 (1): 38–42.

———. 1985. "School Daze: Adolescent Apathy." *Brown University Human Development Letter*, summer.

———. 1984. *Horace's Compromise: The Dilemma of the American High School*. Boston: Houghton Mifflin. An updated version with a new afterword was published in 1985.

———. 1983a. "Essential Schools: A First Look." *Independent School* 43 (2): 7–12.

———. 1983b. "High School Reform: The Need For Engineering." *Phi Delta Kappan* 83 (6): 679–83.

———. 1982. "In Defense of Teachers." *Boston Observer*, Dec. 10.

Smith, Eugene, Ralph W. Tyler, and the Evaluation Staff. 1942. *Appraising and Recording Student Progesss*. Vol. 3 of *Adventure in American Education*. New York: Harper and Brothers.

Smith, John K., and Lous Heshusius. 1986. "Closing Down the Conversation: The End of the Quantitative-Qualitative Debate Among Educational Inquirers." *Educational Researcher* 15 (1): 4–12.

Smith, Marshall, and Jennifer O'Day. 1991. "Systemic School Reform." Pp. 127–54 in *The Politics of Curriculum and Testing: The 1990 Yearbook of the Politics of Education Association*, ed. Susan Fuhrman and Betty Malen. Philadelphia: Falmer Press.

Spindler, George, and Louise Spindler. 1987a. "Ethnography: An Anthropological View." Pp. 151–56 in *Education and Cultural Process*, ed. G. Spindler. Prospect Heights, Ill.: Waveland Press.

———. 1987b. "Cultural Dialogue and Schooling in Schoenhausen and Roseville: A Comparative Analysis." *Anthropology and Education Quarterly* 18: 3–16.

———. 1982. "Roger Harkin and Schoenhausen: From Familiar to Strange and Back Again." Pp. 20–46 in *Doing the Ethnography of Schooling*, ed. George Spindler. New York: Holt, Rinehart and Winston.

Spindler, George, Louise Spindler, Henry Trueba, and Melvin Williams. 1990. *The American Culture Dialogue and Its Transmissions*. Philadelphia: Falmer Press.

Steffens, Heidi. 1990. "Assessing the Central Issue of Schooling. Reform: The Third Wave." *Doubts and Certainties* (Newsletter of the NEA National Center for Innovation) 5 (2 and 3): 1.

Stringfield, Sam, and Charles Teddlie. 1991. "Observers as Predictors of Schools' Multiyear Outlier Status on Achievement Tests." *Elementary School Journal* 91 (4): 357–76.

Task Force on Education for Economic Growth. 1983. "Action for Excellence: A Comprehensive Plan to Improve Our Nation's Schools." Denver: Education Commission of the States.

Terkel, Studs. 1984. *The Good War: An Oral History of World War Two*. New York: Pantheon.

Toch, Thomas. 1991. *In the Name of Excellence*. New York: Oxford University Press.

Twentieth Century Fund Task Force on Federal Elementary and Secondary Education Policy. 1983. *Making the Grade*. New York: Twentieth Century Fund.

Tyack, David. 1990. "'Restructuring' in Historical Perspective: Tinkering toward Utopia." *Teachers College Record* 92 (2): 170–91.

———. 1974. *The One Best System: A History of American Urban Education*. Cambridge: Harvard University Press.

Van Maanen, John. 1988 *Tales of the Field: On Writing Ethnography*. Berkeley: University of California Press.

Wallace, Anthony F. C. 1979. "Schools in Revolutionary and Conservative Societies." Pp. 237–66 in *Anthropology and Educational Administration*, ed. Ray Barnhardt, John H. Chilcott, and Harry F. Wolcott. Tucson: Impresora Sahuaro.

———. 1972a. "Paradigmatic Processes in Culture Change." *American Anthropologist* 74:467–78.

———. 1972b. *The Death and Rebirth of the Seneca*. New York: Vintage.

———. 1966. *Religion: An Anthropological View.* New York: Random House.

———. 1961. *Culture and Personality.* New York: Random House.

———. 1956. "Revitalization Movement." *American Anthropologist* 58: 264–81.

Waller, Willard. 1932. *The Sociology of Teaching.* New York: Russell and Russell.

Wasley, Patricia. 1991. "Stirring the Chalkdust: Changing Practices in Essential Schools." *Teachers College Record* 93 (1): 28–58.

———. 1990a. "Trusting Kids and Their Voices." Studies in Teacher Change no. 1. Providence: Brown University, Coalition of Essential Schools.

———. 1990b. "A Feeling of Uneasiness: A Teacher in the Midst of Change." Studies on Teacher Change no. 2. Providence: Brown University, Coalition of Essential Schools.

———. 1990c. "A Formula for Making a Difference." Studies in Teacher Change no. 3. Providence: Brown University, Coalition of Essential Schools.

Weber, Max. 1978. *Selections in Translation,* ed. W. G. Runciman. Trans. Eric Matthews. Cambridge: Cambridge University Press.

———. 1971. *The Interpretation of Social Reality,* ed. J. E. T. Eldridge. New York: Schocken.

———. 1968. *On Charisma and Institution-Building: Selected Papers,* ed. S. N. Eisenstadt. Chicago: University of Chicago Press.

Wehlage, Gary, Gregory Smith, and Pauline Lipman. 1992. "Restructuring Urban Schools: The New Futures Experience." *American Educational Research Journal* 29:51–93.

Wiggins, Grant. 1991. "Standards, Not Standardization: Evoking Quality Student Work." *Educational Leadership* 48 (5): 18–25.

———. 1989. "Teaching to the (Authentic) Test." *Educational Leadership* 46 (7): 41–47.

———. 1987a. "Creating a Thought-Provoking Curriculum: Lessons from Whodunits and Others." *American Educator* 11 (4): 10–17.

———. 1987b. "An Interim Report on the 'Exhibitions' Project of the Coalition of Essential Schools." Unpub. paper. Providence: Brown University, Coalition of Essential Schools.

Willis, Paul E. 1977. *Learning to Labour.* Westmead, England: Saxon House.

Wolcott, Harry F. 1977. *Teachers versus Technocrats: An Educational Innovation in Anthropological Perspective.* Eugene: Center for Educational Policy and Management, University of Oregon.

Woods, Peter. 1978. "Negotiating the Demands of Schoolwork." *Journal of Curriculum Studies* 10 (4): 301–27.

———. 1983. *Sociology and the School.* London: Routledge and Kegan Paul.

Woods, Peter, ed. 1980. *Pupil Strategies.* London: Croom Helm.

Worsley, Peter. 1968. *The Trumpet Shall Sound.* New York: Schocken.

Yates, Paul. 1987. "A Case of Mistaken Identity: Interethnic Images in Multicultural England." Pp. 196–220 in *Interpretive Ethnography of Education at Home and Abroad,* ed. G. Spindler and L. Spindler. London: L. Erlbaum.

Zook, Jim. 1993. "10 Years Later, Many Educators See Little Progress for the 'Nation at Risk.'" *Chronicle of Higher Education,* Apr. 21, A19, A24–25.